A2-Level Contents

Editors: Polly Cotterill, Rob MacDonald, Jennifer Underwood

Contributors: Najoud Ensaff, Tony Flanagan, Heather Haynes, Rachael Powers, Chris Reynolds, Elisabeth Sanderson, Michael Southorn, Luke von Kotze, Emma Warhurst

Proofreaders: Paula Barnett, Katherine Reed, Glenn Rogers and Elisabeth Sanderson

Acknowledgements

Page 109, Text B:	With thanks to iStockphoto® for permission to use the images on p.109
Page 126, Text B:	www.growingkids.co.uk
Page 135, Text B:	Jean Aitchison, The language web, 1997 © Jean Aitchison 1997, published by Cambridge University Press, reproduced with permission
Page 150, Text F:	www.allotment.org.uk

Every effort has been made to locate copyright holders and obtain permission to reproduce sources. For those sources where it has been difficult to trace the copyright holder of the work, we would be grateful for information. If any copyright holder would like to make an amendment to the acknowledgements, please notify us and we will gladly update the book at the next reprint. Thank you.

ISBN: 978 1 84762 425 3

Published by Coordination Group Publications Ltd.

Groovy website: www.cgpbooks.co.uk
Jolly bits of clipart from CorelDRAW®
Printed by Elanders Hindson Ltd, Newcastle upon Tyne.

Based on the classic CGP style created by Richard Parsons

AS-Level

English Language

Exam Board: AQA B

Language Frameworks

On the next two pages are the essential tools you need for describing and analysing spoken or written language.

You should aim to Analyse all Texts in a Similar way

If you have to analyse a piece of language or discourse, there are several things to think about:

1) **Genre** — **what kind** of language it is. Written discourses could be **instruction booklets** or **adverts**, and spoken discourses could be **formal speeches** to an audience or **casual conversations** between friends.

2) **Register** — a type of language that's appropriate for a particular audience or situation, e.g. the language of a political party or the language of the justice system. Register also includes the level of **formality** in a discourse.

3) **Audience** — the **listener** or **reader**. When you're analysing language, think about how the audience is **addressed**. It might be **formal** or **informal**, **direct** or **indirect**. For example, in advertising the audience is often directly addressed as *you*.

4) **Subject** — what the discourse is **about**. This will be reflected in the **lexical choices**, e.g. a discussion about healthy eating may contain words like *low-fat*, *diet*, and *nutrition*.

5) **Purpose** — what the speaker or writer is trying to **achieve** through language (e.g. to persuade, instruct, etc.).

6) **Mode** — whether the language is **written or spoken**. You can also get **mixed modes** — e.g. in text messages, where the language is written, but contains many of the informal features of spoken language.

There are Seven Main Language Frameworks

This table is an **overview** of what makes up each language framework (also called **linguistic frameworks**, or **toolkits**) and how they can be used. There are more detailed explanations of each one throughout the rest of the book.

Lexis	• **Lexis** means the **vocabulary** of a language — the total stock of words. • When you're analysing spoken and written language you'll notice words that share a **similar topic** or **focus**. For example, in an advert for mobile phones you'd find words such as *SMS*, *text-messaging*, and *battery life*. Words that are linked together in this way are known as a **lexical field**.
Semantics	• **Semantics** is the study of how **meaning** is created through words and phrases. Sometimes this meaning is **explicit**, but sometimes it's **implicit**. A word will have a **literal** meaning but it can also be **associated** with other meanings. • For example, the word *red* refers to a **colour**, but it can also be associated with **danger**.
Grammar	• **Grammar** is the system of **rules** that governs how words and sentences are **constructed**. There are three parts to this: 1) A system that **groups** words into classes according to their **function** (e.g. nouns or verbs). 2) A system of **rules** about how these types of words function in relation to each other (**syntax**). 3) The individual units that make up whole words (**morphology**).
Phonology	• **Phonology** is the study of **sounds** in English — how they're **produced** and how they're **combined** to make words. • This framework includes **Non-Verbal Aspects of Speech** (NVAS) or **prosody** — features of spoken language such as pace, stress, rhythm and intonation.
Pragmatics	• **Pragmatics** is sometimes called **language in use**. It's about how social conventions, context, personality and relationships influence the **choices** people make about their language. • For example, how you address other people shows **levels of formality** and **social conventions** — a student might address a teacher as *Miss Rogers* or *Lizzie* depending on what the college or school expects, and what the teacher finds acceptable.
Graphology	• **Graphology** is the study of the **appearance** of the writing and the effect this has on a text. • When you discuss a text's graphology you describe and analyse features like the **typeface**, the **positioning** of text on a page and the relationships between **text** and **images**.
Discourse	• **Discourse** is an **extended** piece of spoken or written language, made up of more than one **utterance** (in spoken language), or more than one **sentence** (in written language).

Language Frameworks

Discourse has a **Structure**

The way language is organised is called its **discourse structure**. You need to look out for different features, depending on whether the discourse is written or spoken.

1) In **written discourse**, look at how a text is **put together**. It may have an **opening** section which leads the reader into the text. The following sections may develop a **theme or argument**. The final section may make some kind of **conclusion**.

2) In **spoken discourse** the structure can be less organised. For example, **conversations** are often **unpredictable** and speakers often **digress** (go off the subject). This is because conversations are usually **spontaneous**.

3) Even spontaneous conversation has some structure, though.

There'll often be an **opening sequence**, e.g.

> Speaker 1: *Hi, how you doing?*
> Speaker 2: *Fine thanks. How about you?*

This is often followed by **turn-taking** as the speakers talk about a topic (or topics). There's often a **closing sequence** too, e.g.

> Speaker 1: *Well, nice seeing you...*
> Speaker 2: *You too.*
> Speaker 1: *Catch you later.*

4) You can also look at how the discourse **fits together** — **cohesion**. There are **two types** of cohesion — **lexical** and **grammatical**. One example of grammatical cohesion is using **adverbs** like *furthermore* and *similarly* at the beginning of a sentence or paragraph to link it to the previous one. Lexical cohesion is when the words in the discourse **relate** to each other throughout, e.g.

> *There was no sign of **the car** — **her lift** was obviously stuck in **traffic**. Was it really worth it, just for a **ride** in a **Porsche**?*

There are **Three Main Steps** to discourse analysis

1) The **first step** in **discourse analysis** is to think about **what kind** of discourse you are looking at. To do this you need to think about genre, register, audience, subject, purpose and mode.

2) The **next step** is to look at how each of the **language frameworks** contributes to the discourse. You might not need to use all of the language frameworks, or you might need to give more emphasis to one than another. It depends on the discourse.

3) And finally, don't forget to discuss **discourse structure** (how the text has been organised) and **cohesion** (the devices used to knit the text together).

Keith tried to look busy but his approach had been spotted.

Practice Questions

Q1 Give two examples of written discourse.
Q2 What is the difference between lexis and semantics?
Q3 What is phonology the study of?
Q4 Define discourse.
Q5 What is grammatical cohesion?

Discourse is brilliant — way better than those Science and Maths ones...

Soooo... your first two pages of AS English Language. They weren't so bad, were they? Didn't think so — but they are vital for your exam. It's really important to get into the habit of applying these frameworks to texts that you have to analyse. Think of them as guidelines that are there to help you organise your work. Aww, see? That's nice.

Introduction to Grammar

Grammar is one of the most important language frameworks — it covers everything from bits of words to entire sentences.

Grammar controls how **Language** is **Constructed**

1)   Grammar is the set of **structural rules** that controls the way language works.

2)   There are **three aspects** of grammar that you need to focus on — word classes, syntax and morphology.

3)   **Word classes** define the **roles** that each word can play in a sentence. **Syntax** is the set of **rules** that control where each word class can appear in a sentence. **Morphology** describes the **construction** of individual words.

There are **Eight Main Word Classes**

Words are **categorised** by the **function** they have in a sentence.
There are eight main **word classes** — also called **parts of speech**.

Word Class	Function	Example
Nouns	'naming' words	*London, book, romance*
Adjectives	describe nouns (and sometimes pronouns)	*large, sunny, featureless*
Verbs	'doing' words	*jump, read, return*
Adverbs	describe verbs (and sometimes adjectives and other adverbs too)	*steadily, incredibly, sadly*
Pronouns	take the place of nouns	*you, they, him, me, it*
Conjunctions	'connecting' words	*and, or, but, because*
Prepositions	define relationships between words in terms of time, space and direction	*before, underneath, through*
Determiners	give specific kinds of information about a noun (e.g. quantity or possession)	*a, the, two, his, few, those*

Word classes are **Controlled** by **Rules**

Word classes can take **different positions** in a sentence, but there are **grammatical rules** about how they work with each other (**syntax**). In the following sentence you can see all the word classes working together:

She	*saw*	*the*	*new*	*manager*	*and*	*his*	*assistant*
pronoun	**verb**	**determiner**	**adjective**	**noun**	**conjunction**	**determiner**	**noun**

at	*the*	*store*	*yesterday.*
preposition	**determiner**	**noun**	**adverb**

1)   People **instinctively** know the rules for connecting words together. For example, you know that words in this order — *doctor she the yesterday saw* — are wrong, and you can **rearrange** them into something that makes sense straight away — *she saw the doctor yesterday*.

2)   You also intuitively know **less obvious rules** about word order — you'd always say *the big brown bear* rather than *the brown big bear*, because you know that adjectives of size **come before** those of colour.

3)   Sometimes there are **fewer restrictions** — some sentences mean the same thing wherever a word is placed, particularly with **adverbs**, e.g. *I **completely** disagree* or *I disagree **completely***.

4)   Sometimes the **meaning** of a sentence changes depending on the position of a word:
      *He **quickly** told me to leave* (he said it fast)   **or**   *He told me to leave **quickly*** (he wanted me to leave fast)

Grammatical rules **Affect Word Formation**

Grammar affects word formation (morphology) because extra bits have to be added to words to **change** things like number or tense. The extra bits are called **inflections**. Here are a couple of examples.

•   *-s* is added to *cup* to change a **singular** noun into a **plural** — *cups* (p.6).

•   *-ed* is added to *remember* to change the **present** tense verb into the **past** tense *remember**ed*** (p.8).

Introduction to Grammar

Grammar Choices can Influence the reader or listener

You can influence your **audience** in different ways by **changing** the **grammar** of a word or sentence.

Tense

1) Events that happened in the past are usually described in the past tense. Sometimes however, in both spoken and written discourse, past events are described using **present tense forms**.

> • So she **went** up to the customer and **gave** him a good telling off.   ⟵ past tense
> • So she **goes** up to the customer and **gives** him a good telling off.   ⟵ present tense

2) The first example sentence is in the past tense. There is a clear sense that some **time has passed** since the event actually happened. In the second, although the action happened in the past, the present tense creates a more **immediate** and **dramatic** impact. You'll see this technique used a lot in **newspaper headlines**:

New evidence casts doubt on verdict	*Pop star admits to private hell*	*Cop raid closes nightclub*

Plurals

1) As well as telling you that there's more than one of something, plurals can **increase** the scale of a **scene**.

> • There was a **mass** of fans outside the hotel.   ⟵ singular
> • There were **masses** of fans outside the hotel.   ⟵ plural

2) Using the singular form *mass* creates the impression of a **specific** body of people. Adding the **-es inflection** to form the plural *masses* creates the image of a **big crowd** of people across a **wider area**.

Adjectives

1) Adjectives are a great way to **influence** your **audience** — compare the following two examples:

> • If you're looking for the holiday of a lifetime, simply treat yourself to a **great** resort in Sri Lanka. Relax in **fine** accommodation.   ⟵ simple adjectives
> • Looking for the holiday of a lifetime? Simply treat yourself to the **greatest** resort in Sri Lanka. Relax in the **finest** accommodation.   ⟵ superlative adjectives

2) These are similar **advertising discourses**, but the second example is much more **persuasive** than the first. The writer uses **superlative** adjectives (see p.7) (*greatest* and *finest*) rather than the simple adjectives in the first example (*great* and *fine*).

3) There are some **other grammatical features** that influence the reader in these examples.

- The second example begins with a **question**. This makes the reader feel **involved immediately**.
- The first example uses the **indefinite article** *a* before the adjective *great*, but the second uses the **definite article** *the* before *greatest* (see p. 10). This makes the reference very **specific** in the second example (it is **the** greatest resort), but the first could be referring to any one of **several** resorts.

Practice Questions

Q1 In the following sentence, identify each word according to word class:
> It was a cold winter and the Russian soldiers suffered terribly.

Q2 Define the term syntax.

Q3 Why does this sentence sound awkward?
> My blue old raincoat is now in tatters.

What rule about word order can you deduce from this?

If you don't take precautions, you could get a nasty inflection...

I know — grammar's got a reputation for being a bit stale and boring. But if you don't understand the way language works and how everything is put together, and how important this is in discourse, then you can wave your analysis bye-bye. Luckily for you, we're about to get into a bit more detail, so get ready to become a world-class word-classer...

Nouns and Adjectives

Nouns are often called naming words, but at AS, it's all a bit more complicated than that. Nouns do give the names of places, people and things — but they can also refer to groups, states, emotions and more.

Nouns can be **Divided** into **Categories**

There are different **types** of nouns. They can refer to unique **people** or **places** (**proper nouns**), or identify more general **objects**, **states** or **groups** (**common nouns**). See below for some examples.

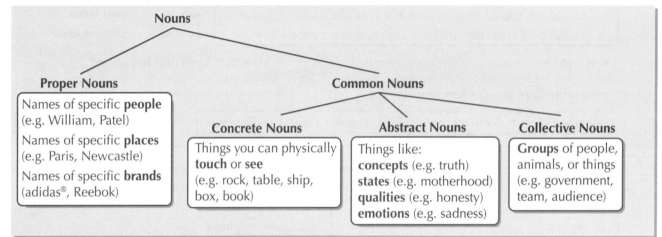

Nouns can be either **Singular** or **Plural**

1) To form the **plural** of a noun you usually add an *-s* or *-es* so that you get, for example, *birds,* or *buses*.

2) Where a noun ends in a consonant and then *-y*, the *-y* is replaced with *-ies* e.g. *lady* ⟶ *ladies*.

3) Word endings that include an *f* like *knife* and *dwarf* often replace the *f* with *-ves* ⟶ *knives* and *dwarves*.

4) Some other nouns form **irregular plurals**, different from the **standard** pattern, e.g.
woman ⟶ *women*   *foot* ⟶ *feet*   *mouse* ⟶ *mice*

5) There are some nouns that **don't change their form** at all, whether they are singular or plurals, e.g. *deer* and *sheep* stay the same even when you are referring to more than one.

Nouns can be classified as **Count Nouns** or **Mass Nouns**

1) **Count nouns** (a bit obviously) can be **counted** — like *brick*. You can have *one brick, two bricks, three bricks*, and so on. Nouns that form irregular plurals can be count nouns too — *one mouse, two mice*, etc.

2) **Mass nouns** can't be counted. Nouns like these **don't** have a **plural**, e.g. you talk about *information* rather than *informations*.

3) Some nouns can function as **both** count and mass nouns, depending on the **context**. For example, in the phrase *war is evil*, *war* is a **mass noun** — it refers to war in general. However, *war* becomes a **count noun** when you use a determiner — e.g. *the war is evil*. This time *war* refers to a **specific** war rather than war in general.

Nouns can be **Modified** to give **More Information**

Nouns **don't usually stand alone**. They're often accompanied by words that **modify** them or that tell you **more** about them. There are two types of modifier — **pre-modifiers** and **post-modifiers**.

- **Pre-modifiers** — these come **before** the noun, e.g. a sign that reads *Dangerous Animal*. The adjective *dangerous* premodifies *animal* and tells you something about it. You can also have **more than one** pre-modifier, e.g. *very dangerous animal* — *very* and *dangerous* are both pre-modifiers.

- **Post-modifiers** — these come after the noun, e.g. *Examination in progress*. The noun *examination* is post-modified by *in progress* — it tells the reader something about the examination.

In **noun phrases**, the noun is called the **head word** — the most important word of the phrase. The other words **modify** it.

determiner	pre-modifier	head word	post-modifier
the	*largest*	*whale*	*in the world*

Nouns and Adjectives

Adjectives *Describe Nouns*

Adjectives are classified according to their **position** — **before** or **after** the noun.

1) **Attributive** adjectives are **pre-modifying**, e.g. *the **sudden** noise*, or *the **red** balloon*.
2) **Predicative** adjectives are **post-modifying**. They're usually **linked** to the noun they are modifying by a form of the verb *be*:

> **Examples of predicative adjectives**
> - *Revision is **brilliant*** — the adjective is **linked** to the noun by a form of the verb *be*.
> - *The food looked **amazing*** — although forms of *be* are the most common links, **other verbs** can link the adjective to the noun (e.g. *looked, seemed, felt*).

Adjectives also make *Comparisons*

Adjectives are **gradable** — they can show **how much** of a certain property a noun displays.

1) **Comparative adjectives** are generally formed by adding an *-er* **inflection**. For example, the simple adjective *long* becomes the comparative adjective *long**er***.
2) **Superlative adjectives** are generally formed by adding *-est*. For example, *long* becomes the superlative *long**est***.

Look back at p.5 to see the effects of gradable adjectives in the holiday advertisement texts. Gradable adjectives make you interpret the sentences and the type of accommodation they advertise differently:

fine accommodation
simple adjective

finer accommodation
comparative adjective

finest accommodation
superlative adjective

3) Some adjectives are **irregular** in the way they form comparatives and superlatives:

Adjective	Comparative	Superlative
good	better	best
bad	worse	worst
much	more	most

4) Some adjectives need *more* and *most* to form comparisons. For example, you can't say *significant**er*** or *significant**est***. You use ***more** significant* or ***most** significant* to make the comparison.

Practice Questions

Q1 In the following list of common nouns, identify three concrete, three abstract and three collective nouns:
love, table, purity, family, government, disgust, team, wall, sock

Q2 Which of the following are count nouns and which are mass nouns?
house, isolation, monkey, furniture, rat, gratitude, hall, courage, jug

Q3 Identify the determiner, pre-modifier, head word and post-modifier in the following noun phrase:
One fine morning in July

Q4 Identify the attributive adjective and the predicative adjective in the following phrases:
The storm was terrible   The terrible storm

Be Here Noun — and other great language albums...

Like 'Noun That's What I Call Music... 88'. Or 'Urban Hymns', by The Verb. Or... never mind. Remember that nouns don't just name specific objects like pencils or sheds — they can refer to states or emotions as well. Get that idea firmly wedged into your head, and then you can go back to making up amusing grammar-based band names. If you want to, obviously.

Verbs and Adverbs

Without verbs, everything in language would stand still. That's why they're sometimes called 'doing' words.

Verbs tell you exactly What Happens

The base form of a verb is called the **infinitive** — it normally follows 'to', e.g. to *be*, to *laugh*, or to *think*. You can describe verbs in two ways:

1) **Main Verbs** (lexical verbs) identify the action of the sentence — e.g. *she sings like a hyena, he gave me his shoe*. The verbs *sing* and *gave* tell you the **action** which is taking place.

2) **Auxiliary Verbs** go **before** the main verb in a sentence. They give **extra information** about the main verb and can affect the **meaning** of the sentence. There are **two** types of auxiliary verb:

Primary auxiliaries
There are three primary auxiliaries — *do*, *have*, and *be*.
- *I **do** like you*
- *I **am** leaving tomorrow*

Primary auxiliaries can also be **main verbs**:
- *I **have** a surprise for you*

Modal auxiliaries
Modal auxiliaries can **only** occur with reference to a main verb. There are 9 modal auxiliary verbs:

| can | could | will | would | must |
| may | might | shall | should | |

- *I **can** play the drums*
- *I **must** do something*

Verbs can Change their endings depending on Who is Doing the Action

The **endings** of verbs can alter depending on **who** is doing the action — the **first**, **second** or **third person**.

Person	Singular Pronoun	Verb	Plural Pronoun	Verb
First	I	play	We	play
Second	You	play	You	play
Third	She/He/It	play(s)	They	play

Only the verb in the third person singular changes its ending — you add an -s to get plays. This rule applies to most of the verbs in English.

Changes to the ends of words that affect the grammar of the sentence are called **inflections**.

Verbs can tell you When something happens

Verbs change depending on whether something is happening in the **past**, **present**, or **future**.

1) **Present tense** tells you about 'now' and uses the **base form** of the verb, e.g. *I write* or *they dance* — unless it's the third person singular (see above), when you need to add the *-s* **inflection**, e.g. *she/he/it talks*.

2) **Past tense** tells you about the past (obviously), e.g. *I danced yesterday*, or *He missed the bus*. For most verbs, you form the past tense by **adding -ed** on the end — another **inflection**.

3) **Future tense** — Some people say that there's no future tense in English. This is because there **isn't** anything specific (like *-s*, or *-ed*) that you can **add** to a verb to show that the action will happen in the future. The future is expressed in **other ways** — often by using **modal auxiliary** verbs like **will** or **shall**.
    e.g. *I **shall** see you tomorrow.*   *I **will** pick you up at eight.*

4) You can also use the **present tense** to talk about **future events** — e.g. *Rachel is **playing** hockey on Saturday*.

Verbs Don't always change in the Same Way

1) Most verbs are **regular** — they follow the same patterns outlined above.

2) Some verbs are **irregular** — they don't change like you'd expect, e.g. *I drink* becomes *I **drank***, not *I **drinked***. Other verbs with irregular past tenses include ***run**, **sing**, **write***, and ***speak***.

3) The verb *be* is very irregular — the forms it can take are the infinitive *to be*, plus *am, are, is, was,* and *were*. It changes more than any other verb according to **person** (first, second or third), **number** and **tense**.

Verbs and Adverbs

Verbs can create an *Active* or *Passive* voice

Sentences that involve an **action** can focus on either the **subject** or the **object** (see p.12 for more on this).

Active Voice

The **active voice** is when the **subject** is the focus and **performs** the action described by the verb, e.g:

- *Ahmed **kicked** the ball.*

The subject, *Ahmed*, acts **directly** upon the object — *the ball*. The object **receives** the action of the verb.

Passive Voice

The **passive voice** is less direct. It focuses on the **object**. The **order changes** so that the object comes first, followed by the subject, e.g:

- *The ball **was kicked** by Ahmed.*

The passive voice makes sentences seem more **formal**.

Verbs can change depending on the *Aspect*

Aspect shows whether the action described by the verb has **finished**, or is still **being performed**.

PROGRESSIVE ASPECT

1) The **progressive** (or **continuous**) aspect refers to actions that don't have a definite end.
2) It's made up of one of the auxiliary forms of *be* and the **present participle** of a verb, which is the **base form** + *-ing*.
3) For example, in the sentence *They **are doing** well, are* is an auxiliary form of *be* and *doing* is the present participle of *do*.

PERFECT ASPECT

1) The **perfect aspect** tells you about an action that has a definite end.
2) It's made up of one of the present forms of *have* (has/have) and the past tense form of the verb, e.g. *They **have bought** a car.*
3) The **past perfect** aspect is formed in the same way but with the past tense of *have* (had), e.g. *I **had missed** it.*

Adverbs are used to *Modify* verbs

Adverbs are mostly used to modify verbs, but they can modify nouns and adjectives too. Most people recognise adverbs as '**-ly** words' but many have different endings. Here are a **few ways** that adverbs **modify meaning**:

- Adverbs of **manner** — how something is done — e.g. *He talks **incessantly**.*
- Adverbs of **place** — where something is happening — e.g. *The book is **here**.*
- Adverbs of **time** — when something is happening — e.g. *The exam is **tomorrow**.*
- Adverbs of **duration** — how long something happens for — e.g. *The journey took **forever**.*
- Adverbs of **frequency** — how often something takes place — e.g. *Mandy visits **sometimes**.*
- Adverbs of **degree** — the extent to which something is done — e.g. *We **completely** understand.*

Some adverbs **express feelings** or opinions — ***Hopefully**, we'll find out where the garage is.*
Adverbs can also **link** sentences together — *The man was a great athlete. **However**, he didn't have a clue about adverbs.*

Practice Questions

Q1 Name the three primary auxiliary verbs.
Q2 What are inflections?
Q3 Give three examples of verbs with irregular past tenses.
Q4 What's the difference between the active voice and the passive voice? Give examples.
Q5 What's the difference between the progressive aspect and the perfect aspect? Give examples.
Q6 What is the function of adverbs?

All these verbs are making me feel a bit tense...

Verbs might seem dull, but they're actually really important. I mean, just think where we'd be without them — we wouldn't really be able to communicate at all. Or should I say, we not really at all. See what I mean? Anyway, everything on this page probably seems quite familiar, but make sure you go over it properly and learn the correct terms for everything.

Pronouns and Determiners

Pronouns and determiners are both related to nouns, but you never see them in the same place at the same time. They're like Bruce Wayne and Batman — and only a teensy bit less exciting.

Pronouns **Take** the **Place** of **Nouns**

Pronouns are a **sub-class** of **nouns**. They can identify subjects and objects, just like nouns do.

1) **Personal** pronouns can replace people or things who are the **subject** of a sentence.
   They're classified in terms of **person** and are either **singular** or **plural**:

	Singular	Plural
First Person	I	we
Second Person	you	you
Third Person	he, she, it	they

e.g.　　Sarah thanked Sanjay
　　　　　　↓
　　She thanked Sanjay
(3rd person singular subject pronoun)

2) Pronouns can also be used to replace the person or thing who is the **object** of the sentence:

	Singular	Plural
First Person	me	us
Second Person	you	you
Third Person	him, her, it	them

e.g.　　Graham thanked Adam
　　　　　　↓
　　Graham thanked **him**
(3rd person singular object pronoun)

Pronouns are used in **Other Ways** too

1) **Interrogative** pronouns are used to **ask questions**. They are *which, what, who, and whose*. As with other pronouns, they help you **simplify** your sentences by **replacing nouns**, e.g:

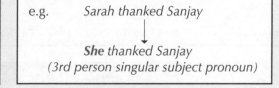

   - *Give me the name of **the person** you're looking for.* ⟹ **Who** *are you looking for?*
   - *Tell me **the thing** you are going to do.* ⟹ **What** *are you going to do?*

2) These aren't the only words you use at the start of questions. *Why, where, how* and *when* are also interrogatives, but they are **adverbs**. Interrogative pronouns and adverbs are usually **classed together** as *wh-words*.

3) **Demonstrative** pronouns like *this, that, these* and *those* can **replace** people and things in a sentence where there's some **shared understanding** of what's being referred to, for example:

   - If you're in the kitchen, you might ask *is this my coffee?* — only people who are also in the kitchen will be able to tell you.
   - You use different demonstratives depending on the **distance** of the object from the speaker — *this* and *these* are objects **near** the speaker. You use *that* or *those* for objects **further away**.

Determiners show what the noun is **Referring To**

There are several determiners, which all **go before** the noun and show what it's referring to.

1) The **definite article** *the* and the **indefinite article** *a* refer to nouns. The definite article indicates something **specific**. The indefinite article indicates something more **general**, for example:

   *Is that **the** frog?* (we are looking for, specifically)　**or**　*Is that **a** frog?* (or is it a toad?)

2) **Numerals** such as *one, two* and *three* (cardinal numbers) and *first, second* etc. (ordinal numbers) are determiners.

3) **Possessive determiners** like *my, your, his, her, its, our* and *their* are **possessive pronouns** used as determiners. They're used before a noun to show **possession**, e.g. **my** *car*, **his** *friend*, **their** *problem*.

4) **Quantifiers** are determiners that show **quantity**, like *few, many* and *enough*.

5) **Demonstrative adjectives**, e.g. *this, that, these*, and *those* are also determiners. They **look the same** as demonstrative pronouns but there is a **significant difference** between them. They refer to specific objects or people that the participants are close to, rather than replacing them like pronouns do:

   *I like **those**　　　　　　**or**　　　　　*I like **those** shoes*
   *(those **replaces** the noun — pronoun)*　　*(those **precedes** the noun — adjective / determiner)*

Prepositions and Conjunctions

Prepositions show Relationships between things

Prepositions show the **relationship** between things in terms of **space**, **time** or **direction**. The preposition usually goes before the determiner and noun.

- *The books are **underneath** the bed* (spatial)
- *She left **before** the end* (time)
- *He moved **towards** the door* (directional)

Sometimes there's no determiner e.g. ➡
- *See you **at** breaktime.*
- *We'll talk more about it **on** Friday.*

Conjunctions are Linking Words

There are **two types** of conjunction — **coordinating** conjunctions and **subordinating** conjunctions.

1) **Coordinating conjunctions** are words like *and*, *but* and *or*. They **connect** single words or longer units of language (phrases and clauses) that have **equal status**:

> Robert **and** Bethany

The **coordinating conjunction** *and* connects the two names — neither is given more importance.

> A white shirt **or** a pink shirt

The **coordinating conjunction** *or* links **two phrases**.

> He kissed her on the cheek **and** she ran away

The coordinating conjunction *and* links two **equal statements**.

2) **Subordinating conjunctions** are words like *since, although, because, unless, whether* and *whereas*. They link a main clause to one that's **less important** to the subject of the sentence:

There's more about clauses on p. 12-13.

> Some people find Maths really difficult, **whereas** others find it easy.

The main clause is *Some people find Maths really difficult*. This is the main point of the sentence. The **subordinating conjunction** *whereas* introduces a less important clause *others find it easy*.

Subordinating conjunctions give **different meanings**. Some, like *after, before* and *until* are to do with **time**. Others, like *where* and *wherever* are about **place**.

1) Conjunctions are an important **cohesive device** — they help a discourse to flow smoothly.
2) A discourse **without** conjunctions seems very **disjointed** — e.g. *Last night I went out. I bumped into my friend Hayley. We talked for a while. She had to leave early. She was babysitting for her auntie.*
3) If you add **conjunctions**, the discourse is much more **fluent** — e.g. *Last night I went out **and** I bumped into my friend Hayley. We talked for a while **but** she had to leave early **because** she was babysitting for her auntie.*

Practice Questions

Q1 What is the function of pronouns?
Q2 What's the difference between the pronouns *we* and *us*?
Q3 Name five types of determiners and give an example of each.
Q4 What do prepositions show? Give an example.
Q5 What are coordinating conjunctions? Give an example.
Q6 What are subordinating conjunctions? Give an example.

If pronouns take the place of nouns, what do protractors do?

Phew, there's lots to learn on these pages, but it's all useful stuff. The problem with all this is there are just so many terms to learn. But I'm afraid you're just going to have to keep reading these pages and testing yourself on them until you're sure you know your numerals from your quantifiers and your possessive pronouns from your demonstrative adjectives. Lucky you.

Phrases and Clauses

Sadly, this isn't a page full of useful phrases for when you go on holiday. So if you need to know how to ask the way to the bus station in Greek, or how to reserve a table in Japanese, I'm afraid you'll have to buy a different book.

Phrases are **Units** of **Language** that have a **Head Word**

Phrases are units of language built around a **head word** that identifies the type of phrase, e.g. in the noun phrase *the empty house*, the noun *house* is the head word. Basic sentences are created from a combination of phrases.

1) The simplest noun phrase (NP) possible is just a **noun itself**.
   It can be accompanied by a **pre-modifier**, a **post-modifier**, or both.

Pre-modifiers come before the noun. They're often a determiner, followed by an adjective.	Pre-modifiers		Head Word	Post-modifiers		Post-modifiers come after the noun.
	determiner	adjective	noun	preposition	noun	
	the	*new*	*mayor*	*of*	*Bradford*	

2) A very simple verb phrase (VP) has **one verb**, but you can also make up a verb phrase from the head word (a main verb) and one or more **auxiliary** verbs.

Auxiliary	Auxiliary	Head Word
should	*have*	*passed*

A **Clause** is a **Unit** of a **Sentence**

1) Sentences are made up of **clauses** — the **simplest meaningful units** of the sentence.

2) A **sentence** can be made up of **one clause** — e.g. *Katherine likes going walking*.

3) Or it can be made up of **more than one** clause. When there's more than one clause in a sentence, the clauses are usually separated by **conjunctions** — e.g. *Katherine likes going walking **but** she doesn't like running*.

4) **Clauses** can be made up of a **subject**, **verb**, **object**, **complement** and **adverbial**.

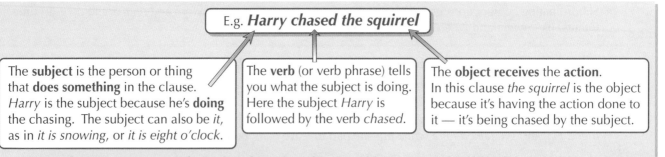

E.g. *Harry chased the squirrel*

The **subject** is the person or thing that **does something** in the clause. *Harry* is the subject because he's **doing** the chasing. The subject can also be *it*, as in *it is snowing*, or *it is eight o'clock*.

The **verb** (or verb phrase) tells you what the subject is doing. Here the subject *Harry* is followed by the verb *chased*.

The **object receives** the **action**. In this clause *the squirrel* is the object because it's having the action done to it — it's being chased by the subject.

A **complement** gives more **information about** the **subject** or **object**. It **completes** the **meaning** of the sentence it appears in, for example:

- In *Harry is a great guitarist*, the noun phrase (NP) *Harry* is the subject. The second NP in the sentence, *a great guitarist* is a **subject complement**. It **completes** the meaning of the sentence by giving information about the subject.

- In *Harry found the film appalling*, *Harry* is still the subject. But the adjective *appalling* refers to *the film*, which is the object, so *appalling* is the **object complement**.

An **adverbial** is a word or group of words that **refers back to the verb**. The simplest adverbial is just an adverb e.g. *Harry kicked the ball **quickly***. In *Harry is playing on Sunday*, the adverbial is *on Sunday* as it relates to the specific time that Harry will play. Adverbials usually describe **time**, **place** or **manner**.

5) The verb, complements and adverbials of a clause or sentence are sometimes also called the **predicate**. The term 'predicate' refers to any part of the clause that is **not the subject**, but that **modifies** it in some way. The verb is sometimes referred to as the **predicator**.

Phrases and Clauses

There are **Seven** Common Types of **Clause**

These are created by **different combinations** of subject (**S**), verb (**V**), object (**O**), complement (**C**) and adverbial (**A**):

S + V	Harry + played
S + V + O	Harry + played + a game
S + V + C	Harry + was + great
S + V + A	Harry + played + on Tuesday
S + V + O + O	Harry + gave + him + a drink
S + V + O + C	Harry + thought + his performance + disappointing
S + V + O + A	Harry + passed + the ball + quickly

Harry + fluorescent trunks + chest wig = one hot look.

Clauses are defined by **Status**

The **status** of a clause depends on its **constituents** and whether it can **stand alone** as a meaningful unit of language.

1) **Main clauses (independent clauses)** can stand alone and still make sense:

> Harry played.

2) **Coordinate clauses** occur in sentences where there are **two or more** independent clauses.
   - They're joined together by a **coordinating conjunction** like *and* or *but*. For example:

   > The band played for two hours **but** I had to leave early.

   - The clauses could **stand alone** and still **make sense** — *The band played for two hours. I had to leave early.*

3) **Subordinate clauses** can't stand alone. They have to be with a **main clause**.
   - A subordinate clause gives **extra information** about the main clause.
   - In most cases, a subordinate clause is led by a **subordinating conjunction** (like *since, although, because, unless, if, whether, while, whereas etc.*). This links it to the main clause. For example:

   main clause ⟹ *Will you pop in to see me **while** you're here tomorrow?* ⟸ subordinate clause (the clause can't stand alone in a meaningful way)

   subordinating conjunction

4) **Combining clauses** — you can combine coordinate and subordinate clauses in the same sentence:

   > He went to London **and** she went to Manchester **because** of a terrible row.

   coordinate clause — coordinating conjunction — coordinate clause — subordinating conjunction — subordinate clause

Practice Questions

Q1 Identify the head word, pre-modifiers and post-modifiers (where applicable) in the following noun phrases:
the gold bracelet   *a cold, frosty morning in spring*   *fish and chips from the shop*

Q2 Identify verb phrases in the following clauses:
Joshua should tell her   *You should have seen it*   *I will be leaving early tomorrow*

Q3 Which is the main clause and which is the subordinate clause in the following sentence?
It was still dark when the travellers rose from their slumbers.

Don't let all this stuff get on top of you... it'd be dead clause-trophobic...

To get the hang of how these phrases and clauses work, practise identifying them — have a look at some articles or listen to the news and see if you can work out how the sentences all fit together. Refer back to these pages if you need to, and just keep going until it's a piece of cake. Mmm cake... Almost as much of a treat as learning about clauses, but not quite.

Sentences

So far you've seen how word classes, phrases and clauses fit together. Now for the big surprise. It turns out that they're all building blocks in sentences — the largest grammatical units. Well who'd have thought it...

Sentences can be anything from very Simple to really Complex

There are **five** types of sentence — **minor**, **simple**, **compound**, **complex** and **compound-complex**.

1) **Minor sentences** are complete and meaningful statements that **don't have** a subject and verb combination. Lots of everyday sayings are minor sentences, e.g. *Be quiet. Goodbye. Sounds good.*

2) A **simple sentence** must have a **subject** and a **verb**. It should express a **complete thought**, e.g. *The snow falls.* *Snow* is the **subject**, *falls* is the **verb**.

3) A **compound sentence** is an independent clause linked to another independent clause by a **coordinating conjunction**. Either one could be a main clause in a different sentence.

independent clause ⟹ *I went to Manchester **and** I went to Liverpool.* ⟸ independent clause

↑ coordinating conjunction

One too many clauses for Mr. Barrett.

4) A **complex sentence** consists of a main clause and a subordinate clause (or subordinating clauses). A **subordinating conjunction** connects the clauses together:

main clause ⟹ *The workers left the building **when** they heard.* ⟸ subordinate clause

↑ subordinating conjunction

5) A **compound-complex sentence** is made up of at least two **coordinate clauses** connected by a **coordinating conjunction**, and **at least one** subordinate clause.

*Some of the children went home early **but** the others remained **because** they had no transport.*

first coordinate clause — coordinating conjunction — second coordinate clause — subordinating conjunction — subordinate clause

The Structure of Sentences tells you about the Target Audience

1) The length and complexity of sentences can be varied according to the **content** and **audience** of a text.
2) A good example of contrasting sentence structures is the difference between **broadsheet** and **tabloid** newspapers.

BROADSHEET NEWSPAPER

The scientific community is under the microscope as it nears hybrid embryo creation.
(Complex sentence: main clause + subordinate clause)

This is a serious ethical issue since it questions the very nature of what it is to be human.
(Complex sentence: main clause + subordinate clause)

The intention to find new ways of treating diseases that have so far proved untreatable is clearly laudable, but the magnitude of the moral issue can't be ignored, as the procedure will involve destroying live embryos after fourteen days.
(Compound-complex sentence: main clause + main clause + subordinate clause)

TABLOID NEWSPAPER

Mad scientists are on the verge of creating monsters.
(Simple sentence)

They will take the sperm and eggs of humans and animals and mix them up.
(Compound sentence: coordinate clause + coordinate clause)

Living embryos will be trashed after fourteen days.
(Simple sentence)

3) The writers create a different **mood** and **tone** depending on the types of sentences they use. They're intended to appeal to different **audiences**.
4) The first example is more complex — it has a **measured** and **serious tone**. The second, relatively simple set of sentences is more **emotive** and **subjective**.

Sentences

You can **Classify Sentences** by their **Function**

Sentences have **four** functions.

1) DECLARATIVES

- **Declarative** sentences are statements that **give information**, e.g. ⟶

> *This summer was the hottest on record.*
> *I don't like cheese.*

2) IMPERATIVES

- **Imperative** sentences **give orders**, **instructions**, **advice** and **directions**.
- They **start** with a **main verb** and **don't** have a **subject**, e.g. ⟶

> **Go** *left and it's first on your right.*
> **Answer** *one question from each section.*

3) INTERROGATIVES

Interrogative sentences ask **questions**.

- Some questions are formed by **inverting** (swapping round) the **verb** and the **subject** of a sentence.

E.g.
> *You are coming out tonight.* ⟶ *Are you coming out tonight?*

Subject   Verb   Main verb   Verb   Subject   Main verb

- Interrogatives can start with **wh- words**, e.g. ⟶

> **Wh**ere are you going?
> **Wh**en will you be back?

- They can also be added to the **end of a statement**. These are called **tag questions**, e.g. ⟶

> *It's cold, **isn't it**?*
> *She said she was on her way, **didn't she**?*

- In **spoken discourse** you can turn **declarative statements** into questions using **stress** and **intonation**. This is called a **rising inflection**, e.g. ⟶

> *He will get better?*

4) EXCLAMATIVES

- **Exclamative** sentences have an **expressive function** — they convey the force of a statement, and end with an **exclamation mark**, e.g. ⟶

> *I will not do this any more!*
> *That was fantastic!*

Practice Questions

Q1   Identify whether the following sentences are minor or simple:
Good afternoon   the doctor is here   the band was late   your turn

Q2   Identify the coordinate clauses and the coordinating conjunction in this compound sentence:
Ravina is going to Delhi but I will stay in Calcutta.

Q3   Identify the main clause, the subordinate clause and the subordinating conjunction in this complex sentence:
I will stay in bed today because I'm not feeling very well.

Q4   In this compound-complex sentence, identify two coordinate clauses and one subordinate clause:
The band played brilliantly and the crowd screamed for more until the lights went out.

<u>Minor sentences — great if you're down 'pit, rubbish if you're in an exam...</u>

Brilliant. That was sentences. Learn this stuff and you'll be OK. It's very important because sentence structure can help identify a target audience. It might seem tedious, but you need to do it, because knowing all this syntax malarkey is useful. Ah, grammar — the most fun you can have in an empty room with no windows, lights, friends or board games.

Morphology

If you were hoping to learn how to make cool figures out of modelling clay, you're about to be disappointed. Morphology is about the internal structure of words — basically, how they're formed and how this can affect their meaning.

Morphemes are the Basic Units that make up words

1) **Morphology** is the study of **word formation**. It looks at how the **form** of a word **changes** because of **grammar**, and how the **meaning** of a word can **change** by adding an **affix** — a **unit** of a word like *un-* or *-ness*.

2) The separate units that make up words are called **morphemes**.

- Simple words are **morphemes** in their own right, such as *man, dog, ignore* and *journey*. They **can't** be **broken down** any further (e.g. *ig+nore*). They're called **free morphemes**, or **base**, **root** or **stem** forms.

- **Bound morphemes** are morphemes that are **not** words on their **own**. They're things like *-ful, -s, -ness* and *-est*, which can be added to **free** morphemes to create words like *thankful, cups, darkness* and *largest*.

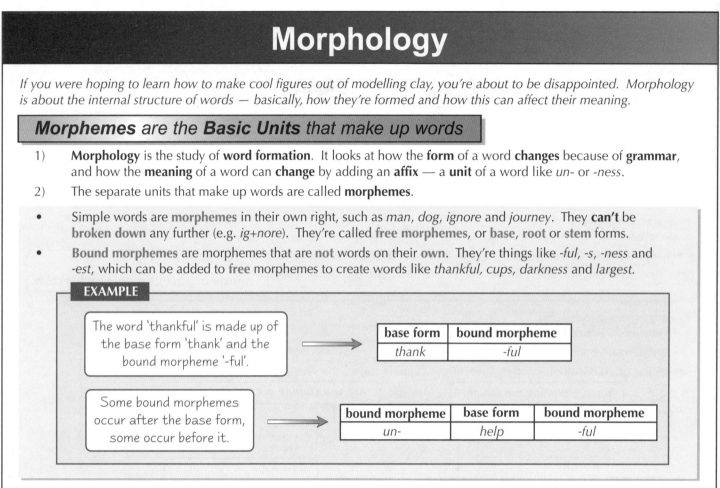

EXAMPLE

The word 'thankful' is made up of the base form 'thank' and the bound morpheme '-ful'.

base form	bound morpheme
thank	*-ful*

Some bound morphemes occur after the base form, some occur before it.

bound morpheme	base form	bound morpheme
un-	*help*	*-ful*

Prefixes can create New Words in the same Word Class

Prefixes are **morphemes** added to the start of a word. They change the **meaning** of nouns, verbs, adjectives and adverbs.

prefix	noun	new word
dis- →	*parity* →	*disparity*

prefix	verb	new word
inter- →	*act* →	*interact*

prefix	adjective	new word
ir- →	*relevant* →	*irrelevant*

prefix	adverb	new word
super- →	*naturally* →	*supernaturally*

Suffixes can change a word's Class and Meaning

Suffixes are morphemes added to the end of a word.

The tables below show how you form different words and word classes by adding **different suffixes** to the **base form**.

1) Base form is a **noun**:

noun	adjective	verb	adverb
type	*typical*	*typify*	*typically*

2) Base form is an **adjective**:

adjective	noun	verb	adverb
legal	*legality*	*legalise*	*legally*

3) Base form is a **verb**:

verb	noun	adjective	adverb
explode	*explosion*	*explosive*	*explosively*

Mixing up words is nowhere near as dangerous as whatever this lady is doing.

Morphology

Adding Morphemes to existing words is called Affixation

Affixes are **bound morphemes** that are added to words. There are **two** kinds of affixation — **inflectional** and **derivational**.

Inflectional affixation

1) **Inflectional affixation** changes the **grammar** of the word — e.g. its **number** or **tense**.

2) Inflectional affixes are always **suffixes** (they go after the base).
   For example, *pushed*. The bound morpheme *-ed* attaches to the verb *push* to change the action from the **present tense** to the **past tense**.

3) Here are some common kinds of inflectional affixation:

Plural -s (also -ies, -oes)	*dogs, ladies, tomatoes*	**Past participle** -ed	*He has recovered*
Possessive -'s	*Bernie's car*	**Present participle** -ing	*He is recovering*
Third person singular -s	*She says*	**Comparative** -er	*Quicker*
Past tense -ed	*He recovered*	**Superlative** -est	*Quickest*

Derivational affixation

1) Derivational affixation has a **semantic function** — it changes the **meaning** of a word.

2) The **noun** *player* is formed by adding the **suffix** *-er* to the **verb** *play*. The word changes from being an **action** to the **performer** of the action.

3) **Prefixes precede** (go before) the **base form**, **suffixes** come at the end — both **change** the meaning of a word:

Prefix	Meaning	Example	Suffix	Meaning	Example
auto-	self	**auto**biography	-archy	leadership	hier**archy**
inter-	between	**inter**active	-less	absence of	shame**less**
un-	not, opposite	**un**necessary	-phobia	fear	claustro**phobia**

Morphology and Coining Words

Coining is the general term for creating words. Many new words are formed through **derivational affixation**. There are **four main ways** that new words are coined:

1) **Clipping** — sometimes prefixes or suffixes are **dropped**. For example, *the gymnasium* is now usually referred to as *the gym*, and you're more likely to say *phone* than *telephone*.

2) **Compounds** — new words are created by **combining** two free morphemes, e.g. *mankind*, *blackbird* and *sleepwalk*.

3) **Back-formation** — this involves a free morpheme that **looks like** it has a suffix, like *editor*, being adapted to create a word like *edit*. **Historically** the word *editor* is a **free morpheme**, but the verb *edit* has been created **from** it. This is also true of *writer* (historically a free morpheme) producing the verb *write*.

4) **Blends** — new words are also created by **fusing** two words into one. These words are referred to as **blends**. For example, *alcoholic* has been fused with *chocolate* to form *chocoholic*, and with *shopping* to form *shopaholic*.

Practice Questions

Q1   Divide the following words into individual morphemes, identifying the base form and the bound morpheme:
     singer   information   atomic   friendly   incomprehensible   brotherhood

Q2   Identify prefixes and suffixes in the following words:
     inconsolable   undemonstrative   inconceivable   antidisestablishmentarianism

Q3   Which of the following words contain inflectional morphemes and which contain derivational ones?
     singing   delightful   unnecessary   smartest

Blending words seems a bit harsh — and a total waste of equipment...

Couldn't you just have a smoothie instead? Anyway — it's too late to worry about that now, because this is the end of section one. By now you should be pretty clued up on the delights of word classes, phrases, clauses and sentences, and how they're all gloriously linked under a big grammatical umbrella. Although it's not very waterproof and it won't keep you dry. Sorry.

Lexis

Not to be confused with the luxury Japanese car firm, lexis is just a fancy word for words. If you're thinking that words is a perfectly good word for words, then you'll be eating your words after you've read these words. No word of a lie.

Lexis means Words

1) **Lexis** is the linguistic term for **vocabulary** — the words of a language.

2) When you're **analysing language**, you'll start by looking at the lexis.

3) It's divided into **word classes** — also called the **parts of speech** (see p.4), e.g. nouns, verbs, adjectives.

4) Lexis can also be analysed in chunks or phrases, known as **lexical phrases**. These are well-known groups of words like *on the other hand* and *once upon a time*. There are hundreds of these phrases and they're used all the time.

English has been Influenced by Other Languages

1) A lot of the most frequently used words in the English vocabulary come from **Old English**. They're mostly **everyday** words like *that, house, on, be, bread*.

2) English developed from Old English with lots of borrowings from **French** and **Latin**.

3) This is one of the reasons why English has lots of **synonyms** (different words for the same thing, see p.21) — some are from one language, some from another.

4) Words with **Latin** origins tend to feel more **formal** than Old English ones — e.g. *chew* comes from Old English, *masticate* comes from Latin.

English is always Changing

1) English is still influenced by other languages. Words that are **borrowed** from other languages are called **loan words** — e.g. *shampoo* from Hindi, *bluff* from Dutch, *schmooze* from Yiddish. They become part of English through contact with other cultures.

2) Words also enter the language through advances in **science** and **technology**, which creates the need for **new words** (**neologisms**) — e.g. *email, genome*.

3) Once a word has entered the language, it can become part of **everyday English** in different ways:

Adding an affix

1) **Suffixes** are put **after** the root or stem of a word. These can alter the meaning of the word they're attached to and change its **word class**.

2) **Common** English suffixes are *–tion, -ness, -ish* and *–able*.

3) When nouns from other languages become part of **everyday English**, the plural is made by adding an -s. For example, the German word *Kindergärten* (meaning *more than one Kindergarten*) becomes *kindergartens* in English.

4) **Prefixes** are put **before** the root or stem of a word. They alter the meaning of the word, often **reversing** the original meaning.

5) Common English **prefixes** include *multi-, dis-, trans-* and *sub-*.

Conversion

1) This is where the **word classes** of existing words are **altered**.

2) For example — *gift* can be a **noun** (*the gift*), but it can also be used as a **verb** (*to gift*).

3) *Empty* is an **adjective**, but it can also be converted to a **verb** (*to empty*).

Creating compound words

1) **Compound words** are created by **joining** two or more words together.

2) For example, *rainbow* joins *rain* and *bow*.

3) The separate words are combined to create a **new meaning**, which is **different** to the meanings of the original words — e.g. *laptop* specifically refers to a computer you could rest on your knees.

Lexis

The **Lexis** people use depends on the **Situation**

Lexis has different **levels** of **formality**.

1) **Informal lexis** is relaxed, familiar and conversational.
2) It's **colloquial** and often **non-standard**, so it will contain **dialect** words and **slang** (see p.34-35 and p.40-41) — e.g. you might describe someone as being *tapped* or a *loony*.
3) It tends to be **smaller** than **formal lexis** and contain more **monosyllabic** words (see p.24) like *nice* and *grub*.
4) It contains lots of **abbreviations** like *can't, you'll* and *would've*.
5) Informal lexis for **ordinary** things often has **Old English** roots — e.g. *house, home*.

1) **Formal lexis** is more serious and impersonal.
2) It tends to be made up of **Standard English** words, so it's unlikely to contain **dialect** words or **slang**, e.g. someone might be described as *mentally ill* or *not in possession of their faculties*.
3) It's bigger and more complex than informal lexis, so there are more **polysyllabic** words (see p.24) like *enjoyable* and *comestibles*.
4) Words are less likely to be **abbreviated** — e.g. *do not* will be used rather than *don't*.
5) Formal lexis often has **Latinate** roots (it comes from Latin) — e.g. *residence, habitation*.

The **Lexis** of **Written** and **Spoken** English is very different

1) As a general rule, **written** language is **more formal** than **spoken** language.
2) The most **informal** language is found in **speech** between friends and family. The most **formal** language is found in **writing** between people who don't know each other — e.g. essays, business letters and broadsheet newspapers.
3) One of the main reasons for this is because **speech** tends to be **spontaneous**, so the lexis is **smaller** and there's lots of **self-correction** — speakers notice their own errors and correct them in mid-sentence.
4) Speech also tends to contain lots of **abbreviations**, like *shan't* and *gonna*. This is even the case with **planned speech**, which can sound strange and stilted if the speaker doesn't abbreviate some words.
5) However, there are situations where **speech** is more **formal** than **writing**. This is especially the case when it's **planned** — e.g. a politician's speech, or in a formal situation like a job interview.
6) Likewise, there are situations where **written language** is informal, e.g. an email between friends.

Practice Questions

Q1 What is lexis?
Q1 Outline how English has been influenced by other languages.
Q3 What is conversion?
Q4 Outline two differences between informal and formal language.

Essay Question

Q1 Outline how English has developed through the influence of different languages, and how it continues to change.

Lexis a nice name — short for Alex you know...

I've got that thing now where I've read the word 'word' so many times that it's started to look ridiculous. Word word word word word. It looks a bit gross somehow, like 'worm'. If this happens to you in the exam you may be forced to replace it with a substitute until the affliction wears off — something neutral like 'gentleman' or 'rice' would probably be best...

Semantics

Another hoity-toity, highfalutin, la-di-da bit of linguistic terminology here, but it's not as tricky as it looks. Semantics just means meaning, so if you've ever understood the meaning of a word then you shouldn't find the idea too difficult to grasp.

Semantics *is the* Study *of* Meaning

Semantics looks at how the **meanings** of words are **constructed** and **interpreted**.

Denotation

1) Denotation is the **straightforward meaning** or **definition** of a word, which you'd find if you looked the word up in a **dictionary**.

2) For example, *red* is *'a primary colour that lies next to orange on the visible spectrum'*. *Cloud* is *'a mass of water or ice particles in the sky'*.

3) It's especially **important** for the denotation of words to be **clear** when people are giving **instructions** and **information**, e.g. in safety notices and scientific documents. Writers have to be careful to **avoid ambiguity** (see below), otherwise people might not understand the meaning properly.

Connotation

1) Connotation refers to the **associations** a word has, or the **emotions** raised by a word.

2) For example, *red* can be associated with love and passion, or with blood and danger. *Cloud* can be associated with fluffiness, blue skies and rainbows, or dreariness and sadness.

3) The **connotations** of words can be **ambiguous**, so **interpretations** can **vary** from person to person.

Implication

1) This is when the meaning is **suggested**, rather than being stated directly.

2) For example, if a child arrives home late from a party, their parents might say *'You're late!'*. Literally, all they're saying is that the child was expected home earlier. But the **implication** behind the words is *'You're in trouble — explain why you're late'.*

Ambiguity

1) This is where a word, phrase or argument can be **understood** or **interpreted** in **more than one way**.

2) For example, *men can't bear children* could mean *men can't give birth to children*, or *men hate children*.

3) Sometimes this is **unintentional**, and a case of the writer not checking carefully. Sometimes it's done **deliberately** to raise questions in the readers' minds.

Structural Semantics *is about the* Relationships *between* Words

Structural semantics looks at the different ways that **words relate** to **each other** through **meaning**.

1) Semantic Fields

1) **Semantic fields** (also called **lexical fields**) are **groups** of words that are **connected** in **meaning**.

2) E.g. the words *classroom*, *teacher*, *assembly*, *lesson* and *homework* are all in the **semantic field** of '**school**'. Although the **meaning** of each word is different, they're all part of the same **framework**.

3) The words (lexis) that make up the semantic field are known as **field-specific lexis**.

Here are some more examples of **semantic fields** and **field-specific lexis**...

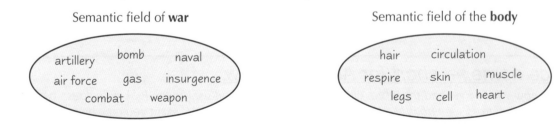

Semantic field of **war**

artillery bomb naval
air force gas insurgence
combat weapon

Semantic field of the **body**

hair circulation
respire skin muscle
legs cell heart

2) Synonyms

1) **Synonyms** are words that have **similar meanings**, e.g. *grub* and *comestibles* are synonyms for *food*.

2) Synonyms can have different **connotations**, so their meaning isn't identical, e.g. *grub* is informal and suggests that the food is quite plain, *comestibles* is more formal and old fashioned. Talking about someone's *children* has different connotations to talking about their *brats*.

3) Using a particular synonym over another can be a **regional variation** (see p.34), e.g. saying *bairn* instead of *child*, or *mardy* instead of *grumpy*.

4) You use different synonyms depending on the **situation**, e.g. in a formal letter you might write about *working*, but in informal speech you might talk about *slogging away*.

It seemed that Max thought 'girlfriend' was a synonym for 'foot rest'.

3) Antonyms

1) **Antonyms** are words with **opposite meanings**.

2) For example — *hot / cold, male / female, day / night, sweet / sour*.

3) Antonym **pairs** are often used together as **comparisons** — e.g. *I'm always tired during the day but I wake up at night*, or *you're blowing hot and cold with me*.

4) They tend to be quite **rigid**, so they don't necessarily work with **other synonyms** — e.g. you wouldn't say *hot / cool, male / feminine, day / evening*.

4) Hypernyms and Hyponyms

This can be a bit confusing at first, but bear with it because it becomes clearer once you've seen some examples:

1) Basically, a **hypernym** is a **general** word. A **hyponym** is **specific** word with a meaning that's **linked** to the hypernym.

2) For example, *school* is a **hypernym**. Words describing more **specific types** of school, such as *primary*, *secondary*, *grammar*, *comprehensive* are **hyponyms**.

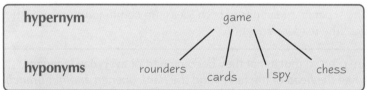

3) Words can be **hypernyms** in one context and **hyponyms** in another, e.g. *fruit* is a **hyponym** of *food*, because it's a **specific type** of food. But it's also a **hypernym** for *melon*, because *melon* is a **specific type** of fruit.

Practice Questions

Q1 Which semantic fields could these words belong to — bed, wine, wicket?

Q2 Explain the difference between a synonym and an antonym.

Q3 Explain the difference between a hypernym and a hyponym.

Essay Question

Q1 Place the word **adult** into each of the categories on these pages, and explain how it fits there.
E.g. its connotations, how it's ambiguous, which semantic fields it fits into, and some synonyms for it.

Relationships between words can be very meaningful...

Lots of technical words to get to grips with here, but it'll look really good if you can use some of them. All this hypernym / hyponym stuff can be a bit of a nightmare, but a handy way of remembering which is which is that hypernym is a longer word, for a bigger, more general thing. I'd like to say that antonyms had something to do with ants, but that would be a lie.

Semantics

You can get your meaning across literally (he's ugly), or you can inject a bit more interest with figurative language (he fell out of the ugly tree and hit every branch on the way down). This kind of language lets writers be a bit more creative.

Figurative Language isn't Literal

Figurative language (or **figures of speech**) **isn't** meant to be taken **literally**.
It's used to add colour to the language, and is classified into **different types**.

Figurative language	Explanation
Similes	1) Similes are comparisons that use the words 'like' or 'as'. 2) For example — *his hair was as white **as** snow, she can swim **like** a fish*. 3) The comparison is always stated **explicitly**, e.g. in the example above, she isn't **actually** a fish, she's just said to be **like** one.
Metaphors	1) Metaphors are comparisons that **don't** use 'like' or 'as'. 2) They describe a person, object or situation as if it actually were something else. 3) For example — *there was a **blanket** of snow on the ground*. The snow isn't actually a blanket, it's just **like** one. Because the comparison is **implicit** it's more **powerful** than a simile. 4) An **extended metaphor** is when the same metaphor is continued throughout a text to create a chain of images — e.g. if the *rain* is referred to as *tears*, then it's also referred to using other words relating to crying, e.g. *weeping, miserable*.
Personification	1) Personification is a type of **metaphor**, where an object or situation is given **human qualities**. 2) For example — *the wind wailed* creates the image of the wind having a mouth and being able to wail like a human.
Metonymy	1) Metonymy is using a **part** of something to describe the **whole** thing. 2) For example — the term *the crown* can be used to mean the *monarchy*, because one of the **attributes** of monarchs is that they wear a crown.
Oxymoron	1) An oxymoron brings two **conflicting ideas** together. 2) E.g. *bittersweet, living death, gentle tyrant*. 3) The separate meanings of both ideas are **combined** to create a new one, and to grab the reader's attention.

1) Some **figurative expressions** are used so much that they become part of **everyday language**, e.g. metaphorical expressions like the **head** of the table, and the bank opened another **branch**.

2) These are known as **dead metaphors**, because they're not seen as comparisons any more, but just expressions in their own right.

3) When a figurative expression is **overused** then it can lose its impact or novelty value and become a **cliché**, e.g. the **similes** *as good as gold* and *as plain as the nose on your face*, and the **metaphors** *it's a piece of cake* and *I'm all ears*.

Jargon is the Specific Language people use at Work

There's loads more about **jargon** on p.42-43 and p.54, so this is just a quick glance at how it fits in with **semantics**.

1) Jargon is **specialist vocabulary** associated with a particular **occupation** or activity.

2) It tends to be more **formal** than everyday language, because it refers to **specific, technical** things.

3) This means it can be **difficult** for **non-specialists** to **understand**.

4) **Existing** words can take on **new meanings** within a specific environment.
For example, online advertisers might talk about *spiders* and *sticky*. These words have completely **different meanings** in the **context** of online advertising — a *spider* is a software program that automatically follows links, a *sticky* website is one that people stay on for longer than usual.

Semantics

Rhetorical Language is designed to Persuade

There are loads of **rhetorical devices** — here are some of the most common ones.

Three-part list

1) This is where three elements are used in a list to give **emphasis** and build to a **climax**.

2) E.g. *blood, sweat and tears* is a list of three **nouns**, *he came, he saw, he conquered* lists three **verbs**.

Repetition

1) **Repetition** is when a word or phrase is repeated for **emphasis**, for **emphasis**.

2) E.g. *it's not good enough, simply not good enough*.

Hyperbole

1) Hyperbole means using **exaggeration** for **effect**, e.g. *I've told you a hundred times*.

2) The **media** use hyperbole to make stories seem more important, interesting or entertaining, e.g. describing a football referee's unfair decision as the *crime of the century*.

Rhetorical questions

1) A rhetorical question doesn't require an **answer**, because it's phrased in a way that **assumes** the answer is obvious.

2) E.g. *how would you like to be in this position?*

Meaning depends on Context

1) Words can have different **meanings**, so readers have to rely on **context** to understand which meaning applies.

2) For example — the word *book*. When it's on its own, it's impossible to know whether it's the **noun** *book*, as in 'printed pages bound in a cover', or the verb *to book*, as in 'to book a hotel room'.

3) Writers sometimes take advantage of **double meanings** to suggest different ideas and make their work more layered. For example, in the sentence *Jonathan was trying*, *trying* could be a **verb**, suggesting that Jonathan was *trying* his hardest, or it could be an **adjective** suggesting that his personality was *trying* (irritating).

Practice Questions

Q1 Outline the difference between similes and metaphors.

Q2 What is the purpose of rhetorical language?

Q3 Why is hyperbole frequently used in the media?

Essay Question

Love's not Time's fool, though rosy lips and cheeks
Within his bending sickle's compass come:
Love alters not with his brief hours and weeks,
But bears it out even to the edge of doom.
If this be error and upon me proved,
I never writ, nor no man ever loved.

Sonnet CXVI, William Shakespeare, 1609

Q1 Analyse the use of figurative and rhetorical language in this extract.

These linguists seem to get up to sem very silly antics...

A good way to remember the difference between a simile and a metaphor is that a simile *says something is* similar *to something else, because it uses 'like' or 'as'. But if you really can't decide which one it is then you can just say that the language is figurative and leave it at that. What a great topic. And to top it all, simile looks a bit like smile — awww...*

Phonology

These seem like a couple of exciting pages. Look at them, all poised like a coiled spring to tell you everything you could ever wish to know about phonology — what the language sounds like. And I know one thing it sounds like — fun...

Phonology and Phonetics are Different

Phonology

1) **Phonology** is the study of the **sound systems** of languages, in particular the **patterns** of sounds.

2) It focuses on **units** of sound, called **phonemes** (see below).

3) Unlike phonetics, in phonology you **don't** look at **differences** of **articulation**, e.g. if someone pronounces *stupid* as *shtupid*, the *s* and *sh* are still classed as the **same phoneme**, because the different pronunciation doesn't create a **different meaning**.

Phonetics

1) **Phonetics** is the study of how speech sounds are **made** and **received**.

2) It covers all **possible sounds** that the human vocal apparatus (vocal chords, tongue, lips, teeth, etc) can make.

3) It focuses on **differences** in **articulation**, e.g. different accents.

Phonemes are Units of Sound

1) The **smallest units** of **sound** are called **phonemes**. There are only about **44** phonemes in English, and combinations of them make up **all** the **possible** words and sounds in the language.

This is the International Phonetic Alphabet (IPA). It's used for writing all the possible phonemes (sounds) that humans can make in any language. Slanting brackets are used to distinguish between phonemes. See p.154-155 for more on this.

2) For example, the word *cat* has **three** phonemes — /k/ (like the *c* in *coat*), /ae/ (like the *a* in *bat*) and /t/ (like the *t* in *toy*). By **changing** one of these phonemes (e.g. /f/ for /k/) you can create a new word, *fat*.

3) The 26 letters of the **alphabet** can express **all** the possible sounds in English, e.g. **pairs** of letters (**digraphs**) like *sh-* and *ch-* can be used to represent **single phonemes**.

4) The study of phonemes is divided into **vowel sounds** and **consonant sounds**.

Vowel Sounds

1) There are about **twenty vowel sounds** in English, even though there are only **five** vowels in the alphabet.

2) E.g. the vowel *a* has a different sound depending on the word in which it appears. In *ape* it sounds different to when it's in *sat*, *care* and *saw*.

3) Vowel sounds are usually in the **centre** of a **syllable**, e.g. *bag*, *coat*.

4) When a vowel sound is spoken, the **vocal tract** is always **open** — the airway is clear and your **vocal chords** rub together to 'voice' the sound. Vowel sounds are made by **altering** the **shape** of the **mouth**. The way vowel sounds are **pronounced varies** in **different** regions. This is how people can tell the difference between accents (see p.34-35).

Consonant Sounds

1) The number of **consonant sounds** in English is close to the **actual** number of **consonants** in the **alphabet**.

2) Consonants are mostly found at the **edges** of **syllables**, e.g. *boys*, *girls*. Sometimes they can appear in **sequences** of three or four consonants **together**, e.g. *string* or *twelfth*.

3) Unlike vowels, they're mostly articulated by **closing** the vocal organs.

4) Some consonants are formed by **vibration** of the vocal cords, e.g. /b/ and /n/. The amount of vibration depends on the **position** of the consonant within the word. At the end of the word, the consonant is less pronounced. Other consonants don't use the vocal cords at all, such as /p/ and /s/.

Words are made up of Syllables

Syllables are a word's **individual units** of pronunciation. They are normally **combinations** of consonants and vowels.

1) The **centre** of a syllable is usually a **vowel sound**, e.g. *bun*, *tyke*.

2) Syllables can have one or more **consonants before** the **vowel**, e.g. *be*, *slow*.

3) Many syllables have one or more consonants **following** the **vowel**, e.g. *ant*.

4) They can also have consonants before **and** following the vowel, e.g. *play*, *read*.

5) **Monosyllabic** words have **one syllable**, e.g. *plate, car*. **Polysyllabic words** have **more than one** syllable, e.g. *amazing* (a-maz-ing), *cryogenic* (cry-o-gen-ic).

Phonology

Words Sound Different when they're Connected

Words are often pronounced **differently** than you'd expect when you see them **written down**.
This is because spoken language **combines** and **runs** sounds together.

Elision is when sounds are **left out**.
1) It happens especially in **rapid speech**, with words that have **clusters** of **consonants** or **syllables**.
2) For example, *library* is usually pronounced *libry*, and *everything* can become *evrythn*.

Assimilation is when sounds that are next to each other become **more alike**.
1) This happens especially in **rapid speech**, because it makes the words **easier** to say quickly.
2) For example, in the word *handbag*, *hand* becomes *ham*, to make it **easier** to **pronounce** with the syllable *bag*.

Liaison is when a **sound** is **inserted between** words or syllables to help them run **together** more smoothly.
1) For example — pronouncing /r/ at the **end of words**. When a word ending with *r* is **followed** by a word that **begins** with a **vowel**, the /r/ is **pronounced**, e.g. *mother ate* sounds like *mother rate*.
2) This is to avoid a gap between the words, known as **hiatus**.
3) Sometimes it's easier to link words with /r/ even if there's no r in the spelling — e.g. *media(r) interest*.

Phonological Frameworks are used to Analyse Sound Patterns

Part of **phonology** involves looking at how sounds can convey **meaning** and **association**.

1) **Rhythm** is very clear in **poetry**. Lines are often **constructed** so that the **stress** falls on **important** words, emphasising their meaning, e.g. *But to go to school in a summer morn, / Oh! it drives all joy away*. **Advertising** also uses rhythm, particularly in **slogans**, to help the audience **remember** the **product**.

2) **Rhyme** is when words have **similar endings**. It's usually associated with poetry and songs, but it's also used in planned speeches and in advertising. The rhyming words in a speech or text always **stand out**, and their meanings are often **linked**.

3) **Alliteration** is where two or more words close to each other **begin** with the **same sound**, e.g. *six sizzling sausages*.

4) **Assonance** is when the **vowel sounds** in the middle of two or more words are similar, e.g. *spoke* and *hope*. When vowel sounds **clash** with each other it's known as **dissonance**.

5) Alliteration and assonance are used in **creative writing** to **emphasise** words and show that the **meaning** is **linked** in some way. They're also used in **persuasive writing** to make phrases catchy and more memorable.

6) **Onomatopoeia** — this is when a word **sounds like** the noise it describes, e.g. *buzz, pop, bang, snap*.

7) Sometimes sounds can appear **symbolic** for other reasons, e.g. **closed vowels** in words like *chip* and *little* can suggest smallness, while **open vowels** in words like *vast* and *grand* can suggest largeness. It's not always the case, but it's worth noting **sound symbolism** like this when you're analysing a text.

Practice Questions

Q1 What is a phoneme? Give examples.
Q2 Give three features of consonants.
Q3 How can pronunciation be affected when words are connected?
Q4 What is the difference between alliteration and assonance?

Essay Question

Q1 How can the techniques of phonetics and phonology be applied in the analysis of a text or speech?

Mobiles, ringtones, texting — this phonology lark is pretty easy...

Apparently when phones were first invented, Alexander Graham Bell thought the best thing to say when you picked up was 'ahoy hoy'. But his rival Thomas Edison didn't like this so he used 'hello' instead, and that's what stuck. I reckon it's about time 'ahoy hoy' made a comeback — remember it next time you answer the phone, and make a poor dead inventor happy.

Cohesion

Cohesion is about connections. Different ideas in a text need to be linked together, otherwise it won't make sense as a whole and you may as well have just smeared some alphabet spaghetti onto the page and claimed it was a short story...

Cohesion *refers to the* Structure *of a Text*

1) Cohesion **links ideas** in different parts of a text together.

2) Sometimes texts don't need to be particularly **cohesive** because they rely on **prior knowledge**. In this case the reader is expected to **fill in the gaps**, e.g. *The winter was one of the wettest on record. York was bracing itself.* These sentences don't appear to be connected — they rely on the reader to make a **link** between them. For them to make sense, the reader would have to know that heavy rain often causes flooding, which York is very prone to.

3) Generally, though, if a text isn't cohesive then it won't **make sense**. Cohesion is especially important in texts containing **complex arguments** or **development** of ideas.

4) Spoken language is also **cohesive**. See p.64 for how ideas are linked in prepared and spontaneous speech.

Grammatical Cohesion *is about* Linking Sentences

There are **five** main types of **grammatical cohesion**.

Reference

1) This involves **third person pronouns** (*he, she, it, they*) and **demonstrative pronouns** (*this, that*).

2) An **anaphoric reference** refers **back** to something that has already been mentioned, e.g.

- *My grandmother went to university.* ***She*** *wanted to be a teacher.*
  The word *she* is the cohesive link between these sentences, because it refers back to the *grandmother*.

- *He just couldn't stand ducks.* ***That*** *was the big problem.*
  Here, the cohesive word *that* refers back not to just one word, but the whole previous sentence.

3) References **forward** to something in the **future** are called **cataphoric references**, e.g.

- *The goat gave* ***the following*** *reasons for its decision.*
  The sentence refers to something that has not actually been said yet, and will follow in the next sentences.

4) Reference to something **outside** the text is called an **exophoric reference**. The demonstrative pronouns refer to something in the **immediate**, **present context** of the utterance e.g. *that* tree over *there* (see p.10).

Identification

1) This is when **determiners** like *the, this* and *that* are used to show that a **noun** has already been mentioned, e.g.

- *A large lorry blocked the road.*
  The *lorry had broken down.*

2) The **indefinite article** *a* is used the first time the lorry is mentioned. After that the **definite article** *the* is used to show that the clause is referring to the same noun.

Ellipsis

1) This is where words are **left out** of a sentence.

2) It's still cohesive if the **earlier** part of the text enables the reader to **supply** the **missing information**, e.g.

- *His jeans were stained, his jacket was ripped and blood dripped down his face. What a state.*

3) The information given in the first sentence allows the reader to understand the second **incomplete** sentence: *What a state (he was in).*

Conjunctions

1) Conjunctions are words that **connect** different words, phrases and clauses, e.g. *and, because, then, although.*

2) They can be used to **link together** parts of a text and show the **relationship** between them, e.g.

- *They'd been promised roast chicken* ***and*** *they were looking forward to it,* ***but*** *they were sadly disappointed.*

3) The conjunction *and* connects the second clause with the first clause — it shows that what they were *looking forward to* was *roast chicken*. The conjunction *but* qualifies what was said in the previous clause.

Adverbs

These connect clauses by referencing **space** and **time**, e.g.

- *We're leaving London* ***tomorrow*** *morning,* ***before*** *the traffic gets bad.*

Cohesion

Lexical Cohesion *is about* Linking Words

Lexical cohesion links words through **meaning** and **association**, rather than through **grammatical structure**:

Repetition

1) Using the **same word** more than once can link separate sentences, e.g.

   *All we could see was **rain**. Anything would have been better than **rain**.*

2) Ideas can also be linked by using **synonyms** (see p.21) rather than exactly the same word, e.g.

   *He **wandered** slowly towards the building, then **ambled** down the corridor before **loitering** outside the door.*

3) This connects different events in the text, but ensures that there's still **variety**.

Collocation

1) Words that commonly appear together in lexical units are called **collocations**.

2) All **native speakers** of English understand its collocations easily, but non-native speakers might find them a bit bizarre. They are related by **association** rather than through any grammatically based rule.

3) Some words produce predictable collocations — you know what word will follow to complete a phrase because the collocation is so **familiar**, e.g. *neat and tidy*.

4) Collocations like this can't be **rearranged** — you'd always say *neat and tidy* rather than *tidy and neat*.

5) Collocations become well known phrases that are seen as **normal** and **acceptable**, e.g. it's perfectly normal to say *fast asleep*, but not *fast awake*, and *wide awake*, but not *wide asleep*.

6) Some words collocate more **broadly** but can still cause confusion for foreign speakers, e.g. the **verbs** that accompany certain phrases — you *make a mistake* rather than *perform* or *do* one.

7) Collocations aren't usually linked together by **meaning** — only by **familiar association**. You can be *green with envy*, but there's nothing green about envy.

8) Collocations are cohesive because they're **recognisable patterns** to the reader. If a word is paired with one that it doesn't collocate with then the **cohesion** and **fluency** of the statement is lost, e.g. you'd have to **stop and think** about the phrase *diamond clear* if you came across it in a text, because the collocation *crystal clear* is much more familiar.

Layout *and* Presentation *can make a text* Cohesive

This is a nice easy one to finish with...

1) **Graphological cohesion** is about making a text **look** cohesive.

2) It's particularly important in writing that's designed to be **persuasive**, e.g. adverts. The aim is to draw the reader's eye to the most important points, and make sure that the text looks **consistent** as a **whole**.

3) This is usually achieved by using the same **typeface** for running text, captions and headings, and by using a cohesive **colour scheme**.

Practice Questions

Q1 List five types of grammatical cohesion.

Q2 Explain how repetition has a cohesive effect on a text.

Q3 Explain what collocation is.

Essay Question

Q1 Find a newspaper and look at the front page. How has cohesion contributed to the meaning of the text?

I'm feeling strangely attracted to this page — must be the links effect...

This cohesion stuff is quite simple really, and these pages are a nice reminder of what to do in your essays too — if they don't have cohesion then they won't make any macaroni sense as a whole cheese. And nobody wants shoes like that he laughed. That might well be the case but there's no need to go on about it now. Good. Glad we've sorted those badgers out.

Pragmatics

It'd be a lot easier if everyone just said what they meant. Although not much fun if it turned out that what everyone meant to say was that they think you smell and they hate your shoes. That's kind of what pragmatics is about.

Pragmatics *is about how* Language *is used in* Social Situations

Pragmatics is the study of the part that language plays in **social situations**.

1) The meaning of what people say **isn't** always as **clear-cut** as it might seem.

2) There are lots of **unwritten social rules** that **prevent** people saying certain things,
   e.g. you probably wouldn't ask the Queen to '*put the kettle on, love*'.

3) There are also social conventions that make people say things in particular situations,
   e.g. saying *thank you* when somebody gives you something.

4) Pragmatics looks at **how** people get their **meaning** across within different **social contexts**.
   People often have to **imply** meanings rather than state them **directly**, so pragmatics concentrates
   on the meaning **behind** what's actually being said — the **subtext**.

5) It's good to point out when speakers don't address each other as you might **expect** them to,
   e.g. if family members address each other formally then it might suggest they don't get on and
   feel uncomfortable around each other.

Prosody *is the* Non-Verbal Aspects *of* Speech

Prosody is about **how** you say things, rather than what you say.
These **non-verbal aspects** of **speech** help **communicate** attitudes and meaning.

'Non-verbal aspects of speech' just means all the aspects of speech that aren't words.

1) **Pitch** — the **level** of the voice is most noticeable if it's particularly **high** or **low**. People might speak with a low pitch if they're relaxed, or depressed. They might speak in a high pitched voice if they're excited or frightened.

2) **Volume** — loudness can show **excitement** or **anger**. **Confident** speakers tend to speak more **loudly** than **nervous** speakers. Speaking quietly can also be a politeness strategy.

3) **Pace** — the **speed** of speaking is another example of non-verbal communication. Slow, controlled speech conveys a sense of calm and authority. Rapid speech can suggest excitement or panic.

4) **Pauses** — pauses can often be **awkward** in conversations, so people often try to fill them. They can show that speakers are **thinking** about what they say, or are **unsure** of themselves.

5) **Intonation** — the same words can mean different things depending on how you say them, so **variation** in **tone** is important for getting the right meaning across. E.g. you could say something angrily or sarcastically.

6) **Stress** — each word or phrase has a pattern of **stressed** and **unstressed syllables**. This is called **natural stress**. **Changing** the way these words are usually stressed can **change** the **meaning** — **emphatic stress**.

7) **Rhythm** — this is similar to **stress**. Prepared speech often has a more strict rhythmic pattern of **stressed** and **unstressed** syllables than spontaneous speech. This is especially true if the speech has a **persuasive** purpose.

Prosody *can* Change *the* Meaning

1) The way that something is said can completely change its meaning,
   so looking at **prosodic features** is really important in **pragmatics**.

2) E.g. there are loads of ways of saying this sentence that would **change** its **meaning**:

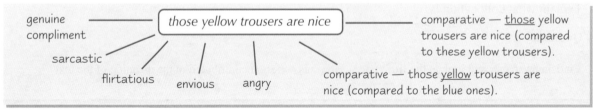

3) It can be really **difficult** to convey **prosodic features** in **writing**. Writers sometimes use **bolding**, underlining or *italics* to show where the emphasis should be. In fiction, they often have to **explain** how a character says something, e.g. *He answered quickly and angrily.*

Pragmatics

Politeness Strategies ensure speakers Don't Cause Offence

1) There are lots of **different ways** to communicate an idea. The way you do it depends on the **situation** — where you are and who you're with.

2) You might need to be **tactful** and **diplomatic**, or very **forceful**.

3) People use different **politeness strategies** depending on how they want to come across, even if the **underlying meaning** is still the **same**.

4) Here are some of the possible strategies for saying *no* in response to the question *would you like to go and see a film tonight?*:

No one knew how to tell Liz that the all-in-one body stocking wasn't a good look.

Politeness Strategy	Example
Definite with negative word (e.g. *no, not, never*)	*No / no way / not a chance.* This sort of direct response would normally just be used with friends or family, because it's generally thought to be a bit rude.
Definite without negative word	*Are you serious? / I'd rather die.* These could be used for humorous effect, or if you really didn't care about being offensive.
Excuse	*I'd love to but I'm busy / Tonight isn't a very good night.* Excuses are used to justify why the answer is no.
Evasive	*Can we talk about this later / Now's just not a good time.* Evasive responses are used to avoid having to say no.
Apologetic	*Sorry... / I'm afraid...* People often apologise when they're saying no to soften their negative response.
Inarticulate	*Erm / Ah / Hmm* This usually shows that the person feels awkward and is trying to think of an excuse or a way to say no politely. If they stall for long enough, the meaning will become clear anyway.

5) People often use **more than one** politeness strategy in their response, e.g. if they were saying no, they might say *erm sorry no I can't tonight, I'm really busy.*

6) Politeness strategies also act as **conventions** for what to say in certain situations, e.g. it's normal in the UK to hear shop assistants and customers saying *thank you* to **each other** when a transaction is carried out at a till. Some politeness strategies like this are used **more** in the **UK** than in other countries.

7) Sometimes following the rules of politeness can lead to strategies being used in **strange ways**, e.g. people often say *sorry* when someone else bumps into them in the street.

Practice Questions

Q1 How do social conventions affect the way we speak?

Q2 Describe how prosody can affect meaning.

Q3 Name and describe the six politeness strategies you could use to turn down an invitation.

Essay Question

Q1 Explain how and why people alter the language they use depending on the social situation they're in.

Pragmatics — make sure you Czech your meaning...

This stuff can sound quite obvious, but until you start learning about all these social rules you often don't notice how weird they are. There's no actual law against going up to a stranger, giving them a hug and telling them how much you've missed them, but most people don't do it. It's a shame really — you never know, you might end up making a lovely new friend.

Graphology

Graphology is about what pages look like, and how things like the layout can help get the meaning of the text across. It's a lovely little topic, cos it gives you the chance to talk about pretty doodles and colours and borders.

Layout and Presentation can Emphasise Meaning

1) Text and images can be placed **next to** each other in **effective** ways. This is called **juxtaposition**. For example, **newspapers** might place **similar** stories next to each other on the page. They might also put **adverts** next to stories that they **correspond** with, e.g. an advert for an airline next to an article about holiday destinations.

2) If the **text** is **broken up** with **borders** or **boxes** then it's designed to draw the reader's **attention** to a particular section. It also makes the text seem more **appealing**. **Colour** and **graphics** can have the same effect.

3) It's good to mention whether the layout fits in with the **form**, e.g. you'd expect a newspaper article to have a bold heading and text set out in columns. Sometimes texts adopt the conventions of **different forms** for **effect**, e.g. a newspaper article might be set out like a letter or a diary.

Typeface is often called Font

This is a bit of a confusing one — until everyone started using computers, **typeface** and **font** were seen as completely **different** things.

1) **Typeface** was things like Arial and Times New Roman, and **font** just referred to the size of the text and whether it was **bold** or *italic*.

2) But now the terms tend to be used **interchangeably**, and most people would call these **different fonts** ~~not~~ ~~different~~ typefaces.

3) When you're talking about the style of the lettering in the exam, it's probably best to stick to saying **typeface**.

Magda had never seen such a gorgeous typeface.

There are some general things to look out for:

Ascenders and Descenders
- These are the '**stems**' of letters.
- The bits that extend **upwards** are the **ascenders**, on letters like 'd', 'h' and 'l'.
- The bits that extend **downwards** are **descenders**, on letters like 'j', 'q' and 'y'.
- **Long** ascenders and descenders could be used to indicate **sophistication** or **elegance**.

Leading
- This is the amount of **vertical space** between **lines** of type.
- It can affect whether the text is dense and difficult to read, or very spaced out.

Serif
- These are small **strokes** on the **ends** of letters.
- Typefaces that don't include them are called *sans serif* (**without serifs**).
- Typefaces with serifs tend to seem **traditional**, while *sans serif* typefaces are considered more **modern**.

A — serif

A — sans serif

Typeface is used to create Different Effects

In any text the **typeface** has been chosen for a particular **reason**, so you need to consider the **effect** it has.

1) The choice of **typeface** tells you about the **tone** of the text. Typefaces can seem traditional, informal, youthful, elegant, etc. They can be can be made to look like handwriting, for example.

2) Bold, italics and underlining can place **emphasis** on certain parts of the text to show that it's **important**.

3) The use of **upper** and **lower case** letters can also be significant. Words can be **capitalised** to draw attention to them. Sometimes the typeface is all **lower case**, which can appear **stylish**, **modern** or **experimental**.

Graphology

Graphemes are Units in a Writing System

1) **Graphemes** are the **smallest units** that can create **contrasts** in **meaning**, e.g. letters of the alphabet like <f> and <e>, and symbols like <,> and <&>.

2) For linguistic analysis they're usually written in **angle brackets** — e.g. <m>, <?>.

3) They can appear in loads of **different** forms, depending on things like **typeface** and **handwriting style**, e.g. <a> can be written as A *A* **a** *a* etc.

4) A different form of a grapheme is called a **glyph**. When **different glyphs** can be used for the **same grapheme**, e.g. A *A* **a** *a* for the grapheme <a>, then they're called **allographs**.

5) Most **graphemes** don't mean anything on their own — their role is to **combine** and **contrast**.

6) However, some **graphemes** can be **interpreted** in **more than one way**, so the **context** they're used in is important:

For example, <*x*> has many uses — it can mean:

> **EXAMPLE:**
> - A **kiss** at the end of a letter.
> - An **incorrect answer**.
> - For **adults only** — X-rated.
> - 'Illiterate' when it's used on a form in place of someone's name.
> - 'Location' — X marks the spot.
> - An indication of **choice**, e.g. when a **ballot paper** is marked with an x.

Graphics can Convey Meaning

1) Graphics can be cartoons, illustrations, tables, photographs and diagrams.

2) Graphics can **break up** the layout of **dense text**, making it more accessible and less formal.

3) They're usually **visual representations** of the text, which help to **illustrate** and **develop** its meaning.

4) They might have the simple **function** of making the meaning **clearer**. This is especially true of **instructional texts** which often use diagrams, and **children's texts**, which might be illustrated to help children learn to read.

5) They could also be used to set the **tone** of a piece, e.g. a cartoon might be used to add humour.

6) Sometimes a graphic will be a deliberate **contrast** to the text, e.g. in a parody or satirical piece of writing.

Don't dwell on graphics for too long — make sure you talk about language by linking your analysis to the text.

Practice Questions

Q1 Give four effects that using different typefaces can create.

Q2 What is a grapheme?

Q3 What function can graphics have in a text?

Essay Question

Q1 Look at two different newspapers, one tabloid and one broadsheet. Analyse the effect of graphological features like typeface and graphics, and the relationship they have with the text.

This is a nightmare — I can barely remember how to draw a bar chart...

It's one of those cruel ironies — you can harp on all you like about how colours and borders can help emphasise meaning, and how a picture paints a thousand words, but the minute you choose to answer your exam in cartoon form, or perhaps create a little flip book in the corners to help get your point across, suddenly everyone changes their tune...

SECTION TWO — LANGUAGE FRAMEWORKS — MEANING

Register

A couple of quite straightforward pages to end this section with. It's really all stuff that you already know just from being aware of different types of language, and generally being alive. So go forth and state the obvious...

Register *is the* Type *of* Language *used in different* Situations

Registers are the different **varieties** of language used in different **situations**. Deciding which register is **appropriate** to use depends on several factors.

Audience
- This is to do with the **relationship** between the speaker or writer and the audience.
- For example, if the speaker or writer knows the audience personally, the **register** they use will usually be quite **informal**. It might include informal lexis, like slang and abbreviations.
- This may be more apparent in informal speech than in informal writing.

Purpose
- For example, a **report** will use a **formal register**, as its **purpose** is to convey information accurately.
- When the purpose is more **persuasive**, e.g. an advert, the register will often be more **informal** as the text needs to get the audience's attention in order to persuade them.

Field
- This is the subject being talked about.
- For example, if the topic is **football**, the **lexis** will include words linked to football, like *match, penalty*, etc.
- Some fields have a large specialist lexicon (stock of words), like **biochemistry**. Most workplaces have their own lexicon connected solely with that field, from car repair shops to hospitals.

Form
- For example, business letters will be written in a **formal register**.
- Text messages, on the other hand, tend to use a more **informal register**.

> Whether the register is **appropriate** depends on the **context** it's used in — using an **informal register** in a **formal situation** is **inappropriate** because it could seem **disrespectful** or **rude**. Using **formal language** in an **informal situation** could sound **unfriendly** and **stuffy**.

Registers Vary *in terms of* Lexis, Grammar *and* Phonology

Different **registers** use different **lexis** and **grammar**, and the way they're **pronounced** can **vary** too. For example:

Lexis
- A conversation between two **specialists** would contain **technical vocabulary** that they would both understand.
- For example, the lexis in the registers used by **mechanical** and **medical** specialists would be very different.

Grammar
- **Register** can affect syntax — the **structure** of clauses and **complexity** of sentences.
- Some registers even have grammatical constructions that are **specific** to them, like the legal register (known as **legalese**), which uses lots of clauses and mainly passive sentences.

Phonology
- This is to do with how the words in a particular **register** are **pronounced**.
- The **informal register** people use when speaking to friends often involves things like dropping the <h> from words like *have* and missing a <g> off words with the *ing* suffix, like *thinking*.
- Generally speaking, the more **formal** a situation is the more likely people are to **modify** their **accent** so it's closer to **Received Pronunciation** (see p. 37).

Modes

Modes can be Written or Spoken

Written modes

1) Written modes include letters, essays, novels, recipes and reports. Written modes tend to be the **most formal**.

2) In written modes the words have to make the **meaning** clear, because there's no opportunity for **non-verbal communication** between the writer and the reader.

3) Sometimes writers try to convey **prosodic features** like tone, intonation and pitch to make the meaning clearer, using **features** like *italicising*, underlining, CAPITALISATION, and **punctuation** like exclamation marks.

Spoken modes

1) Spoken modes are things like interviews, broadcasts and presentations. Spontaneous speech (like a conversation between friends) is normally the **least formal** mode.

2) In **spoken modes** speakers can rely on **non-verbal communication** like gestures and **prosodic features** to get their point across.

3) The grammar of informal speech is often **disjointed** — it contains lots of **interruption** and **incomplete sentences**. It also contains **non-fluency features** (things that interrupt the flow of speech) like **self-correction**, **pauses**, **repetition**, **fillers** (*you know, sort of, I mean*) and **false starts**.

4) Speech also tends to contain **phatic expressions** (small talk expressions that have a **social function**, so their meaning isn't particularly important, like *hello* and *how's things?*).

Multi-Modal Texts contain Features of both Speech and Writing

Lots of texts are a **mixture** of **spoken** and **written** modes, especially electronic texts like **emails** and **text messages**.

1) These are **written modes** that can contain elements of **spoken language**, e.g. **phatic communication** like *hello* and *bye*.

2) Very **informal** emails or messages between friends contain **phonetic spellings**, like *b4* for *before*, and *u* for *you*.

3) **Formal** business emails still tend to be **less formal** than **letters** — they tend not to use **conventions** like writing the sender's address at the top. **Paragraphs** and **sentences** tend to be **shorter**.

Modes can be Classified in Different ways

Different modes can be **grouped** according to the following **approaches**:

1) **Continuum classification** — position on a **scale** that places written Standard English at one end and spoken informal speech at the other. In the middle are multi-modal texts like email.

2) **Typology** — grouping together genres that have **characteristics** or **traits** in common, e.g. sports commentaries, music reviews, formal interviews, novels, poems, etc.

3) **The dimensions approach** — looking at different aspects of modes, e.g. lexis, grammar and structure to analyse the level of formality in a certain text.

Practice Questions

Q1 What impact can audience have on register?

Q2 Outline how registers can vary in terms of lexis and grammar.

Q3 Outline four typical features of spoken modes.

Q4 Classify these three types of language by placing them on a continuum from least formal to most formal: text message to family member, business letter, transcript of a conversation between a teacher and a pupil.

Stod moding and ged od wid id...

When I was at primary school, we all thought it was a real treat if we were allowed to go and collect the class register from the office. Weird. Anyway, once you're sure you know everything on these pages, that's the end of the section. So you can give yourself a pat on the back, take a deep breath, and then you're ready to move on to the next section.

Accent and Dialect

English isn't just spoken or written in one way — imagine how boring that would be. Instead, there are loads of different varieties. These pages are all about dialect and accent — basically, what you say and how you say it...

Accents are Variations in Pronunciation

1) **English** words can be **pronounced** in different ways. The different **patterns** of pronunciation are called **accents**.

2) Accents can be affected by the speaker's **regional** or **social** background.

3) An accent can be a feature of a dialect. But it's **different** to **dialect** because it just refers to **how** you say words, not the words themselves.

> You need to consider accents when you look at the phonology of spoken language (see p.24-25).

> 1) Pronunciation and intonation can vary over **large geographic areas** like countries, e.g. the difference between American, Australian and English.
>
> 2) In **England**, most people can tell the difference between **northern accents** and **southern accents**. The main differences are between **vowel sounds**, e.g.
>   Someone with a **northern accent** would say *path* with a short vowel sound, to sound like *cat*.
>   Someone with a **southern accent** would say *parth*, with a long vowel sound.
>
> 3) Sometimes people that live near each other can tune in to **smaller** differences in each other's accents, to the point where you can often tell if someone's from your town or one a few miles away.

Dialects are Variations in Language

1) A **dialect** is a **variation** in a language, with its own distinctive features of **vocabulary**, **grammar** and **pronunciation**. It's different to **accent** because it refers to the **specific words** you use, not just **how** you **say** them.

2) The term **dialect** is usually used to describe language that's particular to a specific **geographical region**.

3) It's also sometimes used as a **general** term for variations in language that are the result of **social background** (**sociolect** — see p.38) or **personal differences** (**idiolect** — see p.39).

> ### Vocabulary
> Different dialects have different words for things, e.g.
> > - Someone from Yorkshire might say *anyroad* for *anyway*.
> > - People in Lancashire might call a *bread roll* a *barm*.
> > - In the West Country *acker* means *friend*.
> > - In East Anglia to *mardle* is to *gossip*.

> ### Grammar
> The way that people form sentences can depend on their dialect. Regional dialects often contain **non-standard** grammar (see p.36), e.g.
> > - *them* as a demonstrative adjective — *look at **them** books*
> > - Double negatives — *we **don't** want **none***
> > - Missing plurals — *it costs four **pound***
> > - Missing the *-ly* suffix off the end of adverbs — *I walked **slow***
>
> Some grammatical variations are **specific** to a **particular** dialect, e.g. people from **Yorkshire** might miss out the definite article *the*, so they might say *I cleaned car* rather than *I cleaned **the** car*. The **Scouse** dialect has *youse* as the plural of *you* — e.g. *what are youse doing*?

> ### Pronunciation
> 1) Most regional dialects have an **accent** to go with them. So you'd probably expect a **Geordie** (someone from Newcastle) to say the word *town* like *toon*, or someone from **Cornwall** to pronounce the *r* in *water*.
>
> 2) But don't forget — accents are just **one feature** of a dialect. You can use words and constructions from one dialect but speak in the accent of another.

Accent and Dialect

People Have Different Attitudes towards Accents and Dialects

People sometimes make assumptions about others based on the variety of English they use, e.g. people from the **north** of England often think that people with **southern accents** sound 'posh'.

1) **Workman (2008)** studied people's **perceptions** of different **accents**. Participants listened to recordings of different accents while they looked at photos of people.

2) It was found that participants rated the **intelligence** of the people in the photos differently, depending on which accent they thought they had.

3) **Yorkshire** accents were rated as sounding the **most intelligent**. When a recording of a **Birmingham** accent was played, the people in the photo were rated as being much **less intelligent**. Obviously this **isn't** actually **true**, but it shows how strong the **stereotypes** about different accents can be.

Someone's **accent** or **dialect** is often a good indication of **where they're from**. But it can also provide clues about their **social background** and **education**.

1) **Standard English** (p.36) is a **social dialect**. It's usually associated with **educated**, **middle** and **upper class** people. It's the way that you're taught to use English at school, and the language of **formal speech** and **writing**.

2) Some people **assume** that people who use **regional dialects** are **less well educated**, or **lower class**.

3) On the other hand, **regional varieties** of English are often associated with being **down-to-earth** and **modest**, e.g. there are now lots of TV presenters with regional accents, because their accents are seen as being more **accessible** to audiences (see p.37).

You need to look at Written Language as well

Dialect and accent don't just apply to **spoken language**.

1) **Transcripts** of speech can show features of **regional dialects**. Look out for dialect words and grammatical constructions, e.g. *we **seen** her yesterday with her **bairns***.

2) **Literary texts** can contain representations of **accents** as well as **dialects**. The author has included these features for a reason — the way characters speak **reflects** something about them. For example, in *Oliver Twist* by **Charles Dickens**, the Artful Dodger says to Oliver *"I've got to be in London to-night; and I know a **'spectable** old **genelman** as lives there, **wot'll** give you lodgings for **nothink**"*. These features imply things about the character, e.g. that he's from London and he's lower class.

3) Some literary texts are written **entirely** in a **regional dialect**, rather than **Standard English**. This is called **dialect literature**. Authors do this for different reasons, e.g. to make the story seem more **authentic** and **realistic**, or to make a statement about attitudes towards regional varieties of English.

Practice Questions

Q1 What is the difference between accent and dialect?

Q2 Give two examples of how regional dialects can vary from Standard English.

Q3 Outline some of the different attitudes that people sometimes have towards regional accents and dialects.

Essay Question

"I mean as 'appen Ah can find anuther pleece as'll du for rearin' th' pheasants. If yo' want ter be 'ere, yo'll non want me messin' abaht a' t' time."

She looked at him, getting his meaning through the fog of the dialect.

"Why don't you speak ordinary English?" she said coldly.

"Me! — Ah thowt it *wor'* ordinary."

From *Lady Chatterley's Lover*, by DH Lawrence

Q1 Identify some features of regional dialect, and explain what the author is suggesting about attitudes towards them.

Ain't naw use twinin bout revision — quit yer mitherin and gerronwi'it...

It's best to think of English like a family-sized variety pack of crisps, full of different flavours. Scouse and Onion, Salt and Lancashire, Prawn Cockneytail (that's a good one) — they're all here for you to crunch loudly in your dad's ear while he's trying to watch the news. Yes, with its tasty potato-based dialects and crinkle-cut accents, English really is the king of snacks...

Standard English and RP

By now you've probably realised that there are loads of different varieties of English. So many, in fact, that it's a wonder people can understand each other. But they can, and it's down to a little thing called standardisation...

Standard English is a Social Dialect

Standard English is a dialect of English. It has distinctive features of **vocabulary**, **grammar** and **spelling**.

1) A **standard** form of a language is one that is considered to be **acceptable** or correct by **educated** speakers.

2) In **medieval England** people in different parts of the country spoke very different **dialects**. They were so varied that people from different regions would have had **difficulty understanding** each other.

3) The **Standard English** used today started off as the **regional dialect** of the East Midlands. Its influence spread around the country, and it became the dialect that was used in print.

4) As more books were printed, **variations** in **spelling** and **grammar** were ironed out — the language started to conform towards a **standard**.

5) People began to **codify** the language (decide how to write it) in **dictionaries** and books of **grammar rules**. For example, Johnson's dictionary, printed in 1755, aimed to standardise spellings and word meanings.

6) The standard form of the language became associated with **education**, **class** and **power**.

> It's difficult to give examples of **Standard English** as a dialect, because it's what other dialects are usually compared with. As a general example though, this book is written in Standard English, as it contains mostly **standardised vocabulary**, **spellings** and **syntax**.

Standard English is used in Lots of Situations

Standard English is the most widely understood version of English, so it's used in lots of different fields:

1) **Education** — Standard English is the variety of English taught in schools, and it's what people are taught when they learn English as a foreign language.

2) **Media** — it's used in newspapers and by newsreaders on the TV.

3) **Formal documents** — it's the language used in essays, business letters and reports.

4) **Formal speech** — you'd expect people to speak using Standard English in formal situations like business negotiations and public announcements.

People have Different Attitudes towards Standard English

1) As one variety of the language became standardised, other varieties became seen as **less prestigious**.

2) **Regional dialects** were associated with the **uneducated** and the **lower classes**, so it was seen as important to be able to use English '**properly**' if you wanted to be successful.

> **Standard English** is often seen as the '**correct**' or '**pure**' form of the language. Other varieties are sometimes thought to be '**corruptions**' of it. There's a view that if you use another dialect, you're not using English '**properly**'.

> However, most **linguists** argue that all varieties of English should be **valued equally**. There's **no reason** why Standard English should be seen as better than any other dialect. They claim that people shouldn't be thought of as **uneducated** or **lower class** if they **don't** use Standard English.

Received Pronunciation (RP) is a Social Accent

1) **Received Pronunciation** is an **accent**, traditionally associated with **educated** people and the **upper classes**.

2) This means it's **different** from other accents, which normally indicate which **region** the speaker's from.

3) Traditionally **RP** and **Standard English** are linked — the most **prestigious** way of speaking would be Standard English using RP. While lots of people speak Standard English (or something close) with regional accents, you don't generally hear people saying dialect words and phrases in RP.

4) The most recognisable examples of RP are how the **Queen** speaks, and the traditional speech of **BBC presenters**. Because of this, people sometimes refer to RP as the **Queen's English**, or **BBC English**.

5) Because RP has been seen as the standard, accepted way of speaking English, it's the accent many people are taught to use when they learn English as a **foreign language**.

Emma had just received some very juicy pronunciation.

> **Some features of RP**
> - **Long vowel** sounds in words like *grass* (grarss) and *castle* (carstle).
> - **Long vowel** sound in words like *come* and *under*.
> - Pronouncing **hs** and **ts** in words like *hat* and *letter*.

RP has Changed Over Time

Language is always changing, and nowadays very few people actually use RP in its 'original' form, e.g. BBC newsreaders use **Standard English**, but they speak it in a range of **regional accents**. Even the Queen's accent has changed a bit from when she was first crowned 50 years ago.

> **Estuary English**
>
> 1) Some linguists claim that **RP** is being replaced as the most 'acceptable' English accent by **Estuary English**. This is an **accent** that has roots in the speech found around the **Thames Estuary** in **London**.
>
> 2) It contains many similar features to the **Cockney** accent, e.g. dropping **hs** at the beginning of words (pronouncing *hit* like *it*), and pronouncing **th** like **f** (so *mouth* becomes *mouff*).
>
> 3) It's used by a lot of people in the **entertainment industry**, as it's seen as a **commercially acceptable** accent.
>
> 4) Because of the **influence** of the **media**, Estuary English is becoming increasingly common **outside** of London. You can't necessarily tell where someone's from if they use Estuary English — it's become a **widespread accent**.

Practice Questions

Q1 Identify which of the following statements are in Standard English and which aren't. Explain why.

'I were going home when I spotted 'im.'

'The circumference of the circle ain't 54.'

'Turn left at the end of the road. Then take a sharp right.'

Q2 What factors contributed to the rise of Standard English as the accepted dialect?

Q3 Name four instances when you might use Standard English.

Q4 What is RP?

Essay Question

Q1 The use of Standard English and RP in the media has changed over the last 50 years. Identify some of these changes and comment on why they might have taken place.

wivowt stndrd inglish we cudnt undrstnd eech uvver...

Aha, I've done something rather clever there — I've shown that we can still understand each other even without Standard English. That's OK, there's no need to applaud, it's all in a day's work. It does make you wonder why people bang on about using 'good English' so much though, and whether it's right that one variety should be seen as better than the others...

Every individual uses language in a slightly different way. You don't spend all your time talking to yourself in the bathroom mirror, so it makes sense that the way you speak is affected by who you're with and what you're doing.

Sociolect *is the* Language *of* Social Groups

Sociolects (or **social dialects**) are **varieties** of language used by particular **social groups**, e.g. middle-aged lawyers speak differently from school children. The sociolects of different groups help to give them their own **identities**.

The language people use depends on different social factors:

Socio-economic status

- Studies have shown that **middle** and **upper class** people tend to use more **standard forms** (see p.36-37) than **lower class** people.
- The language of lower class people is more likely to contain features of **regional dialect** (p.34-35).

> *The points in this section are generalisations, so they're not true for everyone.*

Education

- Studies show that **well-educated** people are more likely to use **Standard English** and **RP** (see p.36-37) than less well-educated people.
- They're usually less likely to use words and sentence structures from **regional dialects**.

Age

- Sociolects used by teenagers tend to include more **non-standard** forms and **slang** (p.40-41) than language used by adults.
- They also include more influences from, and references to, **popular culture**.

Occupation (there's more on language and occupation on p.42-43)

- Every occupation has its own specialist terms and technical vocabulary, known as **jargon**.
- You might expect a lawyer to talk about *tort* (a civil wrong) or *GBH* (grievous bodily harm), and a doctor to talk about *prescriptions* or *scrubs*.
- Sometimes these **sociolects** also have distinctive **grammatical** features, e.g. legal documents often contain **complex** sentences with lots of subordinate clauses.

Belief system and culture

- **Religious groups** use lots of **specialist vocabulary**, e.g. *Diwali* (the Hindu festival of light), *kosher* (food prepared in accordance with Jewish law), *salah* (Islamic daily prayers).
- Because UK society is **multicultural**, lots of words from other languages and cultures have become part of a **wider** sociolect.
- For example, the word *kosher* isn't just used by members of the Jewish community. It's taken on a **broader** meaning in the English language, so people often use it to mean *genuine* or *legitimate*.

The Way *you* Speak *can* Depend *on the* Situation

Language that's **appropriate** in one social group might not be appropriate in another. People **adapt** the way they speak depending on the **situation** they're in, and how they want to present themselves. For example:

1) **Politicians** tend to use **Standard English** when they're making a political speech, because they're in a formal situation. But when they're talking to individuals on the street they might use **non-standard** language and features of **regional dialect**, so that they seem down-to-earth.

2) Lots of people find that the way they speak to their **friends** is different from how they speak to their **parents**. They might use more **slang** with their friends, or speak in the same **regional dialect** as their parents when they're at home.

3) Some people have a **telephone voice** — a different voice that they use on the phone. Usually it involves using more **standard** forms and an accent that's closer to **Received Pronunciation**.

"Hello? Yes, I'd like to speak to a Mr Hugh Jass".

Sociolect and Idiolect

Idiolect is the Unique Language of an Individual

1) The word choices that people make, and the way they form sentences, are specific to them.
2) This means that the way you use language can **identify** you, like a **fingerprint**.
3) Your **idiolect** is the result of a **unique combination** of **influences**.

Where you're from

- Where you're from affects how you speak. You might expect a person from Newcastle to have a Geordie **accent** and use **dialect** words like *gan* for *go*.
- But not everyone from the same **area** speaks in exactly the **same** way.
- A person could have **moved** from somewhere else and so **retained** aspects of **other** regional accents and dialects.

Social background

- The way you speak is also influenced by your **social background** (**sociolect** — see the previous page).
- Your sociolect is the **product** of lots of different **factors** such as socio-economic status, age, religious beliefs, education and gender.
- It's also affected by influences from **smaller** social groups, e.g. schools, sports teams and groups of friends.

"By 'eck, lad, this is a crackin' spread. Now pass us another pikelet."

Personal characteristics

- The language a person uses could be affected by aspects of their **personality**.
- For example, a **nervous** person might use sentences with lots of **fillers** (*um, like, sort of* etc.).

Practice Questions

Q1 What is a sociolect?
Q2 Give four examples of social groups that might have their own sociolect.
Q3 How might the situation you're in affect the way you speak?
Q4 What is an idiolect?
Q5 Give three factors that might influence a person's idiolect.

Essay Question

Q1 What can a person's use of language reveal about their identity?

You could comment on group influence, accent, dialect, slang, and social background.

Idiolect — the opposite of intellect...

You might have realised by now that speech is a bit of a witch's brew — a foul concoction made up of dialect, sociolect and a pinch of accent, all stirred together and simmered gently under the light of the full moon. After twenty minutes take it off the heat, rinse around the gums, gargle, spit, and hey presto! A fun new voice to amaze your friends and family...

Yeah yeah, don't think I don't know what you're up to — these pages are not to be used by people who just want to have a giggle at some naughty words. (I'd suggest that you use the dictionary for that — it's a lot more fun...)

Slang is Informal Vocabulary

1) **Slang** refers to **informal**, **non-standard** words and expressions that tend to be used in **casual speech**.

2) It's often **inventive** and **creative**, and enters the language in lots of different ways.

New meanings for existing words	Shortening existing words	New words
• *cool, wicked* — good • *sad* — pathetic • *chick* — girl	• *telly* — television • *rents* — parents • *mare* — nightmare	• *moolah* — money • *yonks* — a long time, ages • *snog* — kiss

Slang has Different Purposes

1) People tend to use slang to **identify** that they're part of a particular **social group** — it's part of their **sociolect** (see p.38). Using particular slang shows that you **fit in** and suggests **shared values**.

2) Slang can act as a code to **exclude outsiders**, e.g. groups of teenagers might use slang to establish a sense of identity which is separate from the adult world. It can be **exclusive** and **secretive**.

3) Two of the main **purposes** of using **slang** are to be **rebellious** or **entertaining**.

Slang and social taboos

- There's lots of slang for **taboo** subjects — things that are thought of as **inappropriate** or **unacceptable** to talk about in formal social situations, e.g. words for sex, sex organs and bodily functions.
- Some of the most common and most offensive slang words are **swear words**.
- It's seen as **taboo** to swear in some situations, e.g. in class at school. In this case the purpose of swearing is to be **rebellious**.
- In other situations swearing is an **accepted** part of a group's **sociolect**, and people do it to **fit in** and be **entertaining**, e.g. when they're talking with a group of friends.
- Not all **slang** is **taboo language**, but there's a lot **more** slang for **taboo subjects** than for any others.

Slang is Specific to Social and Regional Groups

1) Some slang words are **familiar** to **lots of speakers**, e.g. most people in the UK probably know that **tenner** is short for **ten pounds**.

2) However, slang also **varies** depending on which **region** speakers are from. Sometimes it's difficult to distinguish slang words from regional dialect variants.

3) One example of **regional slang** is **Cockney rhyming slang**, e.g. *butcher's hook* — **look**.

4) The slang a person uses also depends on **social factors**, e.g. a middle class speaker will probably speak something close to **Standard English** and use fewer slang words than a working class speaker.

5) Some slang is only used by very **small social groups**, like a particular school or group of friends.

6) Slang reflects **multiculturalism**, as slang terms can come from lots of different cultures, e.g. **tucker** — an Australian slang word for food.

7) The **media** also influences slang and gives people **access** to different subcultures.

- British **youth** culture has been particularly influenced by African American slang, through popular music and TV.
- **Hip hop culture** has introduced black American slang that lots of English speakers now recognise, e.g. *sick* — good, *bling* — flashy jewellery, *crib* — house.

Slang

Slang is always Changing

Slang changes very quickly as words go in and out of **fashion**.

1) There are lots of slang words that used to be popular, that you don't hear any more, e.g. *cove* — man, *beak* — magistrate, *viz* — face, *cits* — citizens.

2) Slang terms can quickly start to sound **dated**, e.g. *mega* — good, *dweeb* — someone who isn't cool. This happens especially with **teenage slang** that becomes more **mainstream** when adults and young children start using it, which causes teenagers to stop using it.

3) Sometimes slang terms become so widely used that they become part of **Standard English**, e.g. *okay*, *phone* and *bus*. These words were once considered **informal**, but now it would seem formal to say *telephone*, and very unusual to say *omnibus*.

4) The **opposite** can also happen — words can go from being formal or acceptable to being classed as vulgar. An example of this is the word *arse*, which wasn't thought of as informal until the 17th century.

People have Different Attitudes towards Slang

Slang is sometimes seen as **low level**, **vulgar** language, which shouldn't be used in **writing** or in **formal situations**.

1) Some people think that if you use slang you're **undermining standards** by not using the language 'properly'. They assume that people who use lots of slang are lower class and uneducated.

2) Slang is seen as the language of **informal speech**, so it's considered **inappropriate** to use it in a **formal context**, e.g. you'd lose marks if you wrote an essay using slang words and phrases.

3) This is because slang has a reputation for being **rebellious** and **subversive**, so it isn't formally accepted as a variety of English. Some people worry it doesn't follow the 'proper' **spelling** and **grammar rules** of **Standard English**.

4) However, most slang words and phrases **do** follow the rules of Standard English — they're just more flexible.

5) People who are interested in slang argue that it's an **intelligent** and **creative** variety of language, which **changes** and **develops** very quickly. It also serves an important **social purpose** — people use it to **identify** themselves as part of a **group**.

Practice Questions

Q1 Identify which word in each pair is slang, and which is Standard English:
Old Bill / police, upset / gutted, tired / knackered, quids in / wealthy, lucky / jammy

Q2 Give two reasons why people might use slang.

Q3 Explain two ways in which slang can change over time.

It's normal for transcripts not to have any punctuation. Instead, (.) indicates a short pause. Numbers in brackets indicate the length of a pause in seconds.

Essay Question

A: yeah I had a well good time (.) just really chilled (2.0) just sat on my arse all day

B: wish I had (.) Gemma was being a bitch again (.) I had to keep nipping off to phone her

A: it's not on

B: tell me about it (1.0) I wanna be like your attitude stinks but she'll just blank me till I cave in so what you gonna do

A: chuck her (.) she ain't worth it

Q1 Identify the different types of slang used in this extract and comment on the purpose it serves.

Cripes chums — learning about slang is smashingly wizard...

Good old Eng Lang — there aren't many subjects where you get the chance to discuss the ins and outs (oo-er) of swearing like this. Although I suppose the point of rude words is that they're not quite as fun if you're allowed to use them. Few things are likely to raise more of a snigger than slipping words like knockers into an exam answer...

Ever wondered why you never hear plumbers talking about PSHE or teachers talking about siphon-vortex water closets?
No, me neither, but it's something to do with occupational sociolects — the specific language of occupational groups...

Different Occupations *have their* Own Sociolects

1) **Occupational sociolect** is the distinctive language used by particular occupational groups,
   e.g. lawyers or train drivers (see p.38).

2) It's found in **spoken** and **written** forms.

3) The **sociolect** develops to fit the group's **specific purposes** — it's not **everyday** language.

4) **Specialists** in a job use it to communicate **quickly** and **precisely** with other specialists in the **same job**.
   You wouldn't necessarily expect **non-specialists** to understand it.

5) Occupational language can be seen as **elitist** — **excluding** people who **don't understand** it.

Occupational Language *has a* Special Lexis

Occupational words are the **specialist terms** used in specific jobs — often called **jargon** (see p.54).
They can refer to **concepts**, **processes**, **conditions**, **roles** or **objects**. For example:

- **Hairstylists** might say — *perm, feather, spritz, weave, layer, trim.*
- **Electricians** might say — *transformer, faceplate, fuse, amp, earth.*
- **Actors** might say — *role, script, agent, motivation, scene.*

These words might **not** be **familiar** to people **outside** the occupational group.

Police officers might say —
"you put your left leg in, your
left leg out..."

Occupational Language *has* Distinctive Grammatical Features

1) When you're analysing the grammatical features of occupational language,
   focus on elements like **word classes**, **syntax**, and **sentence functions**.

2) The example below is from a **medical report** written by specialists,
   to be read by other specialists:

*A 27-year-old female **presented with** a pneumothorax,*
*which progressed into **rapidly degenerative Bronchiolitis***
Obliterans Organising Pneumonia.

> These aren't general features
> of all occupational language —
> the grammar used in different
> occupations varies.

- **Word classes** — the **past participle** *presented* is used in an unusual way. It's combined with the preposition
  with to create a **prepositional verb** which describes the **symptoms** the patient was showing.

  The **head word** *pneumonia* has **premodifiers** in front of it — the **adverb** *rapidly* and the **adjective**
  degenerative. This makes the sentence grammatically complex.

- **Syntax** — the long **noun phrase** '*Bronchiolitis Obliterans Organising Pneumonia*' is common in this type of
  medical writing. It packs as much complex information as possible into a small space.

- **Function** — the text's **function** is to **give information**, so it only contains **declarative sentences** (see p.15).

Occupational Language *can have* Distinctive Phonological Features

Some kinds of occupational language have **phonological** features like **repetition**, **alliteration** and **rhyme** (see p.25).

1) You usually find distinctive **phonological features** in the language of occupations where it's
   necessary to speak to **large groups** of people, e.g. **politician**, **religious leader**, **teacher**.

2) This example from a **political speech** uses **alliteration** and **phonological patterning** with a **three
   part list**, e.g. *we will bring you **peace**, **pride** and **prosperity** like you've never experienced before.*

3) Teachers' language might have some common **prosodic features** when they're addressing classes,
   e.g. they're more likely to raise their voices or say *shh.*

Language and Occupational Groups

Occupational Language Varies depending on its Form and Function

1) **Written** occupational discourse has lots of different **forms**, e.g. legal contracts and business letters.

2) **Spoken** occupational discourse also takes different **forms**, e.g. a counsellor might use gentle questioning, a sergeant major might shout out imperatives, and a politician might use rhetorical questions.

3) Occupational discourse also has a variety of **functions** depending on its **context**. For example:

> • **informative discourse**, e.g. a manager explaining a task to an employee.
> • **persuasive discourse**, e.g. a charity worker asking for donations.
> • **instructional discourse**, e.g. an experienced plumber advising an apprentice.
> • **transactional discourse**, e.g. a retailer buying from a wholesaler.

4) Some discourse has a **mixture** of functions, e.g. a factory's health and safety manual might be designed to **inform**, **instruct** and **persuade**.

Occupational Discourse can follow a Specific Structure

This sounds more complicated than it is — basically, it's just looking at the **order** the discourse takes, and how it can be separated by **discourse markers**. For example:

1) **Scientific reports** have a specific structure — **title**, **introduction**, **method**, **findings**, **conclusion**, **evaluation**. These **standard headings** act as **discourse markers** by organising it in a specific order.

2) A police officer arresting somebody follows a strict **verbal discourse structure**: *you do not have to say anything, but it may harm your defence if you do not mention when questioned something that you later rely on in court.*

> In this example of a teacher's report on a pupil, the discourse is structured in **four parts**:
>
> > *Ferdinand is doing well in Mathematics and has made significant progress. However, he really must apply himself next term if he is to fulfil his potential.*
>
> 1. Present performance — *is doing well* (**present continuous tense**).
> 2. Past to present performance — *has made significant progress* (**present perfect tense**).
> 3. What he has to do — *he really must apply himself* (**use of modal**).
> 4. Success depends on him doing this — *if he is to fulfil his potential* (**conditional clause**).
>
> Here the **adverb** *however* acts as a **discourse marker**. It gives the text an **order** by **linking** what's happened in the **past** with what needs to happen in the **future**.

Practice Questions

Q1 What is meant by the term occupational sociolect?
Q2 Give three examples of 'occupation-specific' lexis.
Q3 Give three types of grammatical features you should analyse in occupational language.
Q4 Name three kinds of phonological features that can sometimes be found in occupational language.
Q5 Give an example of one form and one function of occupational discourse.

Essay Question

Q1 Outline the main features of occupational language, and the specific purposes it serves.

You could focus on lexis, grammar, phonological features, form, function and structure.

At least all this revision will keep you occupied...

This is another topic where it can feel like you're stating the obvious quite a lot — you wouldn't really expect, say, doctors to spend much time talking about leather uppers and shoelaces. Well, not while they were at work. Unless someone had had a bizarre accident with a pair of brogues... But that's beside the point. This is all nice simple stuff, so fear not.

Sources and Exam Questions

This is an exam-style question, based on sources like the ones you'll get in the real paper.

Texts A–E illustrate different varieties of language use.

Discuss various ways in which these texts can be grouped, giving reasons for your choices. [48]

Text A — from *Lady Windermere's Fan,* by Oscar Wilde

DUMBY	Clever woman, Mrs. Erlynne.
CECIL GRAHAM	Hallo, Dumby! I thought you were asleep.
DUMBY	I am, I usually am!
LORD AUGUSTUS	A very clever woman. Knows perfectly well what a demmed fool I am — knows it as well as I do myself.
[CECIL GRAHAM *comes towards him laughing*.]	
	Ah, you may laugh, my boy, but it is a great thing to come across a woman who thoroughly understands one.
DUMBY	It is an awfully dangerous thing. They always end by marrying one.
CECIL GRAHAM	But I thought, Tuppy, you were never going to see her again! Yes! you told me so yesterday evening at the club. You said you'd heard —
[*Whispering to him*.]	
LORD AUGUSTUS	Oh, she's explained that.
CECIL GRAHAM	And the Wiesbaden affair?
LORD AUGUSTUS	She's explained that too.
DUMBY	And her income, Tuppy? Has she explained that?
LORD AUGUSTUS	[*In a very serious voice*.] She's going to explain that to-morrow.
[CECIL GRAHAM *goes back to C. table*.]	
DUMBY	Awfully commercial, women nowadays. Our grandmothers threw their caps over the mills, of course, but, by Jove, their granddaughters only throw their caps over mills that can raise the wind for them.
LORD AUGUSTUS	You want to make her out a wicked woman. She is not!
CECIL GRAHAM	Oh! Wicked women bother one. Good women bore one. That is the only difference between them.
LORD AUGUSTUS	[*Puffing a cigar*.] Mrs. Erlynne has a future before her.
DUMBY	Mrs. Erlynne has a past before her.
LORD AUGUSTUS	I prefer women with a past. They're always so demmed amusing to talk to.
CECIL GRAHAM	Well, you'll have lots of topics of conversation with HER, Tuppy. [*Rising and going to him*.]
LORD AUGUSTUS	You're getting annoying, dear-boy; you're getting demmed annoying.
CECIL GRAHAM	[*Puts his hands on his shoulders*.] Now, Tuppy, you've lost your figure and you've lost your character. Don't lose your temper; you have only got one.
LORD AUGUSTUS	My dear boy, if I wasn't the most good-natured man in London —
CECIL GRAHAM	We'd treat you with more respect, wouldn't we, Tuppy? [*Strolls away*.]
DUMBY	The youth of the present day are quite monstrous. They have absolutely no respect for dyed hair. [LORD AUGUSTUS *looks round angrily*.]
CECIL GRAHAM	Mrs. Erlynne has a very great respect for dear Tuppy.
DUMBY	Then Mrs. Erlynne sets an admirable example to the rest of her sex. It is perfectly brutal the way most women nowadays behave to men who are not their husbands.

Sources and Exam Questions

Text B — a conversation between teenage friends

A: mate you can't be serious

B: do I look like I'm joking (.) seriously he is

A: oh he is really not

B: come on no right (.) right he is though cos he's like

A: // he's proper minging

C: he is he's minging he is

B: // ah come on though I mean it's not like he is like compared to some people

A: compared to some people even more minging than him

B: well obviously compared to that right

A: // well then

B: // but that don't even make sense

C: why not

B: thing is though he's (2) okay thing is he's well fit

C: // [inaud]

B: // but he can be he can be well horrid sometimes

A: yeah right like (.) like exactly right I mean it's not like he's ever tret anyone good is it really

B: well I dunno (.) I dunno like he tret amanda quite good till she chucked him

A: she didn't dump

C: // it was him what got rid right (.) it was him what like got rid of her that's why why erm why she's

A: that's why she's such a mardy cow with him innit though right

B: // mardy cow that's

A: // yeah don't jip me right (3) no stop your giggling right she's well mardy with him

C: it's not like you can go blaming her for that though though (.) I mean bless her though cos fact of the matter is (.) fact is that she didn't do nowt wrong and he he he was he went behind her back and proper messed with her head (.) cos it was when she was supposed to meet him at pub (.) right she was gonna meet him at pub but he said he were doing summat else right so like (.) so like she goes anyway with her sister and he were there just like completely shameless with another bird

A: // no way

C: // yeah I mean bless her right (.) like she just don't deserve that

B: // soz defending amanda all of a sudden (.) I knew I knew

A: // it's dead obvious now though

C: what you trying to say

B: you'll not admit (.) he'll not admit to it like but you well fancy her

A: yep

C: whatever right (2) like I clearly don't but whatever if you wanna (.) wanna say

B: // yeah you do you've proper got hots for her

C: no way though we're just just (.) just get well and we just

B: // course yeah we're just good friends course (1) really good friends

A: yeah I don't (.) you'll not catch me snogging my friends (.) snogging

C: // what I ain't snogged her

Transcription Key

(.) *Micropause*

(2.0) *Pause in seconds*

// *Interruptions / overlapping speech*

[inaud] *An unidentified sound*

Sources and Exam Questions

Text C — an email between two employees at a company selling conservatories

RE: Guarantee query

Tony Craig

To: Jane Hilton

Hi Jane,

This was a common problem with the old gutter sleeve we were using at that time. There was a slant at the join with the abutment, which could cause the box gutter to come free and start to split.

If this was the problem in this case, then it's been usual practice in these circumstances to repair the gutter free of charge anyway as a goodwill gesture, because it's only minor.

You should be able to find most information like this in your I49 starting handbook, but if you have any more questions just give me a shout.

Tony

From: Jane Hilton
Sent: 04 August 2008 16:47
To: Tony Craig
Subject: Guarantee query

Hi Tony,

We've had a customer complaint about a uPVC Georgian Hip conservatory, fitted in 04/07.

We had to fit a box gutter because the roof slopes towards the fascia board. The gutter sleeve has now split and the customer wants it replacing under the two year guarantee.

Just wondering if the guarantee covers this?

Thanks

Jane

Text D — a restaurant review on the website gastronomyweb.com

I started with ham hock and parsley terrine, with a Cumberland sauce, confit onion and toasted sourdough — a really skilfully prepared dish and beautifully presented. My only complaint would be that the mountains of toasted sourdough meant that it was really far too big as a starter, and I had to leave about half a plateful.

With a selection of main courses including ballotine of chicken breast stuffed with spinach and ricotta, served with potato and beetroot gratin and sherry cream sauce; poached line-caught turbot and fresh tagliatelle, with fish velouté with lavender and Ossetra caviar; and their classic bouillabaisse, I really felt spoilt for choice. I opted for the ballotine of chicken breast, and wasn't disappointed. The tender chicken was perfectly complemented by earthy spinach and sweet, creamy ricotta.

Chef's take on sticky toffee pudding was disappointing — huge globs of pale pudding swimming in a sauce so ultra sweet that it completely dominated the palate. It didn't seem in keeping with the elegant, if robust, starter and delicate main — a little more gastropub than haute cuisine somehow. All was forgiven though when I tasted the hibiscus sorbet, which was a sharp and tangy triumph.

Service was prompt and attentive, but the staff seemed to feel the watchful eye of the steely maître d' enough to not hang around for long. The exception to this was the sommelier, who appeared to have very little to do and on one occasion had to be chivvied away from a table of pretty girls who were trying to get stuck into their moules marinières. On the whole, though, the chilliness of the maître d' was sufficiently warmed up by the coral walls, plush furnishings, and ultimately delicious food.

Sources and Exam Questions

Text E — a conversation between two mechanics (A and B) and a customer (C)

A: okay we've had a look and we couldn't pinpoint at first why it was (.) ah here's Greg actually it was Greg who was working on it mostly (.) erm I'll get him over (2.0) Greg

C: // okay

B: hiya (.) all right (1.0) back for the (.) er Range Rover is it (.) two point five diesel

C: yes that's right

A: I'm just saying it's you who was working on it really so do you (.) want to go through it and

B: // yeah yeah (.) no of course (.) great

C: great (.) thanks thank you

A: do you want to erm take him through to have a look at the v5 Greg

B: right yeah (.) yeah okay I'll get the get the v5 and we'll have a look

A: if you'd just like to come through here

C: // okay yes (.) okay

A: // we've had a bit of a problem with it really (.) the engine tone was changing slightly so we scanned it for any fault codes but we weren't getting anything from it

C: okay

A: so we thought it's like maybe (.) maybe your MAF playing up

C: // erm right (.) okay

A: // have you had any problems with that before

C: any problems with the (.) the sorry any problems with the (.) the erm (.) the (1.0) MAF

A: right no no (.) have you noticed any differences with your engine tone (2.0) sounds different (.) ever sound different

C: okay (.) erm no no (1.0) not re- (.) don't think I have really no

A: no problems in the past with that Greg

B: no (.) right no (.) I thought that but it can (.) it can just be it needs a clean (2.0) I mean I erm (.) I thought it was more that probably the injector was (.) yeah injector a bit blocked

A: // well yeah (.) that's what I'm thinking really (.) probably just your injector being a bit blocked up (.) happens a lot with these models so it's

C: // yes (.) right yes okay (2.0) so what do you need to do with that (.) how will you fix it

A: basically what I'm thinking is that it's probably not a big problem

B: right yeah (.) not major like is it really

A: nothing major

C: // okay

A: just keep it in a bit longer so we can (.) I'll get Greg on it when (1.0) Greg when you've finished with that coupe (.) with the rev limiter on that coupe

B: // yeah cool (.) okay

A: // so if we get some Forté* in the fuel system then we'll see if that (.) I mean that could sort it completely (1.0) is that okay then

C: is that okay for (.) is that (.) erm yes no that should be fine (1.0) what I mean is I mean when do you think I can come and collect it

A: well Greg's got to finish this coupe (.) but then erm (.) well well it could be tomorrow morning I reckon

C: okay great (.) that's great (.) as long as you think that'll fix it (.) I really don't want to have to be coming back and forth again really if that's (.) it's just a bit of a pain when

A: // oh no worries yeah (.) yeah no a bit of Forté will do it

Forté™ is a brand of fuel treatment.

Language and Gender

Language and gender is a funny old game. There do seem to be some differences between how men and women use language, but no-one seems to be sure exactly what they are or why they occur. Here goes...

Men *and* Women *use* Language Differently

Studies have shown that women tend to use **accents** from a **higher social class** than men.

- **Trudgill (1983)** studied men and women's **social class accents** (see p.34-37). He found that women's pronunciation was closer to **Received Pronunciation (RP)**, the accent that's usually seen as the most **prestigious**.
- **Cheshire (1982)** studied the speech of adolescent girls and boys, and found that boys tended to use more **non-standard grammatical forms**, e.g. *ain't*, than girls.

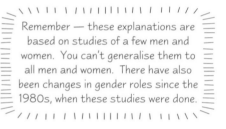

Her parents disapproved of her bit of rough, but Ange couldn't keep her hands off him.

1) Using **Standard English** and **RP** gives a person **overt prestige** — the prestige of being associated with a respectable, well-off section of society. **Women** tend to seek **overt prestige** more than men.

2) Using **non-standard** English gives a person **covert prestige** — they seem a bit rebellious and independent. **Men** are more likely to seek **covert prestige** than women.

Women *may use more* `Prestigious Forms *for* Several Reasons

There are several **possible explanations** for why **women** use more **prestigious** language than **men**.

1) Women might be **less secure** than men in terms of their **social status**. If they feel that they have an **inferior position** in society, then they might use more **prestigious** language to **overcome** it.

2) Society generally expects **higher standards** of **behaviour** from **women** — they're expected to behave like 'ladies' and use 'ladylike' language. This includes things like not swearing or arguing.

Remember — these explanations are based on studies of a few men and women. You can't generalise them to all men and women. There have also been changes in gender roles since the 1980s, when these studies were done.

3) Men already have a **higher social status** than women, so they don't need to use prestigious forms to improve it. Instead, they seek **covert prestige** by using non-standard language that seems tough and rebellious.

4) **Non-standard language** is traditionally associated with **working-class** men, so men might use it to show that they share **traditionally masculine** qualities, like being '**tough**' and '**down-to-earth**'.

Women's *language is usually* More Polite *than* Men's

The researcher **Robin Lakoff (1975)** identified features that she felt were characteristic of women's language:

> **Hedges and fillers** — fragments of language like *sort of, kind of, maybe*.
> **Apologetic requests** — e.g. *I'm sorry, but would you mind closing the door?*
> **Tag questions** — e.g. *this is nice, isn't it?*
> **Indirect requests** — e.g. *It's very noisy out there* (meaning — *could you close the door?*)

1) **Lakoff** also pointed out that women tend to **speak less** than men, use **fewer expletives** (swear less), and use more **intensifiers** (words like **so** and **very**).

2) She argued that these features of women's language reflected women's **inferior social status**, and made it worse by making them seem **indecisive** and **needy**. She said that women's language is **weak** compared to men's language, and this **prevents** women from being **taken seriously**. This explanation is known as the **deficit model**.

3) **O'Barr and Atkins (1980)** suggested an alternative explanation to the **deficit model**. They analysed transcripts of **American courtroom trials**. They found that **male and female** witnesses who were of **low social status** and/or inexperienced with the courtroom practices, both showed many of the linguistic features that Lakoff labelled **female**.

4) This suggests that the kind of language **Lakoff** describes as female isn't only found in women, and might be more to do with individuals feeling **powerless**.

> **Lakoff's** research is quite **old**. More recently, researchers like **Holmes (1984)** have suggested that 'women's language' doesn't show **weakness**, but a desire to **co-operate**. Linguists like **Cameron (2007)** argue that there are actually very **few differences** between men and women's language, and **situation** affects how people speak much more than **gender**.

Language can be Explained in terms of Dominance and Difference

Linguists have come up with other models to explain the **differences** between men and women's language.

1) Dominance model

- **Zimmerman and West (1975)** recorded interruptions in conversations between men and women.
- They found that **96%** of the interruptions were by men.
- This suggested that men are **dominant** in **male-female conversations**. They argued that this reflects male dominance in society.

2) Difference model

Tannen (1990) described male and female conversational style in terms of **difference**.

- **Men** are concerned with **status** and **independence**, e.g. they interrupt a lot.
- They give **direct orders**, e.g. *pass me that*, and don't mind **conflict**.
- **Men** are interested in gaining **factual information** and finding **solutions to problems**.

- **Women** are interested in **forming bonds** — they tend to talk less and agree more than men.
- They usually give polite, indirect orders, e.g. *would you mind passing me that*, and try to **avoid conflict**.
- **Women** aim to show **understanding** by **compromising**, and offering **support** rather than **solutions**.

> The **reasons** for these **differences** in male and female interaction could be to do with the **topics** that they talk about in **single-sex groups**, e.g. traditionally **male** topics of conversation have focused on **work** and **sport**, where **factual information** and **status** are important. Traditionally **female** topics have centred on the **home** and **family**, where **emotions**, **support** and **compassion** are important.

There are Problems with these Explanations

Other researchers have cast **doubts** on some of these explanations of differences in **male** and **female language**.

1) **Beattie (1982)** questioned **Zimmerman and West's** idea that men **interrupting** women was a sign of **dominance**. He suggested that interruptions can be **supportive** and show that the person is listening, e.g. if they **repeat** what the speaker is saying, or say things like *yes* and *mm*.

2) **Cameron (2007)** argues that a lot of research is **biased** because there has been more focus on the **differences** between male and female language, which are actually quite small, rather than the **similarities**.

Practice Questions

Q1   What is meant by the terms overt prestige and covert prestige?
Q2   List the main features Lakoff attributed to female language.
Q3   Why might 'powerless language' be a better term to use than 'women's language'?
Q4   Explain the dominance model.
Q5   List the main features of Tannen's analysis of male and female language.

Essay Question

Q1   Outline the differences in the way that men and women use language. Explain some of the reasons for these differences.

To make your essay more balanced, you could focus on the different explanations that researchers have offered, as well as the problems with some of these explanations.

Try to avoid making genderalisations...

A lot of the stuff people believe about men and women's speech is based on stereotypes about what they think men and women are like. It's possible to think of loads of exceptions to any of these 'rules', and yet still assume that they must be true. Just remember, the way people speak is affected by loads of different factors, and gender is only one of them...

These pages are about the different ways that men and women are spoken and written about in things like adverts, fiction and non-fiction. The basic idea is that the way they're represented shapes how men and women are perceived.

Men *and* Women *are Represented Differently*

1) **Sexist language** is language that **insults**, **patronises** or **ignores** people on the basis of their **gender**.

2) There is a lot **more** sexist language about **women** than men.

3) Some language implies that the **male** version is the **norm**, and the **female** version is **different** or **wrong**:

Marked terms

- These are words that reveal a person's **gender**, e.g. *policeman, wife*.
- **Unmarked terms** don't reveal the person's gender, e.g. *police officer, spouse*.
- Some words are **marked** by a **feminising suffix**, e.g. *actress, usherette, comedienne*.
  The suffix implies that the male version is the **original** or the **norm**, so it seems **superior** to the female version.

Generic terms

- This is when a **marked term** is used to refer both to men and women.
- It's nearly always **masculine terms** which are used to mean **people** in general, rather than just **men**.
- The most common example is the word *man*, e.g. the noun *mankind*, or the verb *to **man** the desk*.
- **Generic terms** refer to everybody, but using them can make **females** seem **invisible** by **ignoring** them. When this occurs, women are said to be occupying **negative semantic space**.

Lexical Asymmetry refers to **pairs of words** that appear to have a **similar meaning**, but aren't **equally balanced**, e.g. *bachelor* and *spinster* (unmarried man and unmarried woman).

- The connotations of *bachelor* are usually **positive** — it's associated with a man living a carefree, independent life.
- The connotations of *spinster* are usually **negative** — it implies that the woman has been unable to find a partner.

Patronising terms are words used by speakers that imply **superiority** over the person they're talking to.

- Terms that imply someone is **younger** than the speaker can be patronising, e.g. *girls, young lady*.
- **Terms of endearment** can be **patronising** in some circumstances, e.g. *love, dear, sweetheart*.
- Whether a word is **patronising** depends on the **context**, e.g. a male employee who addresses a female colleague as *love* could be seen as patronising, but boyfriends and girlfriends calling each other *love* might not.

Grammar *can be* Sexist

The idea that the **male** is the **norm** is also evident in English **grammar**.

1) **Pronouns** — the 3rd person masculine pronoun *he* or *his* is often used to refer both to men and women, e.g. *an **employee** who is absent for longer than five days must obtain a sick note from **his** doctor.*

2) **Syntax** — when one gender specific word is always placed before another, it's known as **order of preference**, e.g. *Mr and Mrs, men and women, Sir or Madam.* Usually the male term comes first.

There are *More Insults for* Women *than* Men

There are a lot **more insulting terms** for **women** than there are for **men**. This is known as **over-representation**.

1) Lots of insulting terms for **women** have an **animal** theme, e.g. *bitch, cow*.

2) There are lots of words to label women as **promiscuous**, e.g. *slag, slut, slapper*.

3) There are hardly any **equivalents** for men. Terms like *stud* tend to have **positive connotations**. Terms like *man whore* or *male slut* tend to be used **comically**, and imply that the **female** version is the **norm**.

4) The **lack** of an **equivalent term** for something — e.g. a male term for *slut* — is known as a **lexical gap**.

Language and Gender

Sexist Language can be Avoided and Changed

1) The **Sex Discrimination Act** was passed in **1975** to **protect** people from sexual discrimination and harassment, especially at work and at school.
2) It reflected the work of **feminist campaigners**, who wanted to promote **equality** between men and women.
3) Part of this campaign was a push to get rid of **sexist language**.
4) The idea is that language doesn't just **reflect** sexist **attitudes** — it helps to **keep them alive**.
5) So if you change **discriminatory language**, then people's **attitudes** might change too.
6) This is often called **political correctness** (more on this on p.55).
7) **Sexist terms** can be avoided by **replacing** them with **gender neutral** ones.

The only surefire way to remove gender issues... get everyone to dress like an idiot.

> **For example...**
> 1) **Marked terms** can be replaced with **unmarked terms**, e.g. *head teacher* instead of *headmaster* or *headmistress*, *police officer* instead of *policeman* or *policewoman*.
> 2) **Feminising suffixes** can be **dropped**, e.g. a female manager is called a *manager*, not a *manageress*.
> 3) Instead of *Mrs* or *Miss*, the title *Ms* is often used, so you **can't tell** whether a woman is **married**.
> 4) The generic use of **man** can be replaced by gender neutral terms, e.g. *humankind* instead of *mankind*, *workforce* instead of *manpower*.
> 5) The **generic** use of the masculine 3rd person pronoun (*he*) can be replaced by *he/she*, *s/he*, or *they*. Sentences can be made **gender-neutral** by using the **plural** instead, e.g. ***Employees** who are absent for longer than five days must obtain a sick note from **their** doctor.*

People have Different Views about Avoiding Sexist Language

1) The point of encouraging people to avoid sexist language is to ensure people will be treated **equally**, and not feel they're being **singled out**, or **ignored**, because of their gender.
2) Sometimes there are **problems** with trying to **control language** in this way. People can feel that it's **controlling**, and find it frustrating because they feel they can't speak freely without getting into trouble. Some people argue that this can create **resentment** towards the group of people it's designed to protect.
3) It's hard to **enforce** the use of non-sexist language. Some people think that condemning all sexist language ignores **context** and **intent**, e.g. if everyone understands that a comment is a joke, and nobody is offended by it, then it's **pointless** to have laws that stop people from making it.

Practice Questions

Q1 Outline what is meant by the term negative semantic space.
Q2 Explain the term lexical asymmetry and provide two examples.
Q3 What is meant by the term lexical gap?
Q4 Outline three ways in which sexist language can be avoided.
Q5 Explain one argument for and one argument against changing language to avoid sexism.

Essay Question

Q1 How can language be used to suggest that women are inferior to men?

I'm not sexist — some of my best friends are men or women...

This is one of those topics where it can feel like you're stating the obvious some of the time, but at least it's not really complicated. And it's a good one for having a bit of a debate over as well. Just remember that you have to show you understand both sides of an argument before you start waving placards and holding a sit-in in the exam hall...

There are loads of ways to assert power over someone in a conversation — when stuffing your fist into the other person's mouth isn't an option, try some of these strategies instead...

The **Language** of **Power** is found in **Different Contexts**

The language of **power** tries to exert **influence** or **control**. It appears in various **contexts**, and in both spoken and written forms.

1) Political language

The purpose of political language is to **persuade**. To achieve this, politicians use **rhetorical devices** (**rhetoric** is the **art** of using language **persuasively**).

1) **Repetition** — *Those who **betray** their party **betray** themselves.*
2) **Three-part lists** — *He came, he saw, he conquered.*
3) **First person plural pronoun** (we) — ***We** must strive together for the better health of the nation.*
4) **Figurative language** — *Under our leadership, the **winter of discontent** has become a **summer of prosperity**.*
5) **Rhetorical questions** — *How much longer must our people endure this injustice?*
6) **Hyperbole** (exaggeration) — *Plague would be a better option than the health policies proposed.*

2) Legal language

1) **Legal language** is quite distinctive — it has its own **lexis**. The specific vocabulary used by an **occupational group** is know as **jargon** (see p.42-43 and p.54).
2) The syntax is often **complex**, with lots of **subordinate clauses**. It's also **repetitive**.
3) Because it's so complex, knowledge of this language gives **specialists** a distinct **advantage** over **non-specialists**. This means that lawyers have a lot of **power** — if their clients don't fully understand the difficult jargon, then they have to **trust** that their lawyers understand it and will deal with their case properly.

3) Education

1) The language of power is seen in schools, colleges and universities. The language of **education** reflects the **power structures** in schools.
2) Teachers often use **imperatives** — *open your books*, and direct questions — *what's the answer to question four?*
3) Students use **fewer imperatives** and ask more **indirect questions** — *is it okay if I go to the toilet?*
4) There's often an **imbalance** in **address terms** — students might use respectful address terms to the teacher like **Sir**, or **title + surname** constructions (Ms Smith), while teachers just use the student's **first name**. This shows an **understanding** that the teacher has **authority**.

4) Business

1) **Power structures** in the language of **business** are very similar to those in **education** — **managers** may speak more **directly** to their **employees**, while **employees** may use more **politeness strategies** (see p.29) and fewer **imperatives**.
2) The hierarchical structure of many businesses is shown in nouns such as **subordinate**, **superior**, **team leader** and **chief executive**.

Address Terms show **Power Relationships**

What people **call** each other can reveal **power relationships**. As with everything, they **vary** in different **contexts**.

Context	Form of Address
Politics	*Madam/Mr Speaker, Honourable Member*
Law	*Your Honour, Ladies and Gentlemen of the Jury*
Education	*Sir, Miss, Mr Briggs, Ms Briggs, Dr / Professor*
Business	*Madam Chair, Sir, Madam*

Look out for **imbalances** in address terms, because they can reveal **unequal power relationships**.

There are **Different Ways** to **Exert Power** in a **Conversation**

Power relationships are shown in the way people talk to each other. People **assert** power in different ways.

1) **Initiating a conversation** — this can be a means of **taking the lead** and establishing the **topic** of conversation.

2) **Holding the floor** — this is when one speaker gives little or no opportunity for other speakers to take a turn. Usually conversation involves **turn-taking**, so a speaker can show **dominance** by not letting anyone else in.

3) **Imperative sentences** — giving **orders** and **directions** can be a sign of **dominance**, e.g. *shut the door.*

4) **Interrupting** — some **interruptions** cut into the other person's turn. It shows that the person interrupting has **little interest** in what the speaker is saying.

5) **Unresponsiveness** — this a more **negative** way of asserting control. If the person speaking is ignored or if the **back-channel noises** (*mm* or *uh huh*) of the other participants are half-hearted or hesitant then the **status** of the speaker is **undermined**.

6) **Questioning** — questions direct the **topic** of conversation, and make it clear when the other person is **expected** to talk.

7) **Topic changing** — this can be a technique of **reasserting control**. Sometimes politicians do this when they're uncomfortable talking about a particular topic. By **diverting attention** to a **different topic**, where they may have something more positive to say, they're trying to **gain control** over the **direction** of the conversation.

8) **Closing down a conversation** — this asserts power by not allowing other speakers to carry on talking, e.g. saying *goodbye* or walking away.

Context is Important

It's important to pay attention to the **context** of a conversation when you're looking at **power**.

1) In a particular **situation**, the way power shows itself depends on how people are **'positioned'** in relation to each other.

2) These **relationships** between speakers can **shape** the **conversational strategies** and **type** of language they use, e.g. you'd **expect** a doctor to ask a patient lots of questions.

3) Depending on the context of the conversation, some of the above examples of **dominance** can actually be interpreted as ways of showing **support**.

4) For example, **interrupting** with words like *yes*, or cutting in to **repeat** what the speaker has said can show that you **agree** and you're **listening**. It doesn't necessarily mean that you're trying to assert power over the person speaking.

5) Similarly, **asking questions** can be a sign you want to **control** the topic of conversation, **or** it can be a way of **passing control** to somebody else to **encourage** them to **hold the floor**.

Practice Questions

Q1 What is rhetoric and what are rhetorical devices?

Q2 Why might a teacher prefer to be addressed by title + surname rather than by first name?

Q3 Outline three ways in which a speaker might try to dominate a conversation.

Essay Question

A: it's so funny isn't it darling (1) do you like it (.) it's really clever and //
B: // but it's so unrealistic turn it off
A: you can't say that (.) you've only just seen a bit of it
B: I don't need to realise (.) to see how bad it is (2) it's like //
A: // fine (1) just put something else on

Q1 How do the speakers in this extract exert power over each other?

Forget language — just get down the gym and show 'em who's boss...

This is a handy little topic — you can find evidence of language and power in pretty much any extract you'll have to look at. There are loads of different ways to exert power, so you shouldn't get too bored. Personally, when I want to dominate a conversation I go for the good old-fashioned fingers-in-ears-la-la-la-I'm-not-listening-to-you technique. Works every time...

The language of power is about dominating your enemies and crushing your opponents, so they cower at your mighty presence and quiver in the face of your wrath. Mwahahaha...

Power shows itself in Different Ways

The ways people **exert power** in a conversation aren't just about what they say.

1) **Non-verbal communication** (**NVC**) is using **posture**, **positioning**, **gestures**, **eye contact** and **facial expressions** to convey feelings and attitudes, e.g. crossing your legs away from someone can function as a **barrier** and appear **defensive**. Maintaining eye contact longer than normal can be an attempt to **assert dominance**. **Smiling** at someone and **pausing** as you walk past them can be a way of **initiating conversation**.

2) **Non-verbal aspects of speech** (**pitch**, **intonation**, **volume**, **pace** and **stress**) can also be used to assert control, e.g. when people **argue** they may try to dominate by **shouting**, raising the **pitch** of their voice or speaking more **quickly**.

3) **Standard English** and **Received Pronunciation** (**RP**) (see p.36-37) are the varieties of English that carry the most **prestige**. They're associated with **professional jobs** and a **good education**. Because of this, speakers who use Standard English and RP are often perceived to have more **authority** and **status** than people who speak in a regional dialect or accent.

Bruce didn't need words — he had raw animal strength.

Jargon can be used to Dominate

Jargon is the **specialist vocabulary** used in particular **fields** of **activity**, especially **occupations** (see p.42-43). For example:

- The **medical world** uses terms like *adenovirus, meningococcal,* and *septum*.
- **Electrical engineers** use terms like *chrominance, phase jitter,* and *watchdog circuit*.
- Terms like these aren't generally understood by **non-specialists**.

1) **Jargon** is often **necessary** when **specialists** are talking to **other specialists** — it's a **precise** form of **labelling** objects, processes and conditions, so it means **technical information** can be communicated **quickly**.

2) People who **understand** the jargon have a sense of **inclusion** in a group, which often brings a **higher status**.

3) The **problem** with jargon is that when **specialists** use it to communicate with **non-specialists** it can become a **barrier** to **understanding**, e.g. doctors with patients, mechanics with car owners.

4) **Non-specialists** can feel **intimidated** by the **specialists** and **excluded** from the **high-status group**. In cases like this, the **specialists** have more power and can **dominate** the situation.

5) **Specialists** can exploit this by using jargon with **non-specialists** in order to **impress** them — it makes people feel that they want to be **part** of the high-status group that uses such specialist terms. It can also be used to hide what's really going on.

There are Alternatives to using Jargon

Jargon can cause real **problems** when it's used **inappropriately**, so different measures are taken to avoid it. For example:

1) Since 1999 some of the language used in the **civil courts** has been changed to make it easier for non-specialists to understand.

2) This includes **Latin** terms like *in camera* and *subpoena*, which have been replaced by *in private* and *witness summons*.

3) Using plainer language promotes **equality**, because it means that everyone has more chance of understanding what's being said, and specialists can't use jargon to **intimidate** non-specialists.

- The **Plain English Campaign** was set up in 1979 to **combat** the use of **confusing** and **unnecessary jargon**.
- It **advises organisations** on how they can use **plainer language**.
- Organisations can apply for the **Crystal Mark**, which shows that the **Plain English Campaign** has approved their documents.

Language and Power

Political Correctness aims to *Promote Equality*

1) Political correctness is a term to describe ways that language can be adapted to **minimise social inequality**.

2) It's politically correct to avoid language that **insults**, **marginalises** or seeks to **control** other people or groups of people — in particular language that is **sexist**, **racist**, **ageist** and **ableist** (discriminates against people with disabilities).

3) Political correctness is based on the idea that language doesn't just **reflect** social attitudes, but also helps to **shape** them. So if discriminatory language is changed or avoided, then people are less likely to discriminate against others.

There are always **reasons why** terms are viewed as **politically incorrect**, e.g.

Original term	Alternative	Reason
half caste	mixed race	*half caste* suggests less than whole, incomplete.
stewardess	flight attendant	*stewardess* reveals the person's gender. The suffix **-ess** suggests that the male term (*steward*) is the original, so more important.
disabled person	person with disabilities	*disabled person* is a dehumanising label — it characterises people by their disability. The alternative version takes the focus away from the disability.

There's a lot of *Debate* about *Political Correctness*

Arguments for Political Correctness

* Language helps to **shape social attitudes**. Changing it sends a clear message about what is **acceptable**, which encourages people to change their attitudes.

* It acts as a **symbol** that society is committed to becoming more **equal** and **inclusive**.

* It's often **blown out of proportion** — people focus on **outrageous** examples of political correctness, when most actually have a **reasonable explanation**.

Arguments against Political Correctness

* People feel they're being **restricted**, and can't speak their minds without getting into trouble.

* It's pointless because language only **reflects** social **attitudes**, it **doesn't shape** them.

* Some feel it creates **resentment** towards the groups it tries to protect, so discrimination is just as likely.

* It's pointless because language **always changes** — words that **were** once politically correct eventually become **less acceptable**. For example, *Third World* was replaced by *Developing World*, but now *Majority World* or *Less Economically Developed Country* (*LEDC*) is seen as more politically correct.

Practice Questions

Q1 Give some examples of jargon associated with medicine.
Q2 In what ways can jargon be seen as a positive use of language?
Q3 How is jargon sometimes misused?
Q4 In what way might political correctness be a good thing?
Q5 Why do some people argue against political correctness?

Essay Question

Q1 Outline some of the ways that people can use communication to exert power over each other, and discuss whether it's important to change the language to avoid this.

You could focus especially on the use of jargon, and debates about political correctness.

It's political correctness gone mad...

This stuff is gold, and that's scientific fact. Talking about non-verbal communication might seem a bit weird, but it can be really useful — if you get an extract from some fiction, and it describes a speaker sighing or gesticulating or whatever, then just whack in something about NVC and the marks are yours. Gesticulate. Tee hee hee. Sounds a bit rude somehow...

Language and Power

These pages are about language and power in terms of the media. Sounds tricky, but it's basically just how the language of things like newspapers, magazines, TV, adverts, radio, the Internet and films can be used to persuade the audience.

The **Media** holds **Considerable Power**

The language of the media can have a big influence on people's **attitudes** and **values**. This occurs in a number of ways.

1) **Bias** — the tendency to **take sides** and view things **subjectively**, e.g. only focusing on the positive aspect of a new law or political party, or using **loaded** and **emotive** language to present factual information, e.g. *tragic*.

2) **Prejudice** — a **preconceived** opinion of a person or group that isn't based on **experience** or **reason**. Media texts can **create** and **reinforce** these negative opinions so that an audience begin to associate them with a particular group of people, e.g. describing asylum seekers as *scrounging from the taxpayer*.

3) **Stereotypes** — **simplified** images or descriptions of people and events. The most common are based around **gender roles**, in which men are viewed in a certain way, and women in another (see p.50-51). The media can easily **create** and **reinforce** stereotypes when presenting pictures, information and opinions.

4) The media can also affect an audience's **point of view** by **sensationalising** stories (making a big deal out of them), being **selective** with quotes or information, or using **ambiguous** language.

Adverts are the most **Persuasive** form of media

All adverts aim to **attract** an audience to a particular product, service or cause, by focusing on the following things.

1) **Selling** — advert makers use different approaches to do this, e.g. showing **attractive people** with **luxurious lifestyles** using a product to persuade the audience to buy it.

2) **Form** — written adverts come in different forms, e.g. in newspapers and magazines. They can also be in the form of appeal letters that come through your door, leaflets, posters and e-mails (SPAM).

3) The **target audience** is the audience the advert is aimed at. This could be very **broad** (food shoppers, drivers) or more **specific** (boys who like snowboarding).

4) The **hook** is the device advertisers use to get the audience's attention — it could be **verbal**, **visual** or **musical**.

5) In paper-based adverts the **text** is referred to as **copy**. People who **write** adverts are sometimes called **copywriters**. It's their job to come up with ways to make adverts interesting and grab their target audience's attention.

Adverts use a number of **Creative Features**

1) Adverts **manipulate** language just like any other **persuasive** text. Here are a few examples.

- **Lexis** — comparative and superlative **adjectives** and hi-tech **jargon** make the product seem state-of-the-art.
- **Grammar** — imperatives without subjects are common **hooks**, e.g. *unite, enjoy*, but adverts use all kinds of sentence functions. They also use **disjunctive** sentences (e.g. *elegant but sturdy*) to make **concise comparisons**.
- **Phonology** — adverts often rely on **alliteration**, **onomatopoeia** and **rhyme** to make them unique and **appealing**.
- **Graphology** — the images, colour and typeface are also carefully chosen to make the advert **stand out**.
- **Discourse structure** — the **hook** is normally followed by further **persuasion** or **information**, and then **instructions** on how to get hold of the product, e.g. price, where it's available, how to contact the company, etc.

2) Using **puns** and well-known **collocations** also grabs the audience's **attention**, and sticks in their minds.

- **Semantic puns**, e.g. *Fly with us, the sky's the limit.*
- **Phonetic puns**, e.g. *Hair today, gone tomorrow.*
- **Figurative language**, e.g. *Is there a black hole in your pocket? Start saving now!*

3) Referencing other texts is called **intertextuality**. This can create a more memorable and **accessible** text.

- For example, a **hook** for a mattress advert — *and on the seventh day he rested*. This echoes words from the Bible, so a lot of people will recognise it. This is aimed at quite a general **target audience**.
- Other adverts aim to appeal to a more **specific** audience. They reference lesser-known texts to 'stroke' the audience — they will feel knowledgeable and know that the product will only appeal to an **elite few.**
- E.g. a **hook** for a luxury travel company advertising city breaks in London and Paris — *A Tale of Two Cities*. This references the title of a Charles Dickens novel, which not everyone would be familiar with.

Language and Power

Tabloid Newspapers use *Different* Language to *Broadsheets*

Every newspaper takes a slightly **different political viewpoint**, so their purpose is to **persuade** as well as to **inform**. Newspapers are in **competition** with each other, so they also need to **entertain** readers to keep them interested.

1) **Tabloid newspapers** are ones like *The Sun* and *The News of the World*. They tend to make their viewpoint on a story very clear, and use quite **straightforward language**.

2) **Broadsheets** are newspapers such as *The Guardian* and *The Daily Telegraph*. They're aimed at a **professional**, mostly **middle class readership**.

Features of tabloid newspapers	Features of broadsheet newspapers
Short paragraphs	**Longer** paragraphs
Large font, spread out	**Smaller font**, compact
Large print, sensational headlines (*May Day Massacre*)	**Smaller print**, factual headlines (*PM Defeat at Polls*)
Lots of **large photographs**	Fewer, **smaller photographs**
Short, Anglo-Saxon words (*think, dead*)	**Long, Latinate** words (*cogitate, deceased*)
Simple sentences with few clauses	**Complex sentences** with more **subordinate** clauses
Simple punctuation, exclamation marks	**Complex punctuation**, few exclamation marks
First names or **nicknames** (*Gordon, Macca*)	**Full names** or **surnames** (*Gordon Brown, McCartney*)
Sensationalised news stories, **one-sided** point of view	**Fact-based** news stories, often more **objective** stance
Emotive vocabulary (*Monster rapist gets off with five years*)	**Neutral** vocabulary (*Rapist gets five year sentence*)
Personalisation	**Impersonal** tone
Informal vocabulary (*pal, kids*)	More **formal** vocabulary (*friend, children*)
Use of **phonological features** like alliteration and rhyme. Also **phonetic spelling** (*No Bovver Says Becks*)	Fewer **phonological features** (*No Problem for Beckham*)
Use of **puns** (*Santa's Grotty*)	**Few** puns

1) Newspaper language also makes use of **modifier + headword** constructions.

2) In the case of **tabloids** this is often for **sensational effect**, e.g. emotive modifiers such as *tragic* hero, *incest* fiend, *heartbroken* midfielder, *chilling* image.

3) **Broadsheets** use these constructions less. When they do, they tend to be more factual, e.g. *experienced* manager, *Dublin-born* criminal. For a direct comparison, see p.14.

Practice Questions

Q1 What is prejudice? Give a linguistic example.
Q2 Explain the terms target audience, hook, and copy.
Q3 Describe how adverts use lexis, grammar, phonology and graphology to appeal to their audience.
Q4 Outline three main differences between tabloid and broadsheet newspapers.
Q5 What is the effect of modifer + headword constructions?

Essay Question

Q1 Compare and contrast these two headlines:

More Cash For Single Mum Scroungers   Single Mothers Can Claim More Benefits

ENG LANG STUDENT IN NAP ON DESK SHOCKER...

It's at about this stage that the mind starts wandering — like, how many newspapers would it take to wrap up every surface you could see... Yes it might be a fire hazard, yes it might go soggy when it rains, yes the ink might rub off on your face when you go to bed (details, details). Don't listen to the naysayers. Join me, and together we shall paper the world with news.

Language and Technology

Technology has a huge impact on language. As new things are invented, new words are needed to describe them — proof if ever you need it that life without TV or the Internet really would be boring and utterly pointless...

Radio Language is Different from TV Language

1) **TV language** has the support of **pictures**, **gestures** and **facial expressions**, and sometimes **text**.

2) On the **radio** there aren't any visual clues, so listeners have to rely on **what** speakers say and **how** they say it.

3) This affects the **type** of language used in each medium. For example:

> *The numbers in brackets indicate the length of pauses in seconds. This symbol (.) indicates a shorter pause.*

Radio commentary of a football match
here's Burton making space along the left hand side (1) Peters in support to his right (1) cross hit hard and low (.) Oliver picks it up on the far right side by the corner flag (.) cuts inside (.) passes to Hilton
Linguistic features
- Lots of information.
- Mainly full sentences.
- Lots of adjectives (e.g. *hard*, *low*).
- Short pauses.

TV commentary of a football match
here's Burton (3) Burton's cross (2) Oliver (3)
Linguistic features
- Minimal information.
- Incomplete sentences.
- Long pauses.

Telephone Language is Dialogue

1) Telephone language shares many features with **face-to-face dialogue**. This includes **non-fluency features**, like **fillers** and **false starts**, and **non-verbal** aspects of speech, like **intonation** and **stress**.

2) The **opening sequence** is very formulaic, and generally involves the same **adjacency pairs** — the person answering says **hello**, and the person phoning says **who they are** or who they **wish to speak to**. Differences in this sequence usually depend on the **age** of the speaker — **older** people are more likely to answer with something like *Molesey 326*, while **younger** people tend to be **less formal**, e.g. *All right, Tyler*. How you answer can also depend on **context**, e.g. people tend to be more **formal** at **work** than at **home**.

3) **Mobile phones** are an exception to this. You can usually **see who's calling** before you answer, and the person phoning can be more certain of who's going to pick up, so the opening sequence is more **flexible** and **casual**.

4) The lack of **non-verbal communication** means that telephone language includes quite **strict turn-taking**, because there are no **visual clues** to indicate when a speaker has finished. There are also **few pauses**.

Mobile Phones have had a Big Impact on Language

Probably the biggest influence that mobile phones have had on language is **text speak**.

1) Text messaging is **creative** — it's not **standardised**, so everyone uses it slightly differently. It's a **mixed mode** of communication, because it's a **written** language that contains many features of **spoken** language (see p.33).

2) These distinctive features have come about because of a need to **communicate quickly**. Typing complete words into a mobile phone keypad is time-consuming, so text speak has evolved as a form of **shorthand**.

Feature	Example
acronyms	LOL (Laugh Out Loud)
numbers for words	2 (to)
numbers for phonemes (sounds)	gr8 (great)
symbols for words	@ (at)
phonetic spelling	coz (because)
incomplete clauses	home safe. speak soon
no punctuation	how u doin wana go out 2nite
simple sentences	went to the zoo. it was good.
smileys / emoticons	:-)

Roger hadn't quite got the hang of this texting lark.

Language and Technology

The *Internet* has affected language too

The language used over the internet, e.g. in **e-mail**, **live chat** and **forums,** shares some of the linguistic features of mobile text messaging.

1) E-mails are a **mixed mode**, containing **spoken** and **written** features. The mode that dominates depends on how **formal** the email is.

2) Internet language is dependent on **context**. An e-mail from one business to another business might be set out like a **formal letter** and use **Standard English** (p.36-38). But friends communicating in a chatroom might use **text speak**, and language normally associated with **informal spoken** English — e.g. **slang**, **non-standard grammar**.

3) Internet communication involves certain **conventions**, known as **netiquette**. This includes things like avoiding using all **capital letters**, because this is the equivalent of shouting.

New technology can be baffling.

New Technology has Created New Words and Meanings

Every piece of new technology needs **new words** to describe it. This can involve giving **existing** words **new meanings**, or **inventing** completely new terms.

Way of forming new words	Example
acronyms — the initial letters from a group of words form a new word	radar (**r**adio **d**etection **a**nd **r**anging)
affixation — adding a prefix or suffix to an existing word	hypertext
compounding — combining separate words	spyware
clipping — a shortened word becomes a word in its own right	fax (from facsimile)
blending — parts of two words are combined	netizen (internet + citizen)
conversion — an existing word changes its grammatical function	**the text** (noun) becomes **to text** (verb)

TV also increases people's knowledge of **specialist vocabulary** from **different fields**. Documentaries and the news do this to a certain extent, but programmes about specific occupations also have an impact, e.g. **medical dramas**, **courtroom dramas** and **cop shows**.

Practice Questions

Q1 What is the basic difference between TV and radio and what impact can this have on language use?
Q2 Outline one difference between telephone dialogue and face-to-face dialogue.
Q3 How does text speak differ from standard written English?
Q4 Define each of the following methods of forming new words: affixation, compounding, conversion.

Essay Question

Hey Sweetie!
hows you? what's my favourite sis been up2 — haven't heard from u in AGES, grrrr!! Anyway ive got some dead dead excitin news... I found a photo of you from when ur little in the bath and im gonna post it on the net for all to see... Nah not really lol! Actually, heard that Pat's comin back from australia next month! See, i knew ud be excited! Well, got to go, but see you really soon for a catch up — gimme a text next time ur free xxoxx

Q1 This is an extract of an email an 18 year old girl sent to her sister.
Analyse it in terms of the impact that technology has had on the language.

This was all fields in my day...

If you get an extract from anything that's got even the merest sniff of technology about it, then throw in this stuff and you're laughing. See, it's not such a bad life really — pretty much everyone watches TV and knows about texting, but not everyone gets to talk about it in their exams. Just don't try to do any actual texting in your exams though — it won't go down well.

Sources and Exam Questions

Here are some exam-style questions, with sources like the ones you'll get in the real paper.

1. The text below is a transcript of a conversation between the manager of a shoe shop and two trainees. It is their first day.

   What is the significance of gender in this interaction?   *[48 marks]*

M: right Josh I want you to work in the men's section (.) is that okay

J: cool

M: and you Susie erm I'd like you to man the customer service desk at first (.) that's on the lower floor (.) okay with that

S: yes (.) yes (.) that's fine

M: great (.) now then (.) let me tell what I'll (.) what I'll expect from you

S: mm mm

M: ok you need to be here by eight-thirty every morning (1.0) and I mean eight-thirty yes

J: sure

S: yes but erm er (1.0) sometimes (.) sorry I hope it's okay but my bus is late sometimes so (.) it should be fine

M: no that's okay (.) but if you can see about getting an earlier one if you can

S: mm mm no of course (.) sorry

M: there's not always much you do about it though is there (.) don't worry sweetheart (2.0) now

J: // I live near yours Suzie

S: okay (.) erm

J: I'll give you a lift

S: oh are you sure (1.0) if you're sure that'd be great (.) thank you

M: brilliant (.) good lad (1.0) that's that sorted then (.) okay erm breaktimes for you two are erm ten forty-five to eleven (.) in the morning erm and two forty-five to three in the afternoon (2.0) finish at five

J: what about lunch-time

M: good question (1.0) lunchtime (1.0) we don't want a growing lad like you starving now do we (1.0) one till two (1.0) right (1.0) everything clear

S: yes thank you (.) although I just wondered

J: // fine (1.0) do we work every Saturday

M: no (.) alternate Saturdays erm we'll need to work out which ones I er want you in for later (2.0) but we'll do that later (.) now (1) the till

J: // don't worry about me (.) I were on the tills in me last job

M: great (.) okay what about you Suzie

S: yep no that's fine (.) I've worked in shops before

M: right (2.0) little miss efficient eh

S: mm

M: okay so we'll have Josh (.) you on the tills at first right (2.0) so Susie (1.0) polite at all times (2.0) and don't forget to smile (1.0) you going to be OK with that Susie

S: yep think so (1.0) thanks (.) can I ask for help if I need it

J: cool

Transcription Key

(.) — *brief pause*

(3.0) — *Numbers within brackets indicate length of pause in seconds*

// — *interruption or overlapping speech*

M — Manager

S — Female Trainee

J — Male Trainee

Sources and Exam Questions

2. The text below is a transcript of part of a Chemistry lesson.

What do you observe about the power relationships in this extract?   *[48 marks]*

T — Teacher
A, **B**, **C**, **D** — Pupils

T: settle down now (.) we haven't got all day to get through this stuff (1.0) keep ties on please okay (.) yeah (.) okay and and top buttons done up James (2.0) so can we turn (.) can we turn to what we we were doing last week okay (.) ionic bonding page nine

A: page ten

T: what

A: page ten (.) it's on

B: // yeah it's on page ten

T: okay thanks page ten (.) fine okay now what do we remember (.) remember from last week about

C: // nothing

T: no not nothing (.) what about

B: // no it is nothing sir (.) we had sports day since then didn't we

T: well sports day doesn't wipe everything from (.) from your memory does it now (2.0) so what can you tell me about what happens to atoms (.) what is it that happens to atoms in ionic bonding (4.0) Melanie (1.0) what happens

A: erm (2.0) it's (.) they don't (.) they don't

T: // think about electrons

A: right yeah (.) well with electrons they like they like (.) have them when

B: // no-one remembers nothing about this

T: anything (.) remembers anything about this

B: right

A: // yeah

T: okay no (.) we do remember (.) let's just settle down and focus now right (1.0) if you don't get this it's you who has to do the exams so you really need to get this bit (2.0) in ionic bonding atoms lose or gain electrons to form (2.0) what do they form (3.0) James

B: ions (.) is it (.) ions yeah

T: yep ions (.) great okay (.) yes Tash erm (.) yes

D: sorry but erm (.) it's really hot in here sir (.) please may I (.) can I

B: // yeah

T: // okay well open the window (3.0) right so what are ions please

3. The text below is a chatroom conversation between two school friends.

What do you observe about the influence of technology on the language of this text?   *[48 marks]*

hani_ani:	hey rosie hw u doin? havnt see u for time
Bubblicious:	i no! am cool chik hw u 2? how was tenerife?
hani_ani:	BRILL!!!!!! the guys are soooo hot there!!
Bubblicious:	naughty! u stil seein Billy?
hani_ani:	lol nah, he's weird man! dmped him
Bubblicious:	Ahhh! He wuz cool! Mite giv im a call lol!! nah fair enuff. Lookin fwd 2 going bak?
hani_ani:	Sort of. Gonna ave 2 do sum work this yr tho
Bubblicious:	yeh, cant wait :'-(
hani_ani:	newayz u wanna do somethin l8tr man? Catch up a bit?
Bubblicious:	love 2 bt no dosh :(u could cum round 2 mine?
hani_ani:	Cud do. Wot time?
Bubblicious:	Hw bout 8. cud watch a film or sommat....??
hani_ani:	Cool! I'll be ther @ 8
hani_ani:	bysie byes xxxx
Bubblicious:	xxxxxxxxx

Spoken Language

Joy of untold joys — time to learn all about talking and stuff. Spoken language refers to the patterns and styles of language you use to communicate every time you open your mouth. Unless you're doing that hilarious goldfish impression again.

Spoken language has **Two Main Purposes**

1) **To convey meaning** — when you need to **explain something** to someone, or **give orders** or **instructions**, you use language as a means of **clarification**, so that the listener will **understand** you.

2) **To demonstrate attitudes and values** — language lets you offer **opinions** on subjects, and get your **point of view across**.

Chris promised to give conversation a chance next time.

The **Content** of spoken language **Depends** on its **Context**

Spoken language is usually the most **efficient** way for speakers to communicate with each other. As with written language, the way a spoken text is **constructed** can be affected by **external** features.

1) The **audience** or **person being addressed** — it could be someone the speaker has known for years, or thousands of people that they've never met before.

2) The speaker's **background** — this will affect their **word choices**, **grammatical constructions**, etc.

3) The **location** and **purpose** of the text — speakers use language differently depending on where the conversation is taking place, and what's being talked about.

Spoken language can be **Formal** or **Informal**

1) **Formal** speech is often used in situations when you **don't really know** the people you're talking to.

2) You might also use formal speech in a situation where you want to **show respect**, like a **job interview**.

3) It's most common in **prepared** speeches — the speaker is reading from **planned written notes**.

4) Formal spoken language is more likely to use **complex** and mainly **complete grammatical structures**.

> 1) **Informal** speech is generally used **among friends** or in situations where there's **no need** for formality or preparation.
>
> 2) It includes mostly **colloquial language**, which is casual and familiar.
>
> 3) It has **simpler** and often **incomplete grammatical structures**, **simpler vocabulary**, more **slang** words and **dialect** features.

Speech can be **Individual** or involve **More Than One Person**

Individual speech is often known as a **monologue**. Monologues convey **internal thoughts**, **opinions** or **experiences**.

1) The term 'monologue' is usually used for a **scripted performance** (a dramatic monologue), but it can also include any **individual** speaking for a longer period of time than normal.

2) Monologues are directed at listeners who make **no spoken contribution**.

3) They can be **prepared** or **spontaneous**.

Dialogue is **spoken** language that involves **more than one** speaker.

1) A dialogue is a **conversation** involving two or more people — they use language to **interact** with each other.

2) Dialogue exchanges can be **short**, but in longer conversations one of the speakers may take the **major role**, with the others mainly listening and only **contributing occasionally**.

3) Dialogue can be prepared or spontaneous. Most conversations between characters on TV or in plays or films are **scripted** by a writer, but conversations between you and your friends are **unprepared** — in spontaneous dialogue speakers **respond** to the different **cues and contexts** that come up as the conversation goes on.

Spoken Language

Spoken Language Functions *in different ways*

There are **five** categories of **spoken language**, which are used in different situations.

1) **Interactional language** is the language of **informal speech**. It has a **social** function — its purpose is to **develop relationships** between speakers.

The speakers exchange personal information. →

> **A:** so what're you studying when you get there
> **B:** I'm going to be doing astronomy
> **A:** no way (2) so am I I'll see you in lectures

← Asking a question guarantees a response and keeps the interaction going.

2) **Referential language** provides the listener with **information**. It's used to **refer** to **objects** or to **abstract** concepts. The speaker **assumes knowledge** from the listener. The listener has to understand the **context** before they can make sense of the **references**.

> **the parcel** is being delivered **here** at **two o'clock**

This wouldn't make sense to the listener unless they knew that a parcel was expected.

The listener wouldn't understand this reference unless they knew where *here* was.

This assumes that the listener knows what day the parcel is expected, and whether it's more likely to be delivered at two o'clock in the morning or in the afternoon.

3) **Expressive language** highlights the speaker's **emotions**, **feelings** and **attitudes**. The language shows the speaker's judgements or feelings about another person, event or situation.

> this **really** can't be allowed to continue (.) my friends (3) it's a **total disgrace**

It's likely to contain adverbs to make the statements forceful

Emotive adjectives make the statements subjective

4) **Transactional language** is about **getting information** or **making a deal**, e.g. buying or selling. It has a specific purpose, so it's driven by '**needs and wants**' rather than **sociability**.

A direct request for information is followed by a direct answer.

> **A:** could you tell me where the soup is please
> **B:** it's on aisle 7 (.) right by the croutons

5) **Phatic language** is used for **social purposes** rather than to convey serious meaning, e.g. when someone comments about the weather as a means of **initiating a conversation**. They don't want to have a meteorological discussion with you, but it starts a conversation that (usually) quickly moves on to other subjects. Phatic communication is also called '**small talk**'.

The speaker doesn't expect these questions to be answered.

> did you see that rain before (.) it was unbelievable (2) I'm not too late am I

Practice Questions

Q1   Explain in your own words the difference between formal and informal spoken language.

Q2   What's the difference between a monologue and dialogue?

Q3   Describe the features and function of referential spoken language.

Essay Question

Q1   Describe the different types of spoken language and suggest where each might be used.

What about people that actually want a meteorological discussion with you?

Just leg it. Pure and simple. It does sort of make me wonder what weathermen or weatherwomen talk about after they've had the small talk. Maybe they talk about things they're interested in, like... I don't know... jazz, or European cinema. I don't trust them though, with their funny laser-thumbs, always changing that map on the wall behind them... making it rain a lot.

Who are you calling speech features? Oh... oh right. These pages will give you some all-important features of spontaneous and prepared speech. These are pretty important — more building blocks for your analysis in the exam.

Speech can be **Prepared** or **Spontaneous**

You can either know exactly what you're about to say, or you can make it up as you go along.

Prepared speech

1) Worked out **in advance**.
2) Designed for specific **audience and purpose**.
3) Needs to be **well written** (so is usually **formal** and in Standard English).
4) **Performed** or **delivered** to try and make an impact.
5) Needs to **maintain the interest** of listeners (who may or may not be known to the speaker).
6) Examples include **political speeches** and **sermons**.

Spontaneous speech

1) **Not prepared** or written down beforehand.
2) Delivered **on the spot** as soon as, or shortly after, the idea comes to the speaker.
3) Usually **informal** (depending on context).
4) Usually shared with people **known to the speaker**.
5) Mainly **in response to** another speaker.

Ross probably should've put the vacuum appliance down before starting his speech.

Prepared and **Spontaneous** Speech are **Very Different**

If you apply **language frameworks** to prepared and spontaneous speech, you can see how different they are.

Lexis
- **Prepared speech** — the lexis is likely to be **standardised** and formal. Speakers have time to think about their word choices, so the vocabulary is more **sophisticated** and **technical**.
- **Spontaneous speech** — the lexis is likely to be **non-standard**. The informal context means **slang** and **dialect** forms are used more.

Grammar
- **Prepared speech** — the structure of sentences follows standard **grammatical rules** and pauses in the speech are controlled by **punctuation**. Speakers don't tend to use many **contractions**.
- **Spontaneous speech** — non-standard **agreements**, non-standard or **irregular tenses**, and **double negatives** are common in conversation, e.g. *I done it, We was planning to, I never told him nothing.*

Formality / Audience
- **Prepared speech** — speeches are aimed at an **audience**. The language is carefully chosen to persuade the audience in some way. Prepared speeches usually **address** the audience **directly** (the speaker uses *I* or *we*, and *you*). They're often **formal** to create a feeling of **prestige**.
- **Spontaneous speech** — most spontaneous speech is only meant for the speakers involved. Conversations that take place in **public places** (over a shop counter etc.) or between strangers are usually more **formal** than private ones.

Prepared and spontaneous speech also have some features in common:

1) **Discourse structure** — a prepared speech has a beginning, middle, and end. **Themes** and **ideas** are introduced at different points, and the whole thing is usually written to end on a **positive note**, so that the audience go away with a **lasting impression**. Spontaneous speech also has **formulaic** beginnings and endings (see p.66-67).
2) **Non-verbal communication** — relates to body language, gestures and facial expressions. It **emphasises** certain words or phrases in both prepared and spontaneous speech, but can also be **disruptive** if it's overdone.
3) **Prosodic features** — include stress, rhythm, pitch, tempo and intonation. They're useful in prepared speech, where a speaker can use the devices to keep an audience **interested** over a long period of time.

Spontaneous Speech has many Unique Features

Even though **spontaneous speech** shares some features with prepared spoken English, it has lots of **specific features**. Look at the following **conversation** between two people:

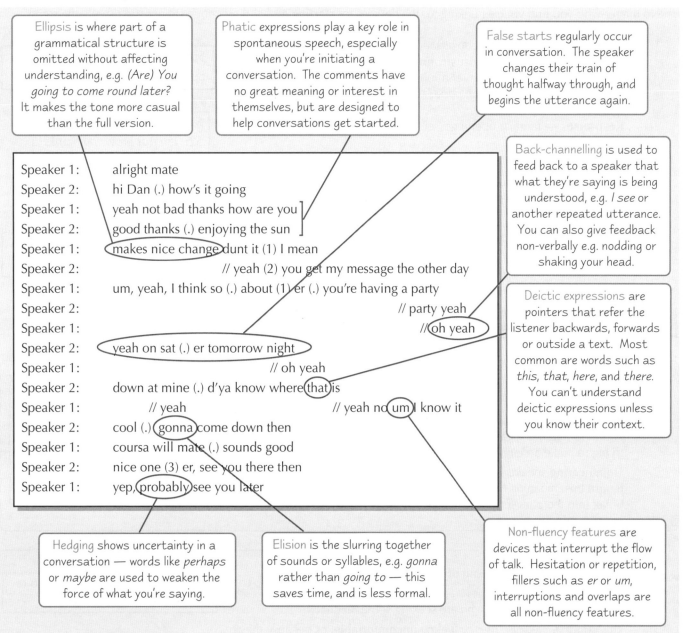

Ellipsis is where part of a grammatical structure is omitted without affecting understanding, e.g. *(Are) You going to come round later?* It makes the tone more casual than the full version.

Phatic expressions play a key role in spontaneous speech, especially when you're initiating a conversation. The comments have no great meaning or interest in themselves, but are designed to help conversations get started.

False starts regularly occur in conversation. The speaker changes their train of thought halfway through, and begins the utterance again.

Back-channelling is used to feed back to a speaker that what they're saying is being understood, e.g. *I see* or another repeated utterance. You can also give feedback non-verbally e.g. nodding or shaking your head.

Deictic expressions are pointers that refer the listener backwards, forwards or outside a text. Most common are words such as *this, that, here,* and *there.* You can't understand deictic expressions unless you know their context.

Speaker 1:	alright mate
Speaker 2:	hi Dan (.) how's it going
Speaker 1:	yeah not bad thanks how are you
Speaker 2:	good thanks (.) enjoying the sun
Speaker 1:	makes nice change dunt it (1) I mean
Speaker 2:	// yeah (2) you get my message the other day
Speaker 1:	um, yeah, I think so (.) about (1) er (.) you're having a party
Speaker 2:	// party yeah
Speaker 1:	// oh yeah
Speaker 2:	yeah on sat (.) er tomorrow night
Speaker 1:	// oh yeah
Speaker 2:	down at mine (.) d'ya know where that is
Speaker 1:	// yeah // yeah no um I know it
Speaker 2:	cool (.) gonna come down then
Speaker 1:	coursa will mate (.) sounds good
Speaker 2:	nice one (3) er, see you there then
Speaker 1:	yep, probably see you later

Hedging shows uncertainty in a conversation — words like *perhaps* or *maybe* are used to weaken the force of what you're saying.

Elision is the slurring together of sounds or syllables, e.g. *gonna* rather than *going to* — this saves time, and is less formal.

Non-fluency features are devices that interrupt the flow of talk. Hesitation or repetition, fillers such as *er* or *um,* interruptions and overlaps are all non-fluency features.

Practice Questions

Q1 Give a key difference in the use of grammar in prepared speech as opposed to spontaneous speech.

Q2 How can paralinguistic and prosodic features help speakers?

Q3 Give three examples of phatic expressions.

Essay Question

Q1 Discuss the differences between prepared and spontaneous speech, with reference to lexis, grammar and formality.

Everyone uses phatic expressions — even if they're not that phat...

Hopefully, you'll recognise some of these features from conversations you've had in the past with people you know (and probably people you don't). If you don't, good work. You're obviously the finest conversationalist since Talky McChatterlot, who never hedged, or false-started, or used phatic expressions or anything. He was dead dull though.

If you've ever had a conversation, you'll know that you can't just rabbit on all the way through... unless it's a conversation with yourself... in which case, sorry for interrupting. But if there are two people involved — learn the rules.

Some features occur in *All Conversations*

No matter who you find yourself talking to, the devices for **starting** and **ending** conversations are usually the same.

1) **Openings** — an informal conversation may begin with a simple **familiar starter**. These are usually **greetings**, such as *hello*, or *alright?* More formal conversations often include **inquiries** like *I wonder if you could help me?* to get someone's **attention**.

> Speaker 1: *good morning*
> Speaker 2: *hello (.) can I help you*

2) **Responses** — familiar openings (see above) invite a particular response.

> S1: *hello (.) can I help you*
> S2: *I'm just browsing thanks*

3) **Adjacency pairs** — **short**, **familiar exchanges** of conversation that follow **predictable** patterns.

> S1: *how are you*
> S2: *I'm fine thanks*

4) **Signalling closure** — speech indicators and other non-verbal signs can be used to show that a conversation is **drawing to a close**.

> S1: *he fell down a manhole once*
> S2: *really (1) well time I was off*

Some features depend on the *Individual Speakers*

Switching and turn-taking

1) The person speaking at any given time may be aware that **someone else** wants to speak.
2) In an orderly conversation they **invite** the switch to another speaker e.g. by **pausing**, or trying to make an **emphatic** final statement.
3) **Domineering** speakers sometimes choose to **ignore** this, meaning other speakers have to break into the conversation by **interrupting**, or just **stay silent**.

> S1: *I can't believe he didn't see it*
> S2: *why not (1) it wasn't a penalty (2) what do you think*
> S3: *I think it probably was*
> S2: *that's why you're not a referee*
> S1: *it's pretty hard to work out*
> S2: *// maybe if you weren't watching*

Tag questions

1) These are attached to the **end of statements**, and **invite responses** from other speakers.
2) They're used by speakers who are seeking some **feedback**.
3) This could be because they're feeling **uncomfortable**, or because they're trying to **control** the conversation by bringing other people into it.

> S1: *this is an issue that we need to resolve quickly isn't it*

Topic Shifts

1) **Topic shifts** are when speakers **change the subject** of the conversation.
2) They move the conversation forward or **change its focus**.
3) They're usually started by the domineering speaker trying to control the **content** and **direction** of a conversation.

> S1: *so I said carbonara*
> S2: *right (2) did you ever hear back from Dave*

Feedback

1) When someone's speaking, people give **verbal** and **non-verbal** signs that they're **listening** to them
2) For example, brief comments, nodding or shaking your head, smiling, frowning, etc.

> S1: *no one told me it was a sponge*
> S2: *mm-hmm*

Conversation and Turn-taking

Different *Techniques* are involved at different *Stages* of a *Conversation*

Getting involved / Initiating conversation

1) Most participants in a conversation will offer a contribution **without waiting** to be asked — if you waited to be asked to speak in every conversation, you might **never** speak at all.

2) You might get a conversation started by showing an **interest** in the other people involved.

3) If you're talking to an **unfamiliar person**, appropriate **phatic expressions** and **questioning** can help get things started, e.g. you can use **tag questions** to initiate **responses**.

Sustaining conversation

1) Fluent speaking (following **adjacency patterns** and **turn-taking rules**), showing an interest (**feedback**) and generally enjoying talking are all factors that help people **sustain** conversation.

2) **Speaker empathy** is important — if people are exploring **shared interests** or **opinions** then the conversation is more likely to be sustained. Listeners might make it clear that they share the speaker's views by using feedback, e.g. *mm* and *yeah*.

Ending conversation

1) **Social convention** makes us not want to appear rude, cut people short or walk away when they're not ready — so **phatic expressions** are used to **signal closure** in a socially recognisable way, e.g. *I should probably get going*.

2) There are also **non-verbal** cues that signal a speaker is about to end the conversation e.g. starting to **get up** from a seat, or increasing the **distance** between the speakers.

The conversation got heated as they tried to work out who'd thought of the fancy dress costume first.

Participants *Manage* and *Control* conversations

In an orderly conversation, you take **turns** speaking with other people. However, not all conversations are orderly and it's rare to find one where each speaker actually waits their turn — it depends on the **individuals** involved.

Prepared / Formal situations

1) These are the types of conversation where there is a defined power relationship between the participants, e.g. conducting an **interview** with someone or being interviewed yourself.

2) **Prepared situations** (like a tutorial, job interview or debate) have a **specific subject** or subject area on the agenda. You may not know precisely how the conversation will go, but you know what is **likely** to be discussed, and the level of **formality** you're expected to use.

3) There's usually a person **overtly** in charge of the exchanges, like a lecturer, interviewer or chairperson, whose **authority** to change the conversation at will is **already acknowledged** before it starts.

Unprepared / Informal situations

1) **Informal** social conversations are less likely to be prepared, and could involve any topic, but these still tend to be **controlled** by certain individuals.

2) People who are **louder**, **quicker** and more **forceful** than other speakers often **dominate informal conversations**.

3) It is easy for less confident and less assertive speakers to be **inhibited** or **intimidated**, and to end up contributing very little (for more on conversations and power, see p.52-55).

Practice Questions

Q1 Give an example of a tag question, and describe its purpose.
Q2 What are adjacency pairs, and how are they used in conversation?

Essay Question

Q1 Discuss the techniques speakers use to initiate, manage, control, sustain and end conversations.

You say potato, I say pipe down for ONE MINUTE so I can get a word in...

Is that too much to ask? Right then. You should now have all the tools you need for analysing spoken language, whether it's prepared speeches (when you need to think mainly about purpose and effect), or spontaneous conversation (where you need to think about features of interaction). And for once, eavesdropping would be really good practice.

Sources and Exam Questions

You'll find plenty of spoken language in the first section of the AQA B exam paper. We've put this question in to help you pick out the important features from different types of spoken language texts, but it's not quite the same as the question you'll get in section A of your exam (see Section 7).

1) Study the three texts below, **A**, **B** and **C**.

Analyse and compare the use of language by the speakers in these texts.

In your answer you should consider:

- the features of spontaneous speech
- the uses of standard and non-standard grammar
- how the texts are controlled and managed.

Text A — Conversation between a customer and a newsagent.

A: now then Sam

B: now then (.) been sent to get the paper

A: yes here we are (.) bit late delivering today

B: oh yeah

A: yeah it's a right pain (1.0) here I saw your lad the other day (.) he back now from

B: // mm   // aye yeah (.) yeah back from university

A: comes round quick doesn't it

B: quick yeah (.) yeah he's back three months now

A: // three months

B: // aye (.) I er I wanted to ask actually (1.0) he's gonna need some er some work you see (.) while he's (.) but he doesn't drive so I mean you don't know anyone in the village who might need (.) need a bit of work done do you

A: oh aye yeah (.) I see (.) long time to go with no work is three months (2.0) I'll have a think

B: // mm I mean I think he's willing for most things (.) odd jobs and

A: // odd jobs like (.) mm (2.0) tell you what (.) some of the older people might need a hand in their gardens (.) you know mowing the lawn and that

B: // yeah that'll be

A: tell you what (.) write his name and a contact number on a card (.) I can put it up there with the others on the board over there

B: oh cheers yeah (.) oh that'll be great yeah thanks (1.0) if you hear anyone mentioning needing help in the meantime give us a nod will you

A: no problem mate

Text B — Extract from a job interview.

X: (*the interviewer*) you must be Matthew (2.0) come in and have a seat

Y: (*the candidate*) yep that's ri- (2.0) oh right (.) thanks

X: you found the office alright then did you?

Y: er (.) yep it was fine (.) I had a map so

X: // good good (.) we'll get started then (1.0) I don't want to keep you too long (.) basically what's going to happen is I'll ask you a few questions about your suitability for the role (1.0) and then we'll have a little chat about the company so you can see if you like us (.) and we can see if we like you (2.0) that sound ok?

Y: yeah grea- (1.0) um (.) yeah that sounds fine

X: excellent (.) so (2.0) I see from your CV and application that you've worked in radio before?

Y: Yep (1.0) yes I

(Text B contd.)

X: // why don't you tell me a little bit about that

Y: OK (3.0) well basically (.) um (.) it was a hospital radio station and (1.0) er I had to go round wards and get requests from people that were going to listen to the show (.) and (2.0) um (.) sort of put it together you know

X: mmm-hmm (1.0) right OK (1.0) and did you get a chance to do any work behind the desks?

Y: Yeah (.) yeah I did (.) er (2.0) at first I was only really allowed to speak on air (1.0) you know, probably a good thing (2.0) but then I started to learn a bit about the presenting and I got

X: // and then you got a shot at DJ-ing?

Y: er (.) yeah (1.0) they let me loose after that

X: good (.) great (1.0) so did you enjoy that or did you prefer producing the shows you were working on?

Text C — Speech by a company director to the company's employees.

ladies and gentlemen (1.0) err ladies and gentlemen (2.0) can (.) can you hear me OK at the back there?

(*indistinct responses*)

err (.) ladies and gentlemen thank you all very (.) very much for coming today (2.0) I (.) I know some of you were only given very short notice of this meeting (.) and I apologise for that but thanks for making the effort to be here (2.0) I wish I had better news to share with you (1.0) but as some of you will already know (1.0) I'm afraid I don't

it's difficult to know how best to put this (2.0) but here goes (.)

many of you will already be aware that the company has been struggling of late to break even (1.0) what with the increasing costs of production (.) the high cost of borrowing (1.0) and so on (2.0) and so (.) management has been forced into the kind of decision that we hoped that we were never going to have to make

(*murmuring from the floor*)

the branch is going to have to close down in order to keep alive the chances of us keeping going elsewhere (5.0) we aim to find work elsewhere for as many of you as possible (.) especially our younger workers (1.0) but we simply can't provide enough for everyone (1.0) so with the greatest regret (1.0) and I assure it <u>is</u> with the greatest regret and we're <u>not</u> smiling behind your backs (2.0) we are going to have to offer redundancy packages to some of you (.)

I want you <u>all</u> to be aware that a redundancy package in <u>no way</u> suggests that we think that you are no longer valued by us (1.0) but we simply <u>can't avoid</u> doing this if we're to have <u>any</u> chance of continuing to hold our place in the market in the future (3.0) we <u>have</u> to be pragmatic about this — we have no choice (3.0)

Les (.) the branch manager (.) will be speaking to each of you individually within the next few days (1.0) I don't envy him this for one moment (1.0) so that you're all in the picture as quickly as possible.

I can't really say very much more (2.0) other than to emphasise once again how much it hurts me to have to stand up and do this (2.0) thank you all very (.) very much

---

Transcription Key

(.) *Micropause*

(2.0) *Pause in seconds*

// *Interruption / overlapping speech*

All the texts you'll see will have been written for a purpose, otherwise there wouldn't have been any point in writing them in the first place. To identify the main reason a text was written you need to analyse the language it uses.

Texts usually have one of **Four Main Purposes**

1) Written texts usually try to achieve one of the following purposes.

> 1. **Inform** e.g. newspaper   2. **Instruct** e.g. cookbook   3. **Persuade** e.g. advert   4. **Entertain** e.g. comic

Not all texts slot neatly into these categories, e.g. a film review might be informative, entertaining and persuasive.

2) Despite this, you can usually work out the primary function of a text by looking at its language and presentation. To find out the **purpose** of a text you need to apply these **frameworks**:

> - **Lexis** — vocabulary / specific words
> - **Graphology** — how the text is arranged
> - **Grammar** — sentence length and structure
> - **Semantics** — meaning (actual or hidden)

Informative Texts are Factual

1) There are many different types of informative text. Informative writing needs to contain **knowledge** or **facts** that readers want to know, like the latest news in a newspaper.

2) Informative texts are **structured clearly** so they're easy to **understand**. They might include presentational features such as headings / subheadings, bullet points, boxes and illustrations.

3) The information is presented in a way that's **suitable** for the **intended audience**. If it's intended for children, the language is **simple** and **less detailed**. An informative text for an older audience might use more **complex** language — assuming that the reader has some **previous knowledge**.

4) The text may include **specialist** or **technical terms**, and explain them.

5) The tone is usually **serious**. Informative texts don't generally include **opinions** or **comments**. Some informative texts simply consist of times and dates, e.g. a train timetable.

6) Informative texts are usually written in the **third person**, using *he*, *she*, or *it*.

Instructional Texts tell you **How** to do something

These texts are similar to informative texts because they include **information**. However, the main function of an instructional text is to show the reader **how** to do something **practical**. They have a **clear**, **structured** style:

> 1) Instructional texts usually include **chronological**, **numbered** sections.
> 2) They use graphological devices such as **bullet points** and **headings**.
> 3) The instructions are often given as **imperative** sentences e.g. *Add the butter, sugar and flour to the mixture.*
> 4) The text may use **second person** forms (e.g. *you do this*) to address the reader directly.
> 5) The lexis is **straightforward** and **uncomplicated**, but can be **subject-specific** (e.g. *beat*, *whisk*, *fold* in cooking).

Persuasive Texts aim to **Change Your Mind**

1) Persuasive texts try to either **influence** the reader's opinions or **persuade** them to do something.

2) They often use **first person address** (*I* and *we*) to communicate the writer's **feelings** and include the readers. Possessive pronouns like *our* and *your* also **personally** involve the reader in the views expressed in the text.

3) They often use **emotive adjectives** and **subjective judgements** to provoke emotional and intellectual responses.

4) They use facts, statistics and other **evidence** to support the main argument, linked together with connectives such as *therefore*, *because*, and *however* to create a **logical route** to a conclusion.

5) They might use eye-catching **graphology** (p.30-31), such as **logos**, **capitalization** and **colour**, to attract the reader's attention and **stress** the importance of a particular point or argument.

There are many **Different Types** of **Entertainment** texts

1) **Entertainment texts** include novels, stories, articles, verses, songs, poetry, plays, biographies and autobiographies.

2) Even though there's a big **range** of entertainment texts, they tend to have **several features in common**:

- **Sophisticated** language
- **Figurative** language
- **Extensive** vocabulary
- Often **complex structure**
- Varied **sentence types**
- Eye-catching **layout**

3) These techniques help the writers of entertainment texts to express personal **feelings** and produce **poetic** thoughts and ideas.

4) Writers also use these features to influence how the audience **experiences** the text. Entertainment texts can help audiences **escape** from reality, **frighten** and **shock** them, affect them **emotionally** or make them **think**.

5) Some writers might choose to **change** or **ignore** these **expected conventions** to achieve **different effects**.

Texts that **Analyse Language** are called **Commentaries**

A **commentary** or **language analysis** (which you'll be asked to produce in your exam) needs to focus on the following areas:

1) The **linguistic choices** made by the writer.
2) **Distinctive features** of the style or genre chosen by the writer.
3) The influence of the **context** upon the language choices.
4) What **effects** were **intended** or **achieved** in the text.

Linguistic terminology is all very well, but sometimes the only appropriate medium is contemporary dance.

As a writer, commentaries enable you to do the following things:

There's more on writing commentaries in the Do Well in the Exam section, on p.86.

1) Communicate your **knowledge** and **understanding** of how language works by applying it to a particular piece of writing or speech.
2) Use appropriate **linguistic terminology** to explain your points.
3) Demonstrate your knowledge of appropriate **frameworks of language**.

Practice Questions

Q1   How can you tell if the purpose of a text is to inform?

Q2   Which type of text (informative, instructive, persuasive or entertaining) is more likely to use sophisticated language and a variety of sentence structures?

Q3   In persuasive texts, why is the reader often directly addressed in the second person *you*?

Essay Questions

Q1   What sort of language would writers use to make their purpose obvious to an audience in the following types of text: reference book, feature article for a magazine and an advertisement for a charity.

Revision guide texts aim to make you really really really smart...

And that's just the start. I also aim to solve the world's climate problems, but I've yet to work out how to do it using only a handful of verbs and some prepositions. I imagine the eventual solution will be glorious and I'll be hailed as a genius. For now, I'll just advise you to try and be a better student by learning everything there is to know about purpose.

It stands to reason that if texts are written for a particular purpose, they're probably going to be written for a particular audience too. You should be able to identify a text's target audience by analysing the type of language it uses.

The **Audience** is the group of people that the **Text** is **Aimed At**

Intended audiences can vary from the very **general** (e.g. 'adults'), to the very **specific** (e.g. 'females over 30 with young children').

1) Writers **tailor** their texts for different audiences and purposes.

2) To work out the audience of a text, you need to be able to **recognise** and **describe** how a text **suits** a particular kind of reader.

3) You can find **clues** about the audience, their age and relative status, and how the writer **feels about them** in the language of a text, e.g. if a text contains simple sentences and basic lexis, it's likely to be for a young audience.

A writer may or may not **Know Their Audience**

A lot depends on **how familiar** the writer or speaker is with their audience:

Known audience

1) The writer might use **personal pronouns** like *I* and *you*. This writing is most often found in memos, personal letters, diaries and stories.

2) The writer may use language that expresses **emotion**, **feelings** or **opinions**.

3) A writer might also have a **target audience** they know quite a lot about e.g. science fiction fans, or film buffs, or supporters of a particular political party. The writer will choose language that they **expect** will be understood and have an effect on members of the target audience.

Unknown audience

Sometimes the text is for an audience that is **unfamiliar**. This type of writing is often found in **academic** or **instructive texts**. The main characteristics are:

1) The writer doesn't **acknowledge** the reader directly as it's usually written in the third person.

2) There is no expression of **personal feeling** and no use of first or second person **pronouns** (*I* or *you*).

3) The text is quite **formal** — it may use formal vocabulary, imperative sentences (in instructive texts) or the **passive voice**. Texts for unknown audiences deal with **serious** subject matter rather than entertainment.

You can **Work Out** the **Intended Audience** of a text

To **identify** the intended **audience** of a text, you need to look at the **style** of the text, its **content**, the choice of **vocabulary** and the **tone**.

1) **Style** — **formal** and **serious** writing is usually for an **older audience**. If the text is **informal** and more **light-hearted** it's often aimed at a **younger audience**. To narrow down the audience further, you need to look at the content of the text.

2) **Content** — the text might be about a **general topic** like global warming, or it might be something **very specific** like the writer's new trainers. The first would have a very **broad** audience, but the second would be aimed at a much smaller audience.

3) **Lexis** — if there are any **complex**, **specialist** or **technical** words, the audience are probably experts — they will already be **familiar** with the jargon. If there are no specialist words, and the lexis is **uncomplicated** and easy to follow, this suggests a **younger** or **less specialist** audience.

4) **Tone** — the tone reflects the purpose of a text, e.g. an informative text would have a serious tone. The tone can also say something about the audience, e.g. a **serious** tone suggests a **mature** or **interested** audience.

5) **Formality** — formal texts (e.g. reports, articles) are usually aimed at **older**, **professional** audiences (with the exception of textbooks, which are aimed at students). Other texts, e.g. e-mails, are more **informal** and **friendly** as the audience is a **known person** or **group**.

Audience

Texts need to *Suit* their *Readership*

Texts are more **accessible** if they are tailored to suit their audience.

1) The text needs to be **tailored** depending on whether it's aimed at children or adults, e.g. different language is used on a **newspaper front page** compared to a **children's comic**.

2) Texts can sometimes be **gender-specific**, aimed at male or female audiences, e.g. the style and content of *Cosmopolitan* is different to that of *FHM*.

3) The **expertise** of the audience is also an important factor — if the audience are experts then the lexis can be more **specialised** than if the text is for a general readership.

Texts can have *Multiple Audiences*

1) Texts may have **more** than one audience, each of which may respond **differently** to it.

2) For example, a children's story is principally aimed at a **young audience**. However it is an **adult** who will decide whether to buy the book — so it needs to **appeal** to the adult as well.

3) If you've ever seen the film **Shrek**® (2001), you'll have seen how a text can appeal to **lots of different** audiences. It's designed to work on **different levels**, with plenty for kids but also jokes that only adults will understand.

Audiences of *Spoken Discourse* vary too

1) The **content** of a spoken discourse can **reveal** the audience, e.g. the **content** of a **university lecture** reveals that it's intended for students specialising in a subject.

2) The talk could be **formal**, like a public speech, or **colloquial**, like a conversation. The level of formality shows the **relationship** of the listener to the speaker, e.g. you speak **respectfully** and **politely** to someone in a position of **authority**, but **casually** with friends.

3) In the same way, **long complex** sentences would be appropriate in an academic lecture or formal context. **Shorter sentences** and the use of **contractions** (like *won't* or *can't*) as well as **interruptions** and **non-fluency** features are more frequently found in informal conversations.

4) Use of a **regional dialect**, or words and grammatical constructions not considered to be '**correct**' English, can help place a target audience **geographically**, **socially** or **ethnically**.

"We've been talking for 3 days now — I should probably get back to work."

Practice Questions

Q1 What are the main differences between a text that is written for a known audience and a text that is written for an unknown audience?

Q2 Name at least two elements of a text that you need to analyse in order to work out the intended audience.

Q3 Explain how analysing the lexis of a text can help you understand the audience.

Essay Question

Q1 What differences would you expect to see between an instruction text for children and an instruction text for adults? Explain your answer with reference to style, content, lexis, tone and formality.

If you're aiming for a target audience, make sure you don't miss...

For some reason people get really uppity about texts pinging around and hitting them in the chops when they're not expecting it. But on a serious note, don't forget that writers identify audiences through the attitudes, beliefs and needs they think a group might have or want. Then they can tailor texts specifically to attract the audience (more on this later).

Boy, do those linguists love sorting things into groups. CDs, clothes, pens — you name it, they'll sort it. But the thing they love to sort more than anything else is texts. Genre is one way of classifying and organising texts into different categories.

Genre *groups texts that have* Similar Features

Similar types of texts often seem to follow a **distinctive pattern**. A group of texts with the same features is called a **genre**.

1) **Genre conventions** make **written** and **spoken** communication more **efficient**.

2) When you read a text from a particular **genre**, you have certain **expectations** about it.

3) Knowing **what kind of text** you're reading lets you **predict** what form it will take.

Knowing about genres means you can **classify** language. It allows a reader to form **expectations** about the text based on their **experience** of the **genre**.

There are Many Different Genres of Written Text

Examples of **written genres** include: letters, reports, poems, stories, advertisements, postcards, recipes, e-mails, cartoons, text-messages etc. Each genre has a different **writing style** associated with it. For example:

Letters

Formal convention:

1) Sender's address at the top

2) Date and *Dear Sir/Madam*

3) Concludes *Yours sincerely/faithfully*

4) Followed by a signature

Postcards

Abbreviated format:

1) Very informal

2) Contractions common (e.g. *won't, can't*)

3) Dashes and exclamation marks

Recipes

Step-by-step instructions:

1) Start with list of ingredients

2) Followed by numbered instructions

3) Short instructive sentences

4) May include some technical words (like *braise, simmer* or *baste*)

Text messages

Extremely informal:

1) Highly contracted language (*lol* or *btw*)

2) Emoticons (e.g. :-))

3) Language based on sound (e.g. *gr8* or *neway*)

Spoken Texts *also follow* Conventions

Spoken text also has its own genres with **distinctive patterns**. Spoken language is broken down into two main areas — **monologue or dialogue** (see p.62). Each spoken genre has different **conventions** associated with it. Some examples are:

Genre	Conventions
Answer-phone message	The message often begins with *"Sorry, I'm not around at the moment"* (or something similar), and is likely to end with *"Please leave a message after the beep"*.
Interview	An interviewer will often ask typical questions such as *"Why are you interested in this company / college?"*, or *"What are your strengths and weaknesses?"*.
Lesson	A lesson might begin with some questions to recap a topic, and may end with the teacher giving out homework to the class.
Radio show	A radio presenter would normally begin a show with *"Hello, and welcome to..."* and then give the name of the show and their own name. They'd typically refer to the listener directly as *you*, and refer to the audience and themselves collectively as *we*.

Genre

You can also **Group Genres**

1) As well as classifying texts into genres, you can group **similar genres** together according to how they use **language**.

2) Each group of genres is called a **field**, e.g. music, literature and conversation.

3) Each field has **field-specific lexis**, or vocabulary, that is used within that particular topic, for example:

Music
Genres — jazz, rock, classical, folk
Field-specific lexis — *CD, album, single, artist, band*.

Literature
Genres — plays, poetry, short stories, novels
Field-specific lexis — *metaphor, stanza, chapter, stage directions*

TV
Genres — game shows, soap operas, dramas, sitcoms
Field-specific lexis — *studio, script, lighting, boom, presenter*

Henry and Jonny couldn't believe they were the only ones in their field.

Genres can be **Broken Down** into **Sub-genres**

As if that's not enough, you can divide genres into smaller groups of texts, called **sub-genres**:

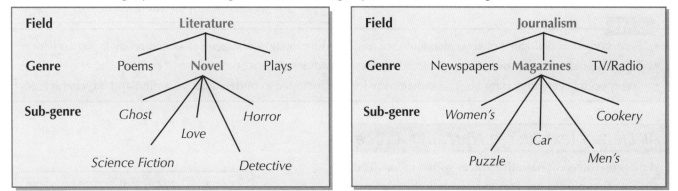

Field	Literature
Genre	Poems Novel Plays
Sub-genre	Ghost Horror Love Science Fiction Detective

Field	Journalism
Genre	Newspapers Magazines TV/Radio
Sub-genre	Women's Cookery Car Puzzle Men's

Each of these sub-genres has developed its own **specific lexis** that relates to that sub-genre in particular. For example, the word *autocue* is specific to the **sub-genre** of **TV presenting**, and *blog* relates to the **sub-genre** of **online publishing**.

Practice Questions

Q1 Why are texts categorised into different genres?

Q2 Give three examples of spoken genres.

Q3 What is a field? Give an example and list some of its field-specific lexis.

Essay Question

Q1 Choose three examples of written genres. Explain the differences between them, focusing in particular on graphology and lexis.

That's where my answerphone message has been going wrong then...

I've been using Hello, *by Lionel Richie. Which I suppose is pretty unconventional, and might be the reason no one leaves me any messages. Or maybe they're not actually looking for me. Make sure you've got your head around the field / genre / sub-genre distinctions here, and learn some written and spoken examples. Then make like a new leaf and turn over.*

Literary Texts

Literary texts are mainly written to entertain — people read or listen to them for pleasure. To keep the audience interested, literary texts usually contain imaginative uses of language, like experimentation with vocabulary and grammar.

Authors of Literary Texts can be very Creative

Literary texts are part of the very broad entertainment field. People read literary texts because they can:

1) **Entertain** or **amuse** the reader.

2) Affect the reader's **emotions**, e.g. make them scared, excited or sympathetic.

3) Describe the **atmosphere** of a place or setting.

4) Examine the **personality** of a **character**.

5) Influence how the reader **looks at the world**.

His wife's shopping list evoked an atmosphere of mild panic.

There are Three Main Types of literary texts

The most common types of literary texts are prose (like books), poetry (like poems), and plays (er... like plays).

PROSE

- For example, novels, short stories, biography, autobiography.
- It's structured as **running text**, and divided into paragraphs and chapters (for novels).
- There are often no subsections, charts, or lists, and **usually no illustrations**.
- It has a **beginning** and usually a **definite ending**.
- The narrative is told from a certain **point of view**.

POETRY

- Poems **vary** in content, structure, style and intention.
- Some present **narrative stories**, some are written to be **performed**, others explore **emotional issues**.
- Poems are organised into **stanzas** (verses) of varying sizes.
- **Line length** can vary considerably and the poem may or may not **rhyme**.
- There are some **traditional forms** poems can take, e.g. sonnet or villanelle.
- There are also traditional **metres** (rhythms) e.g. pentameters.

PLAYS

- Plays consist of **dialogue** between characters, or (if it's a monologue) a character talking **directly** to the audience.
- They also include **stage directions** to instruct the actors and describe actions etc.
- The speech is very important, as it's the main way for the audience to **understand** the **action** and the **characters**.

All literary texts use a Narrative Voice

Writers use different **narrative voices** within literary texts.

1) A **first-person narrator** in a text tells the reader directly about their **feelings and experiences**. The text is viewed through the character's eyes.

> The moment I woke up that morning I just knew that something wasn't right. I was utterly exhausted and Ryan wouldn't stop talking...

2) A **third-person narrator** tells the story from a detached viewpoint, as a voice separate from the characters.

3) A **third-person omniscient narrator** lets the reader see into the **minds** and **thoughts** of **all** the characters.

> Kit explained it to her as gently as he could; there was no point upsetting her even more. But still, poor Sarah was devastated. As soon as she got home she flung herself on the bed and was overcome with sorrow...

Literary texts use lots of Figurative Language

Figurative language adds layers of meaning to texts. There's loads more on this on p.22.

1) **Imagery** creates a scene in the reader's mind e.g. *the sea was wild and stormy*.

2) A **simile** is when something is described in **comparison** to something else, e.g. *The sea is like a savage beast*.

3) A **metaphor** creates a **comparison**, like a simile, but it implies the subject and the thing it's being compared to are the **same**, e.g. *the sea is a savage beast*, rather than comparing them.

4) **Personification** is a kind of metaphor, in which the **attributes** of a person are given to abstract or non-human things, for example *the sea shrieked and roared*.

5) **Symbolism** is where a word or phrase **represents something else**, e.g. the colour *red* could represent danger.

Literary Texts

Rhetorical Language is used to provide Extra Effects or Meanings

There are **two categories** of rhetorical language.

Phonological — manipulates sound. Words or phrases might be used because they sound good.

1) **Rhyme** is particularly effective in poetry because it can contribute to the **musical quality** of a verse. It unifies the poem and can **add emphasis** to certain words. There are different kinds of rhyme, including **half rhyme** — where the vowel or consonant may vary (e.g. *roll* and *tell*) and **internal rhyme** — where rhymes occur within a line itself (e.g. *in mist or cloud, on mast or shroud*).

2) **Alliteration** is the repetition of the **same sound**, usually at the beginning of each word, over **two or more words together**, e.g. *sink slowly into a soothing sleep*.

3) **Assonance** is a similar repetition, but of **vowel sounds** in the middle of words e.g. *a hoover manoeuvre*.

4) **Onomatopoeia** refers to words that sound like the noise they describe, e.g. *buzz, pop, bang*.

Structural — affects the overall meaning of a text by manipulating its structural features.

1) **Repetition** is often used to add **emphasis or persuasiveness** to a text. It can add **power** to a subject, or help a text lead to a **dramatic climax**.

2) **Parallelism** repeats **structural features**, like the construction of a **phrase**, e.g. *She jumped from the bed, and raced to the window*, which repeatedly uses the **past tense** form of the verb with a preposition and noun. An example of **non-parallelism** is something like *He loves films and to eat* — the construction of the phrases *loves film* and *to eat* are different and seem awkward to the reader.

3) **Antithesis** is when contrasting ideas or words are balanced against each other, e.g. *when there is need of silence, you speak, and when there is need of speech, you are silent*.

Dialogue can also be Very Effective

Dialogue is an especially effective device in **plays**.

1) Different characters may speak in **different ways** to influence the audience's opinions of them.

2) Dialogue helps to show the **relationships** between characters — whether they get on, or if there's **tension** between them. It also tells you about a character's **personality** through their **interactions** with other characters, e.g. if they're assertive, nervous, thoughtful, domineering, etc.

3) There are differences between dialogue in **literary texts** and **natural conversation**. In plays and novels, the dialogue tends to be **organised** and **fluent**, e.g. there is strict **turn-taking** and not much **interruption** or **hesitation**. In real-life conversations there are a lot of **non-fluency features** because the dialogue is **spontaneous**.

4) **Dramatic writing** relies on **dialogue** to create and develop **characters**. In **fictional texts**, the writer can **experiment** with **language** to describe these features.

Practice Questions

Q1 What are the main purposes of literary texts?
Q2 Why might a writer choose to use a third-person narrator instead of a first-person narrator?
Q3 What is the importance of rhyme in poetry?

Essay Question

Q1 Read the opening page of a novel that you already know. How does the author use language to convey the setting, characterisation and atmosphere effectively? You should consider:

1) the ways in which the writer's attitudes and values are conveyed to the reader.

2) features of the language such as figurative and rhetorical devices, and dialogue.

Even the simplest texts are still just one thing after anauthor...

Well it's not like there's a good pun for "symbolism", is it? These pages are all about ways of manipulating language, and the effect this has on the audience of a literary text. They've got some great terms to have at your disposal in the exam — being able to pick out these sorts of features and describe their purposes in different texts will get you tonnes of marks.

This basically covers what people think about different texts. Both writers and readers approach texts with their own attitudes. These attitudes affect what the writers write, and how the readers interpret it.

Writers show their Attitudes in their Texts

An ideology is a set of beliefs and ideas.

You can often get a sense of a writer's **opinions** and **ideology** through **how** they write and the **topics** they choose.

1) The **values** and **morals** in a text will probably depend on those held by the writer or speaker, e.g. a politician might speak about their attitude to marriage, based on the views of their particular political party or religion. This is often the case in **fictional** texts too, but not always.

2) Texts can show **prejudice** and **bias**, e.g. a writer might portray British characters sympathetically, and make their foreign characters all appear rather shady. This is an **implicit** meaning — it's not immediately obvious.

3) A writer might also show their **attitudes** quite **explicitly**, e.g. a journalist writing for a liberal newspaper might express their dislike for conservative politics.

4) Writers sometimes draw on **personal experience**, because it's easier to write about what you know, e.g. because he's been through the experience himself, a writer might describe a young gay man struggling to come out to his parents.

5) Writers' attitudes are also influenced by the social or political **environment** they're in. This is often evident in the **representation** of their **characters**, **narrator**, and the **themes** and **issues** that the text tries to deal with.

> **Social and historical context**
> * Texts often **reflect** the **concerns** of a **society** at a particular **time**.
> * For example — the James Bond books often feature Soviet villains being thwarted by Bond, a British spy. They were written during the **Cold War** period of the 1950s and 60s, so they reflect the fear that countries like Britain and America had of the communist USSR.
> * A text is a **product** of the **culture** and **time** it's written or set in — you wouldn't expect a spy novel written in the UK today to feature Russian Communist villains.

Writers can show their Attitudes through their Characters

1) Writers might draw on **stereotypes** when they're **constructing characters**, e.g. they might present a character who is an MP as a middle-aged man with grey hair who wears a suit.

2) A writer may create characters based on how the **media** represents groups of people (see p.56-57). This includes **stereotypes** like portraying a group of young people as a *gang of hoodies*.

3) The writer might **unconsciously** reflect the views or values of **wider society**. Someone from a Western culture, writing nowadays, might refer to a character as '*lovely and slim*'. This would reflect the **broader** attitude in Western society that being slim is beautiful.

4) You can also get an idea of a writer's values and beliefs from how they **subvert stereotypes**, e.g. a feminist author might write about workplaces and homes dominated by women.

A writer's Language Choices can Influence the Reader

The language of a text is often **manipulated** to create certain emotions or reactions in the reader. The **manipulation** of the reader is a frequent tool that writers use to **increase** the **impact** of their texts or even to **subvert conventions**.

> 1) Politicians delivering speeches about social problems want listeners to feel like they **share** their desire to solve the problem. They use **inclusive pronouns** like *we* and *us* to position the listener as a **confidant** and therefore a potential **supporter**.
>
> 2) A charity leaflet might use emotive words like *cruelty* to **represent** the **treatment** of people or groups, or *desperate* to convey the **seriousness** of their situation.
>
> 3) Writers can use **different viewpoints** in novels and articles. First person narrators can bring readers **close** to the text and they can get **emotionally involved**. Third person omniscient narratives give **insights** into characters and allow the reader to step back and be **objective**.
>
> 4) Writers can also **subvert** these conventions to manipulate the reader, e.g. using a first person narrator who turns out to be **completely unreliable**.

Ideology and Representation

Writers still have to Appeal to Readers

Writers know that audiences **approach** texts in different ways so they have to represent ideas and characters that readers can identify with.

1) Members of an audience bring their own **experience**, personality, background, prejudices, beliefs and values to their interpretation of any text. These factors shape how a reader **views** a situation or **feels** about a character.

2) Writers might aim to **appeal** to audiences by writing things that they know they'll **agree** with — e.g. most people buy a particular newspaper because they know it will express **similar views** to theirs. Journalists for that paper know what views will appeal to the audience and make them want to keep reading.

3) Writers might know their readership and try to **influence** or **change** their views in some way, e.g. charity adverts.

4) The meaning of a text can be **ambiguous**. Often the meaning expressed on a **literal** or **explicit level** is different to the one on a **figurative** or **implicit level** (see p.20). Writers can challenge readers to provide their **own** meanings.

5) For example, writers are sometimes **ambiguous** on **purpose**. They leave things **open** for the audience to **interpret**, e.g. in the film *Lost in Translation* (2003), a character whispers something to another character at the end. The audience never find out what he says, and it's left up to them to come to their own conclusion.

Readers Interpret Texts in different ways

Readers **draw on** their own **values** and **experiences** when they **approach** texts.

1) Just like writers, readers bring their individual **backgrounds** and **biases** to texts — each reader's interpretation will be slightly different.

2) A reader's response to a text depends on the influences of social factors like **education**, **religion**, **family** and **the media**. These factors create the reader's **ideological position**.

3) Interpretations of texts are also a **product** of the readers' **historical context**, e.g.

- *Dr Jekyll and Mr Hyde* is a **Victorian** novel about a man who appears to have two sides to his personality.

- The way it was **interpreted** by Victorian readers is quite **different** to the meanings that it's given now.

- When readers at the time first saw the words *shame* and *sin* in the novel, some of them assumed that Mr Hyde was Dr Jekyll's **homosexual lover**.

- This is because **Victorian readers** would have **viewed** such a relationship as shameful and sinful.

- Other readers associated the character with **Jack the Ripper**, a **murderer** who was plaguing London **at the time**.

- Modern readers might see the novel as exploring issues related to the **self**, e.g. good and evil, and are less likely to think of the Victorian interpretations.

"No Hyde — I don't know what's wrong with her, but I don't think that's helping."

Practice Questions

Q1 Give two examples of how a writer might express their personal opinions in a text.

Q2 Explain the different effects created by using a first person narrative or a third person narrative.

Q3 What factors can influence a reader's interpretation of a text?

Essay Question

Q1 Outline the main factors that can influence a writer producing a text.

Apparently, 'Lost in Translation' was actually lost in translation...

I kid you not. When the title was translated into Hebrew, Chinese and Spanish (in South America), it turned up as Lost in Tokyo *instead. So there you go... little bit of Hollywood trivia for you there. And you thought English Language was going to be all about spelling and grammar and endless transcripts. Well it's not. It's actually cool and ultra-glamorous.*

These pages show you what to expect from an exam question on analysing written language. It's important to apply the different parts of analysis that you've learnt in this section methodically in order to get the best marks.

> 1) Study the following texts A - E. The texts illustrate different varieties of language use.
> Analyse and compare the language in these texts and discuss the various ways in which these texts could be grouped, giving linguistic reasons for your choice. *[48 marks]*

Text A — An extract from the novel *The Way of All Flesh* (1903), by Samuel Butler

Old Mr. Pontifex had married in the year 1750, but for fifteen years his wife bore no children. At the end of that time, Mrs. Pontifex astonished the whole village by showing unmistakeable signs of a disposition to present her husband with an heir or heiress. Hers had long ago been considered a hopeless case, and when on consulting the doctor concerning the meaning of certain symptoms she was informed of their significance, she became very angry and abused the doctor roundly for talking nonsense. She refused to put so much as a piece of thread into a needle in anticipation of her confinement and would have been absolutely unprepared, if her neighbours had not been better judges of her condition than she was, and got things ready without telling her anything about it. Perhaps she feared Nemesis, though assuredly she knew not who or what Nemesis was; perhaps she feared the doctor had made a mistake and she should be laughed at; for whatever cause, however, her refusal to recognise the obvious arose, she certainly refused to recognise it, until one snowy night in January the doctor was sent for with all urgent speed across the rough country roads. When he arrived he found two patients, not one, in need of his assistance. For a boy had been born who was in due time christened George, in honour of his then reigning majesty.

To the best of my belief George Pontifex got the greater part of his nature from this obstinate old lady, his mother - a mother who though she loved no one else in the world except her husband (and him only after a fashion) was most tenderly attached to the unexpected child of her old age; nevertheless she showed it little.

Text B — A film review of the *Sex And The City* movie, By Celia Walden

"Everything that happens tonight must stay in this room," said Sarah Jessica Parker to the several hundred guests at last night's world premiere of Sex And The City the movie.

But with the girlish excitement filling the cinema it seemed unlikely anyone would heed her plea.

Just in case none of us remember, the producers of the much-awaited film version of the hit TV series remind fans with a quick recap at the start of the film where the four characters were at the point we left them when the series ended.

Three years on, the two Ls are still carrying the storyline along: labels and love. In the first half-hour we're bombarded by so much brand placement that one might as well be witnessing an extended Vogue photo shoot brought to life.

While love scenes between the happy characters brought not so much as a murmur from the audience, a Vivienne Westwood dress and a Louis Vuitton handbag provoked coos of heartfelt admiration.

The triumph of capitalism is as unabashed as it always was but given, if possible, a greater ironic twist.

In 20 years, Carrie Bradshaw, the lovelorn journalist, has come a long way: she is engaged to a billionaire, who can offer her a walk-in wardrobe and more Manolos than she can ever dream of - but the consumer Cinderella has a crash heading her way.

And as the film progresses, the seemingly adult and perfect lives of the four fortysomethings start to show cracks.

Miranda's husband Steve commits an act she may never be able to forgive him for while Samantha's ego threatens to derail her relationship with Smith Jerrod.

Just Charlotte seems to have escaped the New York clique's curse.

It is only in the last 10 minutes that we find out whether the fairytale has the happy ending the audience so desperately seemed to crave. But one thing's for sure: fans of the series will lap this film up.

It was coarse, sentimental, and outrageously materialistic - just as we hoped and expected it would be.

Sources and Exam Questions

Text C — A web page for an educational children's club

| Who are We? | Teaching | Case Studies | Contact Us |

Why fish?
Instructors
Lessons
Links
Gallery

Welcome to Carp-ey Diem

Carp-ey Diem helps children master the ancient art of carp fishing, whilst building strong learning skills, boosting their confidence, and teaching them respect for nature.

We give your child:

- an opportunity to learn at their own pace
- a positive attitude
- confidence to meet new challenges
- invaluable experience

Realise your child's potential — Join in Now

Carp-ey

Diem

Carp-ey Diem - teaching kids to fish since 1947

Text D — A competition entry form

CAPTION COMPETITION ENTRY FORM

Name
Address Line 1
Address Line 2
Town
Postcode
D.O.B

Please note — this competition closes at midnight on 25/08/2008

Your Caption

I declare that this caption has not been published elsewhere and that I am the original author ☐

You may use my caption in advertising should it be declared the winner of the caption competition ☐

*Please inform me if my caption is **not** successful (see over for Terms and Conditions)* ☐

Send your entries to:
Caption Competition,
P.O Box 4653,
Sheepy Parva,
Nuntonshire,
NU88 9UN

....
....
....
....

Signed:

Text E — A self-diagnosis booklet

Insomnia is best known as the inability to get to sleep, but sufferers are also affected by being unable to stay asleep, or by waking up too early. Experiencing these effects for an extended period of time is called chronic insomnia, whilst short-term sufferers experience what's called transient insomnia.

Chronic Insomnia

You can take some measures to try and alleviate chronic insomnia (see page 17). If these fail to have the desired effect then it may be best to seek medical advice to try and isolate the causes of the sleeping disruptions. On occasions, chronic insomnia is one of the symptoms of depression, but there are also many other potential causes.

Transient Insomnia

Short term insomnia often remedies itself in the space of a few days. Usually it is nothing to worry about but if you start to experience excessive worry about not being able to sleep, and if this in turn keeps you awake, then you might want to seek medical advice. Ultimately though, transient insomnia is fairly common and could be caused by bereavement or stress in your professional or personal life.

For your AS exam, you'll need to understand language frameworks and linguistic concepts, know how to analyse different types of discourse, organise your answers, and write clearly and precisely. If that's all Greek to you, panic ye not. For here is a helpful little section, with some exam and coursework tips neatly crowbarred into a nutshell.

Make sure you know How To Get Marks

You need to think about the **assessment objectives** for the questions — these are the **criteria** the examiners use to mark your answers:

AO1	You get **AO1** marks for using linguistic terminology correctly and writing accurately.
AO2	You get **AO2** marks for applying linguistic approaches to questions, and showing that you understand issues related to the construction and analysis of meaning in texts.
AO3	You get **AO3** marks for analysing and evaluating the influence of context on the language used.

Basically, the examiners want you to show that you understand the way purpose, audience and context affect the ways that language is produced and received.

Make sure you know your Language Frameworks

Language frameworks can be thought of as **headings** to help you to **structure** your **analysis**. You need to be able to **identify them** in different kinds of texts and explain how the features are used to help the text **achieve its purpose**:

Language Frameworks

- **Lexis** (vocabulary)
- **Semantics** (meanings that words convey)
- **Grammar** (word classes and syntax)
- **Phonology** (sounds)
- **Pragmatics** (social conventions surrounding language use)
- **Graphology** (visual appearance and arrangement of the text)
- **Discourse** (how segments of language are developed and structured)

1)   You need to refer to as many of these as possible, as long as they're **appropriate**.

2)   Don't focus on just **one framework** and **ignore** the rest. For example, if you write a lot on graphology (in written discourse) or non-fluency features (in spoken), and don't get chance to mention grammar, you won't **score highly** on the mark scheme.

3)   Don't just be descriptive. You have to relate the frameworks to **meaning** and **purpose**, e.g. *The adjective 'unique' is persuasive [**purpose**], suggesting that the product is special [**meaning**].*

Think about how you're going to Approach the Questions

When you're analysing **non-topic-based discourse** in the exam (section A asks you to group texts according to features you think they share), think about the points on this checklist:

1)	Read the texts **quickly**, just to get a feel for what they're generally about. Then read them again **more carefully**, noting down what the **subject matter** is.
2)	For **written** texts, identify genre, register, the likely audience and purpose.
3)	For **spoken** texts, identify context, the role of the participants, register, pragmatics and conversational theory.
4)	Find **examples** of the language frameworks — be selective and **link** linguistic features to purpose and meaning.

Topic-based questions still give you a **text** to **analyse**, but your analysis has to focus upon a certain aspect of the text.

1)	This sort of question requires you to have a good knowledge of **particular language topics** (like power or gender) as well as being able to apply the language frameworks to the text.
2)	Look for features that **specifically relate** to the topic (e.g. power, gender, occupation, technology, etc.).
3)	The best way to prepare is to **underline key features** in the texts you're given so you can refer back to them when you're writing your answer.

The AS AQA B exam is called **Categorising Texts**.

The exam has **Two Sections**

The **AQA B** paper lasts **two hours** and is split into **two sections** — section A is a question on **text varieties** and section B is a topic-specific question on **language and social contexts**.

Section A — Text Varieties

1)   This section contains **one** compulsory question.

2)   You'll get about **six texts** from **everyday sources** to analyse.

3)   You'll have to discuss the various ways in which these texts can be **grouped together**.

4)   You'll need to write about things like: **purpose**, **genre**, level of **formality**, **mode** (spoken, written, multimodal), **representation** and linguistic features (**lexis**, **grammar**, **phonology** and so on).

5)   There are **48 marks** available for this question.

Think about how to **Organise Your Answers**

1)   It helps if you go into the exam with a **clear idea** about how you're going to organise your answers.

2)   There are various approaches you can take, as long as you're **methodical** and **thorough**. Here are some things to think about when you're preparing to answer the questions.

Written Discourse	Spoken Discourse
The first things to identify are:	Make sure you're familiar with the following:
Genre, purpose, register, formality, likely audience.	Context, content, function, participants.
Then to compare texts, write in **more detail** about: **Graphology** (layout, fonts, use of visual stimuli) **Phonology** (alliteration, assonance, repetition) **Lexis** (lexical fields, figurative language) **Grammar** (word classes, e.g. modals, types of adverb) **Discourse structure** (beginning, how it's developed, end)	Then to compare texts, write in **more detail** about: **Phonology** (pronunciation features) **Non-fluency features** (pauses, false starts, fillers) **Non-verbal** aspects of speech (stress) **Pragmatics** (conversational theory) **Lexis**, **grammar** and **discourse structure**

3)   The exam board might include texts like adverts, conversations, websites, feature articles, comics, instructions or lists, and speech or radio transcripts. Here are a few ways that you could group some of the common texts.

•   Adverts, websites and comics use a lot of **bold graphological features** to stand out and attract casual viewers.

•   Comics, conversations, speeches and radio extracts can be grouped according to their representation of **spoken language** — they could show different levels of **formality** in the language choices, or be grouped because they represent features of **dialects** or **accents** in some way.

•   Feature articles and comics are usually meant to **entertain**, but this can also be true of websites, adverts and instructions, depending on their **tone**, **formality** and use of **figurative language** or **phonetic features**.

Keep your answers **Simple** and **Concise**

1)   Write **clearly** and **concisely** — don't try to impress the examiner with big words for the sake of it.

2)   Write in **paragraphs** and make sure that each paragraph has a **clear focus** (e.g. grouping texts by a certain feature like lexis).

3)   When quoting, make sure that you use **inverted commas**. It doesn't matter if these are single or double as long as you are **consistent**. For example — *the modal auxiliary 'might' adds a degree of uncertainty to whether the athlete will achieve what he has set out to do.*

4)   Avoid using **long quotations**. It's much better to work quotations **into your sentences** rather than present them as big separate chunks.

*The second section of the exam is **topic-specific**.*

You have a choice of **Three Questions**

Section B — Language and Social Contexts

1) In this section you have to choose **one** question out of three.
2) The three questions are on **language and gender**, **language and power**, and **language and technology**.
3) There'll be **one text** to analyse for each question.
4) There are **48 marks** available for this question.

You'll need to make sure you're **comfortable** talking about the following things for this section of the exam.

Gender — How gender is **represented** in texts and how the **roles** of men and women are portrayed in everyday life. How gender roles function and are **conformed** to or **subverted** in mixed and same-sex conversations.

Power — The way power is **communicated** in discourses, e.g. official letters or documents, medical advice, etc. How individuals **exert power** in interactions like arguments, debates or speeches, etc.

Technology — How language has been **changed** by mobiles, the Internet, etc., and how this has affected **social practices**.

Here's an **Example Question** and **Answer** to give you some tips:

4) Read Text 1. How has the language of the text been influenced by technology?

Straight to the point, focusing on the impact of technology.

Good range of examples, supporting the idea of simplification.

Text 1 — text messages from the mobile phones of a 17-year-old boy and his 14-year-old sister.

Simon: *hi sis,ows it goin down in Lndn?*
Trish: *its cool.bin on the EYE*
Simon: *wow bet that was wkd. wot els?*
Trish: *nuffin much.bin hangin round wiv billy*
Simon: *BILLY? aw billy, hes well cool.*
Trish: *yeh*
Simon: *he still doin athletix?*
Trish: *yeh,really into it.trains every nite almos*
Simon: *hows auntie Bett? lol.*
Trish: *lol shes really strick. we don't get away wiv nuffin not even Billy n hes nearly 16*

Comments on lexical / grammatical frameworks with examples.

Comments on conversational features of text messaging.

These text messages show some of the distinctive qualities of text messaging language. The language used is influenced by the need for participants to respond quickly with a limited set of buttons to work with.

For this reason, words are abbreviated, as in *sis*, and spelling is simplified, as in *nite*. Another form of simplification occurs with the omission of vowels (*wkd*, *Lndn*) and with the dropping of final consonants (the final *g* is dropped in *goin*, *doin*, and *hangin*). There is one example where a single consonant is used to replace a consonant cluster (*athletix* rather than *athletics*). Silent vowels at the end of words are also omitted (*els*). In addition to simplified spelling, there are also examples of phonological spelling: *bin, wiv, nuffin, strick*.

Colloquial expressions such as *ows it goin?*, *wkd* (wicked), *hangin round*, and *well cool* suggest an informal conversation between two people who are comfortable with each other. Grammatical structures are incomplete, especially with the omission of personal pronouns: *[I] bet that was wkd*, or subject-verb combinations: *[I've] bin on the EYE*.

The text conversation mirrors some features found in actual spoken conversation. There is an opening sequence with Simon addressing his sister with *hi* and her responding. Brother and sister take turns with Simon driving the conversation forward by asking questions. However, there are also declaratives, particularly from Trish, who tells her brother about Billy's athletics training and the strictness of her aunt.

This is quite a good answer. It **focuses** on the **question**, identifies a **range** of **features** and gives some **good examples**. It explores how text messaging has some of the same features as **spoken conversation** and shows that the student is aware of the **context**.

The student could **improve** the answer by writing about the **function** of the **interaction**, and how the exchanges might fit in with **conversational theory**. If it carried on like this, the essay would get at least **32 marks** out of **48**.

What the **Exam Board Wants**

For your AQA B coursework, you have to do **two** different pieces of **original writing**. They have to be from different genres and written for a different purpose and audience.

The total length for the two pieces together is 1500 - 2500 words. You can pick a type of text from any of the following areas:	
A text to entertain	• an extract from an interview • part of a script from a TV show • a parody or piece of satirical writing
A text to inform	• news coverage of an important event • a piece of travel writing • a press release from a football club
A text to instruct	• a step-by-step fitness regime • a manual for a computer game • a novice's guide to email (or similar)
A text to persuade	• a film, music, car or restaurant review • a political speech • a piece of motivational speaking

Check the coursework tasks with your teacher — there's a chance they might change.

If you need some help, have a look at:

*   Section 2 (terminology and useful language features, p.18-33).
*   Section 4 (language in different contexts, e.g. the media and exerting power, p.48-59).
*   Section 5 (e.g. if you're doing a script, refer to features of spoken language, p.62-67).
*   Section 6 (written language, purpose, genre and representation, p.70-79).

You also have to submit **two commentaries** in total — one for **each** piece of writing (see p.86). The **total** word count for the **two** commentaries together is **1000 words**.

Each type of text shares some **Common Features**

Here are some hints on the main features to include. For more on these features, see Section 6.

1) Entertainment Texts

You can write in several different styles if you pick an entertainment text, but they all share some features:

*   **Structure** — Most entertainment texts have a **fairly complex** structure. For example, a novel usually has a **sophisticated plot line**, and plays need **stage directions** as well as lines for the characters.
*   **Language** — a written entertainment text usually has quite complex language and lots of **figurative devices**. Spoken and written entertainment texts sometimes use **non-standard** language to **subvert convention**.

2) Informative Texts

Informative texts may be **factually based**. Make sure your **facts** are right and the language is **appropriate**.

*   **Structure** — the bulk of the facts you want to get across should be in the **middle** of the **text**. Have a more general introduction and conclusion to **frame** what you're talking about.
*   **Language** — it's important that your language **suits** your **target audience**. If you're writing to inform **children**, you'll have to use quite different language to what you'd use in a text written for your friends or parents.

3) Instructional texts

If you write a set of instructions, you need to guide a reader through the text, step by step.

*   **Structure** — you'll probably need to use numbered or bullet-pointed **lists**. The reader can't go on to the next one until they've **completed** everything the former one tells them to do — they're very **linear**.
*   **Language** — instructions are usually **imperative sentences** (see p.15). Sometimes the word choices are **specific** to the type of task or process that the reader is doing.

4) Persuasive texts

The best persuasive texts manage to get the reader to 'buy into' the idea they're promoting.

1) **Structure** — it's best to steadily **build** your **argument** as you go along and end with an **emphatic conclusion**.
2) **Language** — persuasive texts are meant to be **emotive**, so use lots of **direct address** and **inclusive pronouns**, as well as **emotive adjectives** to promote your subjective judgements.

Commentaries are where you get the chance to **explain** the language choices you made in your **coursework**.

Writing a **Commentary** shows your choices were **Intentional**

1) The commentary shows the examiner that you knew what you were doing in the **writing process**, and that you've thought about the effect that your **language choices** have had on the piece of writing you produced.

> **Your commentary is a review of what you've done and how you did it.**
> It will refer to all or some of the following frameworks, depending on the kind of text.
> **Lexis, semantics, grammar, phonology, pragmatics, graphology** and **discourse structure**.

2) You need to keep to the point and make sure you discuss all the features **equally**.

3) Your commentary should explain how your language choices in your coursework **match** the genre, mode, purpose, audience and subject matter of your text.

4) It should also discuss how planning and reworking has affected the final text, and how what you've written has been influenced by other texts.

5) Commentaries should be **400-500** words.

Your commentary should be **Concise and Well-Organised**

Start by stating what **kind of text** you've written, who it's **aimed at**, and what its **purpose** is. For example:

> I chose to write the kind of unsolicited letter that charitable organisations send out to the public. The purpose of this letter is to persuade adults to donate money to a good cause; in this case, a campaign to end forced child labour in developing countries.

Now describe some of the **specific language choices** you made, making sure that you always refer back to how they helped you **identify with** and get your **message across** to the audience. Here are a few examples of the kind of things you should be aiming to write about:

Mentioning narrative voice is a good way to describe how you're treating the reader.

Throughout the letter I used the second person pronoun *you* to address the reader directly. By doing this, I aimed to involve the reader by making it seem I was talking to them personally...

Try to describe how you've attempted to manipulate the reader's response to the text.

Another technique I used for involving the reader was incorporating a number of rhetorical questions, e.g. *Can we stand by and let this happen?*, and *Would you let this happen to your own child?*. My purpose here was to further personalise the issue and involve the reader by projecting the situation onto their lives...

Discuss the lexis you've used, and why you've chosen certain words (e.g. for their connotative meaning).

To further the personal impact of the text, some of the lexis I used was deliberately emotive as I wanted the reader to be shocked by what they read. For this reason, I gave a short case study of a six-year-old boy called Arjit. I used adjectives such as *fatherless*, *unloved* and *malnourished* to give a sense of his vulnerability, loneliness and frailty. I also used the metaphor *dungeon* to describe the factory where Arjit works to emphasise that his workplace is a dark, harsh and restricted environment...

Grammar can be just as influential as lexis on the tone and style of a text, so make sure you discuss it. Also consider how the complexity of the sentences and words make your text accessible to your reader.

I mainly used simple sentences because it gives the text a shorter, more dynamic tone, making it more assertive and therefore more persuasive. As this is a letter that someone might easily throw away without reading, it was important that the opening sentences in particular were short and to the point, e.g. the very first sentence, which simply states that *Two hundred children died last year*. This is a stark fact and grabs the reader's attention straight away...

Describe how you've organised your text.

The letter has a clear structure. First I paint a picture of the situation focusing on Arjit, then broaden the text to show how forced labour is a worldwide issue which affects thousands of children. Finally, having hopefully influenced the reader, I have urged them to donate money, using modals and adverbs of time to give a sense of urgency: *You must do something now!*

You might want to talk about how the structure reflects or subverts the conventions of the genre you've chosen to write in.

There are **two** important things to remember.
1) **Support** every point you make with **examples**.
2) For every linguistic choice you discuss, say how it **affects** the **audience** or contributes to the **effect** of the text.

Section Three — Varieties of English
Pages 44-47

1   The question asks you to discuss the sources in terms of the varieties of English used, and how they could be grouped. Here are some points you could make in your answer:

Dialect

- Text B contains dialect words like *nowt* and *mardy*, which suggest that the teenagers are speaking a regional dialect.

- It also contains non-standard grammar, which is a feature of regional dialects (*she didn't do nowt wrong, that don't even make sense*).

- The speakers in text B miss out the definite article *the* in constructions like *she was gonna meet him <u>at pub</u>*. This grammatical feature is mostly specific to the Yorkshire dialect, so this is probably where the speakers are from.

Sociolect

- In text B the speakers are a group of teenagers who are friends, so their sociolect is made up of informal, familiar language. This is shown by speaker A's use of the address term *mate*. Their language also includes a lot of slang words, like *minging*, *chucked* and *snogging*, and elision in words like *wanna* and *dunno*. Their language contains informal fillers typical in teenagers' language, e.g. *innit though right* and *like*.

Idiolect

- In text B, Speaker B's idiolect is evident in their use of *well* as an intensifier (*he's <u>well</u> fit, he can be <u>well</u> horrid*).

- In text A, Lord Augustus's idiolect in text A is evident in his use of ellipsis — he misses out the third person pronoun *she* in these clauses: *Knows perfectly well what a demmed fool I am — knows it as well as I do myself.*

Occupational Sociolect

- Text E is a cooperative interaction, with feedback features and turn-taking. However, there's an obvious hierarchy between the speakers, which is often evident in language of the workplace. Speaker A appears to be in authority over B — A addresses him with his first name a lot: *have a look at the v5 Greg*, also using an imperative in this example. A invites B to take control, but then speaks for him, which suggests that A is in charge.

- The lexical field contains references to cars and specific car parts (*two point five diesel, MAF, rev limiter*). Much of the lexis is context-specific jargon — it's referential and deictic (*<u>that</u> coupe*). This is a quick, efficient way for A and B to communicate.

- The problem with A and B's jargon is that the customer is left behind and hardly figures in the conversation, other than when invited to answer questions. It's clear from the customer's use of fillers, hedging and pauses that they don't really understand. Rather than explaining the jargon, A uses this to avoid having to answer the question of when the car will be finished, simply replying *a bit of Forté will do it*.

- Text C also contains occupational sociolect and jargon, e.g. *uPVC Georgian Hip, box gutter* and *fascia board*. The employees use it to communicate quickly and concisely. Unlike the jargon in text E, this is appropriate to the situation because it doesn't exclude any non-specialists. The specialists need to use it for their specific needs.

- The sociolect in text C contains examples of general business language, e.g. *usual practice*. It also contains words that are specific to this occupational field, e.g *abutment*, and words that are specific to the particular company, e.g. *149 starting handbook*. This lexis is part of the employees' occupational sociolect — it's specific to the situation they are in.

- Text D also contains specific technical language, but it is for people who are part of the same interest group, rather than the same occupational group. This sociolect contains lexis from the semantic field of food, and there are lots of detailed descriptions of particular dishes: *ham hock and parsley terrine, lavender and Ossetra caviar*. The text assumes knowledge from the readers, so it doesn't explain technical terms like *palate* or *haute cuisine*.

- Text D contains features that are typical with language that describes food, e.g. French loan words such as *confit* and *sommelier*, and lots of premodifiers: *poached line-caught turbot*.

- The function of text C is to obtain and impart information, so it contains mostly declarative sentences, with one clear interrogative: *Just wondering if the guarantee covers this?* The ellipsis in this question is evidence of some of the features of spoken language in the text. Omitting *I was* also makes the question more concise and to-the-point, which fits with the purpose of the email. Because the text is purely functional, it contains short sentences and doesn't have a complex syntax. Graphologically the layout of the email means that the information is presented clearly — the previous email is there for reference, and information like the date and time is separate from the main text.

- In contrast, the function of text D is to entertain and persuade, as well as to inform. Because of this, it contains a more varied and colourful lexis: *globs, chilliness*, and lots of adjectives: *sharp and tangy*. The syntax is complex, with lots of subordinate clauses. It is designed to entertain and impress the readers.

Standard English

- Text A is an extract from a play script, so the language is more structured and contains fewer non-fluency features than the spontaneous speech in text B. In contrast to the speakers in text B, the characters in this extract use mostly Standard English, e.g. *It is an awfully dangerous thing*. The writer may have used this as a literary device to suggest that the characters are well-educated or upper-class. This is supported by the fact that one of the characters has a title — <u>Lord</u> Augustus.

Formality

- You can tell that Text A is an informal conversation between friends because of the use of informal address terms like *my dear boy* and affectionate nicknames like *Tuppy* and *Dumby*.

- In text A, words like *hallo*, and modifiers like *awfully* and *perfectly* would have been considered informal at the time the play was written, although they seem quite formal to readers today. The text also contains some non-standard slang words like *demmed* and *monstrous*.

- The lexis in text E is also informal and colloquial, as expected in spontaneous speech (*we've had a bit of a problem with it really*). Speakers A and B use more formal language with the customer than they do with each other, e.g. A uses a less direct request with the customer: *if you'd just like to come through here*, than is used with B: *do you want to take him through to have a look.*

- Emails are multimodal texts — they contain aspects of spoken and written language. This is evident in text C, which contains some informal language that you might expect in spoken interaction, e.g. *give me a shout*, and deictic expressions like *Hi*.

- Texts C and D are different to texts A and B because they have a very specific function, rather than just a social one, so the lexis is more technical. They are also different to text E because they are written texts. The language is mostly formal and Standard English is used. Unlike texts A, B and E, there aren't any slang or dialect features. Text D can be grouped with text A because they are both crafted to entertain an audience.

Section Four — Language in Social Contexts
Pages 60-61

1 **Conversation between a manager and two trainees**
The question asks you to analyse a spoken discourse between three people — a manager, a male trainee and a female trainee, in relation to the significance of gender in the interaction. Below are a list of language and gender issues that you should aim to cover in your answer:

- The function of the conversation is referential. The manager provides information and guidelines to the two trainees.

- The context is one where language reveals the power relations between the three speakers involved. The manager speaks the most, followed by the male trainee, then the female trainee. This shows that the manager is the dominant speaker in the conversation, and holds most of the power.

- The manager assumes control by virtue of their knowledge of how the shop operates and what is expected of the trainees. They use emphasis and repetition to reinforce this (*and I mean eight-thirty*). The manager also uses politeness strategies (*I'd like you to work*), in which the use of *I* personalises the manager's request, and probably makes it more likely to be respected by the trainees. The manager's speech also contains filled pauses like *erm* but this is more about creating time to think rather than being nervous.

- The male trainee is the more self-assured. He uses informal terms and slang (words like *cool*) and affirmatives like *sure* and *fine* to look for covert prestige. He asks questions and offers answers without being prompted. His informal language affects the amount of power the manager can assert.

- The male trainee also interrupts the manager at one point to talk about his work experience. This assumes control over the manager in the conversation, and suggests that he's a lot more confident than the female trainee. He offers the female trainee a lift to work, assuming a responsible / controlling role.

- In contrast, the female trainee is less self-assured. She hesitates and aims for overt prestige by using fillers like *yes* rather than *yeh*. Her filled pauses show that she is nervous. Her responses are more submissive, with back-channel noises like *mm*. When she attempts to explain her travel issues she is interrupted by the male trainee.

- Of the two trainees, the male is more dominant than the female. This seems to support Lakoff's deficit model.

- The role of the manager doesn't follow any traditional stereotypes, but their language use displays a lot of sexism, e.g. *growing lad like you*, *don't worry sweetheart*, and *little miss efficient*. This is patronising to the female trainee in particular.

- The lexical field relates to the service industry (*tills*) and working routines (*breaktimes*, *lunch time* and *eight-thirty*).

2 **Transcript of a Chemistry lesson**
This question asks you to look at power relationships. Here are some points you could include in your answer:

- The text takes place in a school classroom, so the environment is immediately more formal than that of a conversation between friends. The context means that there is an acknowledged leader of the interactions, the teacher, who you would expect to be the dominant speaker.

- The power relationships in this extract are most apparent in the address terms used by the speakers. The pupils address the teacher as *sir*, a sign of respect, while the teacher addresses them using their first names (*James*, *Tash*). This shows that he is the authority figure.

- The teacher also shows his authority by using imperatives (*settle down*, *keep ties on*). As a politeness strategy, some orders are given as questions, but in the context of the school lesson the pupils understand that they're not supposed to respond and they don't have a choice, for example *can we turn to what we were doing last week*.

- The teacher uses direct questions (*what is it that happens to atoms*) to elicit a response from the pupils. He also uses the first person plural pronoun *we* to include them, and as an invitation that any of them can respond to his questions. This is common in educational sociolect. When no-one volunteers to answer, he directs questions at individuals to force them to respond (*what do they form (3.0) James*).

- In contrast the pupils use indirect questions to show respect (*sorry but erm (.) it's really hot in here sir (.) please may I*). This apologetic request to open the window involves lots of hedging, fillers, and false starts, which show that the pupil is uncomfortable about having to ask. The teacher's power is evident in his response — he uses the brief imperative *well open the window*.

- Power structures between the pupils are evident in their interaction. They try to act as a powerful group against the teacher — when one interrupts they all join in to disrupt the conversation as much as possible.

- However, it seems like pupil B is more disruptive than the other speakers, as he or she waits until someone else speaks before interrupting in to add an expression like *yeah*, or a non-standard phrase like *no one remembers nothing about this*.

- Pupils A and D seem more hesitant, although A is quite assertive at first when he or she interrupts the teacher to say *page ten*. However pupil A stumbles over language, e.g. *they don't (.) they don't* when put on the spot. Pupil D appears the least powerful, making a hesitant request to open the windows starting with an apology *sorry*.

- The teacher controls the discourse even though the pupils try to assert power by interrupting him and shifting the focus of the conversation. He uses repetition to bring it back to the subject he wants to discuss, e.g. by repeating *what happens to atoms*. Both pupil B and the teacher use tag questions to encourage the other to agree, (*didn't we*, *does it now*). These are used rhetorically to support their argument and force the other to agree.

3 **Chatroom conversation between two friends**
This question asks you to think about the impact of technology on the language used by two friends in a chatroom. Here are some points you could include in your answer:

- The function of the chatroom conversation is mostly interactional, but it also has referential elements in which the speakers exchange information.

- As they're friends, and because they're talking in a chatroom, the speakers communicate very informally, using slang like *cool* and *dosh*.

- Technology has had a big impact on the language they use, stemming from a need to communicate quickly e.g. dropping vowels from words like *hw* (how), *havnt*, or *yr* (year) and having relatively limited options on a keyboard compared to spoken language). They use different typefaces from each other so that it will be easier to distinguish one participant in the conversation from the other.

- They use a range of linguistic features: phonetic spelling (*newayz*), non-standard use of punctuation marks, numbers for sounds (*l8tr*), numbers for words (*love 2*), phonetic spelling (*Cud do. Wat time*), emoticons (:'-(), symbols (*be ther @ 8*), upper case (*BRILL*).

- Sentences are often shortened and function words omitted (*hey rosie hw u doin?*).

- The conversation contains many of the features found in spoken interaction: an opening and closing sequence, adjacency pairs, turn-taking, question and answer and topic shifts, boyfriends, college, plans for the evening).

- Chatroom interaction is less spontaneous than regular conversation, e.g. one participant has plenty of time to decide if she wants to accept the other's invitation before replying.

Section Five — Analysing Spoken Language
Pages 68-69

1 The question asks you to analyse and compare the three source texts. Here are some features of each text that you might want to consider and use to contrast the texts in your essay:

Text A — conversation between a customer and newsagent

- The conversation has a transactional function — one speaker wants to buy a paper and find some odd jobs for his grandson. This can be seen from the fact that most utterances are either suggestions, questions or responses.

- The conversation contains features of informal, spontaneous speech, including dialect expressions (*now then*), slang (*cheers, mate*), ellipsis (*bit late delivering*), elision (*gonna*) and non-fluency features (*he's gonna need some er some work you see (.) while he's (.) but he doesn't drive*).

- It also contains deictic expressions that could only be understood in the specific context of the conversation (*I can put it up there with the others on the board over there*).

- The speakers use adjacency pairs and turn-taking rules, but there are also non-fluency features like self-corrections, false starts and hedging, which are common in spontaneous speech, e.g. *anyone in the village who might need (.) need a bit of work done*. They repeat each other a lot, which suggests they are in agreement.

- The speakers are on first name terms and use phatic conversation (*now then, comes round quick*) before B changes the subject. The control of the conversation mostly lies with A, as B is asking for information. B's speech contains pauses, fillers and hedging, as if he feels uncomfortable about asking for help, and so it might be a politeness strategy.

- In contrast, speaker A appears more confident, e.g. using the imperatives *write his name* and the phrase *tell you what*.

Text B — extract from a job interview

- The interviewer is overtly in charge straight away, opening the conversation with a rhetorical question and then an imperative (*come in*, *have a seat*). Taking control immediately sets the interviewer apart from the candidate who false starts straight away (*that's ri-* (2.0) *oh right*). This unequal power relationship continues throughout the interview as the interviewer regularly interrupts the candidate.

- An interview situation is always very formal despite being spontaneous speech — there aren't many contractions and there aren't any colloquialisms or non-standard grammatical features.

- The interviewer does give the candidate feedback and some back-channelling (*mmm-hmm*) to try and put them more at ease. They also let the candidate know when to speak by asking tag questions at the end of their utterances (*did you?*).

- There isn't much informal language in this extract. The language is standard English. There are some non-fluency features on the part of the candidate as they try to process the question and then answer it after being 'put on the spot' by the interviewer.

Text C — speech by a company director to company employees

- This is an official prepared speech, so it uses standard language and grammar throughout and is mostly very formal. The speaker has immediate prestige.

- The main content of the speech — the redundancy payments — is framed between two emotive apologies. This discourse structure shows that the speaker is delivering news that will directly affect the audience and has obviously been pre-planned with the delivery worked out in advance.

- Despite this, there is the occasional non-fluency feature and repetition of *I* and *can*. Most likely this is due to the awkward content of the speech, rather than any informality on the speaker's behalf.

- The speaker tries to appear as personable as possible by using collective addresses such as *you* and *hold our place*. This is also evident in the emotive language, such as *hurts* and *valued*, and the apologies that are repeated.

- The content is also emphasised by prosodic features as the underlined words like *no way* and *can't avoid* would be stressed in the actual delivery of the speech.

Section Six — Analysing Written Language
Pages 80-81

1 The question asks you to give various ways that texts A to E can be grouped. The texts are listed below with some of the linguistic features that you should try and focus on when comparing the texts and grouping them together.

Text A — Novel Extract — *The Way of All Flesh*

- **Purpose** — to entertain.
- **Audience** — readers of 19th century literature, and later students of English literature.
- **Genre** — literature, novel.
- **Register** — formal.
- **Lexis** — example of 19th century vocabulary, e.g. *disposition, confinement, Nemesis*.
- **Lexis** — references to context by use of *1750, George... reigning majesty*.

- **Grammar** — complex sentences throughout.
- **Grammar** — use of parentheses and semicolons (also complex).
- **Tone** — serious yet with humorous undertones e.g. *who though she loved no one else in the world except her husband (and him only after a fashion).*
- **Narrator** — third person who interjects own personal views, e.g. *to the best of my belief* into narrative.
- **Representation** — depicts a strong woman (abusing the doctor and ignoring advice), though this also makes her seem ignorant when she is in fact pregnant.
- **Representation** — Her apparent inability to have children was considered a *hopeless case,* which reflects the domestic roles of women (i.e. producing children) at the time Butler was writing.

Text B — Film Review — *Sex and the City*

- **Purpose** — to inform / entertain
- **Audience** — predominantly female (*girlish excitement*), those familiar with the TV series as the characters are mentioned by their first names.
- **Genre** — journalism, newspaper, review / critique
- **Register** —mostly standard English but the inclusive first person plural pronoun *we* adds to the chattiness / informality.
- **Lexis** — plenty of figurative language and lots of alliteration, e.g. *clique's curse, walk-in wardrobe, labels and love.*
- **Lexis** — field specific to the fashion industry, e.g. *Vogue, Louis Vuitton, Vivienne Westwood.*
- **Grammar** — mainly compound sentences, lots of punctuation to break up statements and make text less complex. Short paragraphs spread the content out over the page.
- **Narrator** — very subjective, giving opinions and displaying attitudes that the reader is expected to share, e.g. *just as we hoped.*
- **Representation** — represents film audience as females who might be attracted by the fashion labels mentioned (e.g. *coos of admiration*). Females in general are the focus of the review. This gives a certain representation of men as outside the text, and male characters in the film are only mentioned as props to the central characters' relationships.
- The cultural context is also represented by the author making the point that despite capitalism being very prevalent in the film it doesn't necessarily make the characters' lives better when they get what they want materially.

Text C — A web page for an educational children's club

- **Purpose** — to persuade.
- **Audience** — parents of young children.
- **Genre** — advertising.
- **Register** — formal.
- **Graphology** — lots of information in a small space, links to different parts of the website in frame and borders, separated by headings and bullet points. Stand-out link to *Join now.*
- **Graphology** — pictures to support information and act as persuasive images for parents / potential customers.
- **Graphology** — Logo for name of company indicates professionalism.
- **Lexis** — emphasises achievement and success, e.g. *learning skills, confidence, respect, invaluable experience.*
- **Grammar** — imperatives: *Realise your child's potential — Join in now.*

Source D — Entry form for a caption competition

- **Purpose** — to instruct.
- **Audience** — prospective competition entrants.
- **Genre** — entry form.
- **Graphology** — businesslike, with brief, essential text. Bold headings for sections that need to be filled in.
- **Grammar** — imperative sentences, e.g. *See over for Terms and Conditions*, *Send your entries to.*
- **Lexis** — no figurative or rhetorical language, only standard vocabulary and grammar.

Text E — Self-diagnosis booklet

- **Purpose** — to inform and instruct.
- **Audience** — adults concerned about health, specifically insomnia sufferers.
- **Genre** — medical, self-help.
- **Register** — formal.
- **Graphology** — headings to highlight subjects being discussed, e.g. *Transient Insomnia.*
- **Graphology** — short sentences and short paragraphs, so as not to overload the audience with information.
- **Lexis** — specialist medical terminology e.g. *chronic, symptom, depression.*
- **Tone** — reassuring, explains symptoms and treatment so the reader feels they have nothing to worry about.
- **Grammar** — use of second person *you* e.g. *you can take some measures*, to include the reader.

A2-Level

English Language

Exam Board: AQA B

Early Language Development

Language development is a long process, so get cracking, else you'll never get those first words out.

Language Development may Begin in the Womb

There is some evidence that suggests language development starts **before** birth.

1) **DeCasper and Spence (1986)** found that babies sucked on their dummies more when their mothers read them the **same story** that they'd also read aloud during the last six months of the pregnancy.

2) **Mehler et al (1988)** found that four-day-old French babies increased their sucking rate on a dummy, showing interest or recognition, when they heard French as opposed to Italian or English. This suggested that they had acquired some awareness of the **sounds** of **French** before they were born.

3) **Fitzpatrick (2002)** found that the heart rate of an unborn baby **slowed** when it heard its **mother's voice**.

> All this suggests that even in the womb, babies become familiar with the **sounds**, **rhythms** and **intonations** of language.

Babies start to use their Vocal Chords Straight Away

1) The period between birth and the first word being spoken is known as the **pre-verbal** or **pre-language** stage.

2) **Crying** is the first main vocal expression a baby makes. It makes the **caregiver** (e.g. parents, sibling, or baby-sitter) aware that the baby needs something. Crying can indicate **hunger**, **discomfort** or **pain**.

3) This isn't really a **conscious act** on the baby's part. It's more an **instinctive response** to how it feels.

Babies then start to Form Sounds — the Cooing Stage

1) At the **cooing** stage (which starts when they're **six to eight weeks old**), babies start making a **small range** of sounds — they get used to moving their lips and tongue.

2) This starts with **vowels** like /u/ and /a/. Then they start linking these to produce **extended vowel combinations** like *ooo* and *aaah*. They start to use **velar consonants** (ones made using the back part of the tongue) like /k/ and /g/ to form sounds like *coo* and *ga*.

3) These sounds don't carry any **meaning** — the baby is just **experimenting** with sounds.

4) Gradually these sounds become more **defined** and are strung together. This **vocal play** is the start of babbling.

Babbling is the next significant stage

1) Babies usually start to babble when they're about **six months** old.

2) At this stage, they start producing repeated consonant / vowel combinations like *ma-ma-ma*, *ba-ba-ba*, *ga-ga-ga*. These sounds are common in babies from many different nationalities. Repeating sounds like this is known as **reduplicated** or **canonical babbling**.

3) Sometimes these sounds are not repeated, e.g. *goo-gi-goo-ga* or *da-di-da*. This is called **variegated babbling**.

4) The **consonants** that you usually get in **reduplicated** or **variegated** babbling are: *h, w, j, p, b, m, t, d, n, k, g*.

5) Research has shown that **deaf** babies who've had some exposure to **sign language** will **babble** with their **hands** — producing consonant and vowel combinations in sign language. This suggests that babbling is an **innate activity**, which is **preprogrammed** to happen in the process of language development.

6) Most people argue that babbling is a **continuation** of the baby's experimentation with **sound creation** (cooing) rather than the production of sounds which carry **meaning**. For example, the infant may produce *dadadada* but they're not actually saying anything referring to *Dad* or *Daddy* at this stage.

7) Some people argue that babbling is the **beginning of speech**:

> **Petitto and Holowka (2002)** videoed infants and noted that most babbling came more from the **right side** of the mouth, which is controlled by the **left side** of the brain. This side of the brain is **responsible for speech production**. Their findings suggest that babbling is a form of **preliminary speech**.

The **Babbling Stage** can be divided into **Two Parts**

1) When babies start to babble, the number of different **phonemes** (sounds) they produce **increases**. This is called **phonemic expansion**.

2) Later in the babbling stage, they **reduce** the number of phonemes they use (**phonemic contraction**).

3) This is the period when the baby starts to concentrate on **reproducing** the phonemes it hears in its **native language**. It **stops using** the sounds that it doesn't hear from its carers.

4) It's at this stage (about **ten months old**) that children of **different nationalities** start to sound different.

> A study at **Bristol University** in **2008** showed that babies who are exposed to different languages in the first nine months of their life are more able to pick out the sounds of these languages as they get older. This is because **phonemic contraction** has occurred less than it would if the baby had been exposed to one language only.

Infants start to show **Intonation Patterns** at the babbling stage

1) Even in the early stages of babbling (at six months) some babies will use **rhythms** that resemble the **speech patterns of adults**. There will be recognisable **intonation** in the strings of phonemes they put together.

2) For example, at the end of a babbling sequence the intonation may **rise**, mirroring the kind of intonation adults use when **asking a question**. Babies can also accompany these sounds with **gestures**, like pointing.

Babbling leads to the production of a **Child's First Words**

1) Eventually, certain **combinations** of **consonants** and **vowels** start to carry meaning. For example, a child might say *Mmm* to show that they want some more food. This is not a word in itself but it **functions** like one. These are called **proto-words**, and sometimes they're accompanied by **gestures** as well.

2) Another example of a proto-word is when a child refers to a cat as /*da*/. This is still just a **sound** rather than a recognisable word, but it **refers** to an **object** and is not just a random utterance. At around **9 months** children start to sound like they're speaking their own **made-up language**. This is called **jargon**.

3) In the later stages of babbling, sound and meaning start to **come together**. At this stage, *ma-ma* does indicate *Mum* and *ka-ka* does mean *car*. This usually happens by the time the baby is **ten months old**.

"AUDREY! Get this checked monstrosity off of me!"

Practice Questions

Q1 Outline a piece of research that suggests language development begins in the womb.

Q2 When does the cooing stage usually start?

Q3 What's it called when babies produce repeated consonant / vowel combinations?

Q4 What evidence is there to suggest that babbling is the beginning of speech?

Q5 Outline what happens in the two parts of the babbling stage.

Q6 What are proto-words?

Essay Question

Q1 With reference to research, outline the different stages that babies go through up to and including the babbling stage.

All this revision is making me go a bit ga-ga...

I don't know how babies get their tiny little heads around proto-words and extended vowel combinations. They must be smarter than they look. It's hard enough learning about them learning about this learning about... but don't mind me and my canonical babbling. Get learning all the important information on this page and you can be as clever as a baby.

Once babies have moved on from the babbling stage, they start trying to pronounce words. They don't always get them right first time but they can still make themselves understood. Experts claim that this is when they start to get really cute.

Phonological Development *depends on the* Individual

1) Children learn **vowels** and **consonants** at different speeds. They learn to use some **phonemes** earlier than others.

2) Most children will be able to use all the **vowels** in English by the time they're two-and-a-half years old.

3) They might not use all the **consonants** confidently until they're **six** or **seven** years old. The earliest consonants that they master tend to be /m/ and /n/ (known as **nasals**), and /p/, /t/, and /k/ (known as **voiceless plosives**). The last ones tend to be the /th/ sounds in words like *thought* (the /θ/ **phoneme**) and *this* (the /ð/ **phoneme**), and other sounds known as **fricatives** like /v/, /tʃ/ and /dʒ/ as in *very*, *church* and *jack*.

4) Children find using consonants at the **beginning** of words (**word-initial**) easier than consonants at the end of words (**word-final**). For example, they'll find it easier to say the /t/ in *teddy* than the one at the end of *sit*.

Simplification *helps children* Communicate

1) Learning to **pronounce** things properly is difficult, but children can still **communicate** — if they can't pronounce a word as adults do, they use a simpler version. Simplification mainly applies to **consonants**.

2) There are three main kinds of phonological simplification — **deletion**, **substitution**, and **cluster reduction**:

> **Deletion** Sometimes a child **drops** a consonant altogether, particularly at the **end** of a word. For example, they might say *ca* rather than *cat*.

> **Substitution** Instead of dropping a consonant, a child might **replace it** with one that's easier to say. For example, they might say *wegs* rather than *legs*, or *tup* rather than *cup*.

> **Cluster Reduction** Where there are **consonant clusters** (two or more consonants together in a word), a child may **drop one** of the consonants. For example, the child will say *geen* rather than *green*.

> **Berko and Brown (1960)** reported what they referred to as the ***fis phenomenon***. A child referred to his plastic fish as a *fis*. When an adult asked *Is this your fis?*, the child said no, stating instead that it was his *fis*. When the adult then asked *Is this your fish?*, the child replied *Yes, my fis*.
> This suggests that children can **recognise** and **understand** a **wider range** of phonemes than they can **produce**.

Other Features *are common in phonological development*

1) **Addition** is when a vowel is added to the end of a word, e.g. *dog* is pronounced *dogu*.

2) **Assimilation** is when one consonant in a word is changed because of the influence of another in the same word, e.g. *tub* becomes *bub* because of the influence of the final /b/.

3) **Reduplication** is when a phoneme is repeated, like *moo-moo* (for *cow*), or *bik-bik* (for *biscuit*).

4) **Voicing** is when voiceless consonants like *p, t, f, s* (sounds produced without using the vocal chords) are replaced by their voiced equivalents *b, d, v, z*, so instead of saying *sock*, a child might say *zok*.

5) **De-voicing** is when voiced consonants (sounds produced using the vocal chords as well as the mouth / tongue / lips), are replaced by their voiceless equivalents, so instead of saying *bag* a child might say *pag*.

It takes longer to Develop Intonation

1) Even at the babbling stage, babies begin to demonstrate **intonation** patterns. When they start to put words together, it becomes even more obvious, e.g. they put stress on certain words, e.g. *that's mine*.

2) It takes a long time for children to understand the complexities of intonation and stress. For example, **Cruttenden (1985)** found that ten-year-olds had difficulty distinguishing between:

> a) *She dressed, and fed the baby* (she dressed *herself*, and fed the *baby*), **and**
>
> b) *She dressed and fed the baby* (she dressed the *baby* and fed it too).

Children's Language has a range of Different Functions

1) At first, a child can get responses or reactions by using **proto-words**. After a while they start to use **recognisable** words, which have **different functions** depending on their context. For example, the word *dummy* could be an order (*get my dummy*), or a question (*where's my dummy?*).

2) **Halliday (1975)** states that the early language of children has **seven functions**:

Instrumental	to get something (e.g. 'go toily' meaning 'I want to go to the toilet').	These four are about the child satisfying their social, emotional and physical needs.
Regulatory	to make requests or give orders (e.g. 'Not your teddy' meaning 'Leave my teddy alone').	
Interactional	to relate to others (e.g. 'Nice Mummy').	
Personal	to convey a sense of personal identity and to express views and feelings (e.g. 'naughty doggy').	
Heuristic	to find out about the immediate environment (e.g. 'What boy doing?').	These two are about the child coming to terms with their environment and their place within it.
Imaginative	to be creative through language that relates to imaginative play, storytelling, rhymes and humour (e.g. 'One day my Daddy came home and he said...').	
Representational	to convey information (e.g. 'I'm three').	

Children quickly learn to Interact With Others

1) Babies learn about **social conventions** even before they can speak. For example, the game of "peek-a-boo" familiarises the baby with **turn-taking** and is an early form of social interaction.

2) Even at the babbling stage, a child's carer might respond to their babbling as if they were having a **conversation** — so there's some basic **interaction** between child and caregiver.

3) As a child's **pragmatic** development continues, they can interact in more **sophisticated** ways. They will **start conversations**, use a full range of **speech functions** and show **politeness features**. They start to use more adult forms of interaction like **turn-taking**, **adjacency pairs** (e.g. saying *hello* when someone says *hello* to you) and **opening and closing sequences** (e.g. *hello* and *goodbye*).

4) **Non-verbal communication** (like hand gestures and facial expressions) and **non-verbal aspects of speech** (like pitch, volume, intonation and pace) also become increasingly **sophisticated** as children grow up.

Practice Questions

Q1 Which phonemes do children usually learn to pronounce last?

Q2 Outline the three different kinds of simplification.

Q3 What is the *fis phenomenon* and what does it suggest about how children acquire language?

Q4 What is meant by assimilation in the context of language acquisition?

Q5 According to Halliday, what are the seven functions of early language? Give examples.

Essay Question

Q1 Explain the phonological features that are found in the speech of young children who haven't yet learned to pronounce all the phonemes correctly.

Phonological development — babies are always looking at their mobiles...

Ah, if only life was as simple as it used to be when you were little. Remember the good old days on the farm playing in the mud and digging for worms. Sadly life's a bit more complicated these days what with revision and exams. Don't worry though, everything you ever wanted to know about phonological development is right here on these pages. Phew.

Children start off by using one or two words to express themselves. As their vocabulary grows, they start using more and more words, and they're able to put them together to form basic grammatical relationships.

Children acquire vocabulary **Very Quickly**

1) This table gives you an idea of how your **vocabulary grows** as you get older:

Age	Number of Words Used
18 months	50 +
2 years	300
5 years	approx. 3000
7 years	approx. 4000

A child's ability to **understand words** will always develop quicker than their ability to **use** them. At 18 months old, a child can **actively** use 50 words, but can **understand** around 250.

The **increase** in vocabulary between age 2 to 7 is so big that these figures can only ever be an **estimation**.

2) Children's first words relate to their **immediate surroundings**. They're connected to things that children can see, hear, taste, smell and touch, or that have a **social function**. Words that express concepts and more abstract ideas start to appear as the child becomes more **self-aware** and **experiences** more of the world.

3) As they get older, children's **vocabulary** continues to **increase**, and their **grammar** becomes more **accurate** and **complex**. It's difficult to know for sure, but it's been estimated that 11-year-olds have a vocabulary of around 40 000 words.

First Words can be put into Categories

Nelson (1973) studied the first fifty words produced by eighteen children and grouped them into **five categories**:

1) **Classes of Objects** — *dog, shoe, ball, car*
2) **Specific Objects** — *Mummy, Daddy*
3) **Actions / Events** — *give, stop, go, up, where*
4) **Modifying things** — *dirty, nice, allgone*
5) **Personal / Social** — *hi, bye-bye, yes, no*

Don't tell me... don't tell me... Dog... No? Table?

Classes of **objects** formed the largest group — it's easier for children to identify things that they can actually **touch**.

Children soon learn to Use Words Creatively

When they're between 12 and 18 months old children will **improvise** if they don't know the word for something. This takes **two** main forms — **underextension** and **overextension**:

1) **Underextension** is when a child uses a word in a very **restricted way**. For example, when a child says *hat*, but means only the hat that she wears rather than any hat.

2) **Overextension** is when a child uses a word to refer to several **different** but **related** things. For example, she might use the word *cat* to refer to anything with four legs, like foxes, dogs, etc.

Rescorla (1980) said there were two types of overextension — **categorical** and **analogical**:

- **Categorical** is when a word is used to refer to things in a similar category, e.g. the word *car* is used to refer to buses, trucks and other forms of four-wheeled vehicle. This kind of overextension is most common.

- **Analogical** is when a word is used to refer to things that aren't clearly in the same category but have some **physical** or **functional relation** to each other, e.g. the word *hat* is used for anything near or connected with the head.

Aitchison (1987) suggested three other Development Processes

1) **Labelling** is when a child links a **sound** to an **object** — they are able to call something by its **correct name**.

2) **Packaging** is when a child begins to understand the **range of meaning** a word might have. They recognise that the word *bottle* can cover different shapes and sizes, but that they all have a similar **function**.

3) **Network building** is when a child starts to make **connections** between words, e.g. they understand that words have **opposites** like *big* and *small*, or know that *little* and *small* are **synonyms**.

Most first words function as **Holophrases**

1)   The stage where a child says their first words is known as the **holophrastic** or **one-word stage**. **Holophrases** are **single words** that express a **complete idea** — an individual word performs the same function as a sentence would.

2)   For example, when a child says *teddy*, the **meaning** of this utterance isn't obvious straight away. It could be *here's my teddy* (like a **declarative** sentence), *where's my teddy?* (an **interrogative**), *get my teddy* (**imperative**), or *here's my teddy, excellent!* (**exclamative**).

3)   Caregivers often need **contextual clues** (e.g. being able to see the objects surrounding the child, intonation and stress) and the child's **non-verbal communication** to interpret holophrases.

The two-word stage is the **Beginning** of **Syntax**

At around **eighteen months** children start to use **two words** in **conjunction**. When they do this they automatically begin to create **grammatical relationships** between words — the start of **syntax**.

There are some common combinations:

baby crying	subject + verb
catch ball	verb + object
daddy dinner (daddy is cooking dinner)	subject + object
dolly dirty	subject + complement

- These combinations show similar patterns to more complex grammatical constructions.
- The phrases use the basic blocks of meaning needed for sentences (subject, verb, object and complement).

complement — gives more information about the subject or object.

The **Telegraphic Stage** combines three or more words

At around **two years old**, children start to use three or four word combinations — the **telegraphic stage**.

These utterances are also formed according to **grammatical rules**:

doggy is naughty	subject + verb + complement
Jodie want cup	subject + verb + object
give mummy spoon	verb + object + object

- Children still focus on the words that carry most meaning.
- They omit functional words e.g. prepositions (*from, to*), auxiliary verbs (*has, do*) and determiners (*a, the*).

By **age five**, children will be able to use a **range** of **grammatical constructions** which include:

1)   **Coordinating conjunctions** (like *and* and *but*) to link separate utterances.

2)   **Negatives** involving the auxiliary *do* (e.g. *don't like it*).

3)   **Questions** formed with *Who, Where* and *What*.

4)   **Inflections** like *-ed* for past tense, *-ing* for present participles and *-s* for plurals.

Practice Questions

Q1   What five categories did Nelson put first words into?

Q2   What is overextension? Outline the two types that Rescorla identified.

Q3   What are holophrases?

Q4   Write down three common grammatical combinations that you find in the two-word stage.

Q5   What happens in the telegraphic stage?

Essay Question

Q1   Discuss children's early language acquisition with reference to the research of Nelson, Rescorla and Aitchison.

Holophrases — words with lots of ho   les in the mid   dle...

Wouldn't it be great if babies could speak English fluently from the moment they were born? It would certainly make your life a lot easier. But then this section would just be a load of blank pages at the start of a book and you'd probably feel a bit ripped off. So learn the wonderful facts on these pages and then at least you've got your money's worth.

Ah, good old grammar — it always pops in to cheer you up when you're feeling a bit jaded. Have a look at the AS Language Frameworks section if you need a reminder of any of the technical terms, then just sit back and enjoy...

Inflections seem to be **Acquired** in a **Set Order**

1) Children start to **add inflections** to their words as early as **20 months old**.

2) Studies have shown that inflections are acquired in a certain order. A study by **Brown (1973)** of children aged between 20 and 36 months suggested that the **order** in which children learn inflections is as follows:

If you're a little rusty on inflections and affixation, have a look at p. 16-17.

	Inflections	A Child Will Say (e.g.)
1	present participle -*ing*	*I going* (although *am* will still be missing)
2	plural -*s*	*cups*
3	possessive '*s*	*Teddy's chair*
4	articles (*a, the*)	*get the ball*
5	past tense -*ed*	*I kicked it*
6	third person singular verb ending -*s*	*She loves me*
7	auxiliary *be*	*It is raining* (or, more likely, *It's raining*)

3) **Katamba (1996)** found that there was **little connection** between the **frequency** with which these inflections are used by parents and the **order** in which children acquire them.

4) *A* and *the* are used **most frequently**, and -*ed* **least frequently**, but they're fourth and fifth in terms of acquisition. This suggests that **imitation** doesn't have a strong influence on how children acquire inflections.

5) The -*ing* inflection is acquired the **earliest** — probably because it represents the **present tense**, and the child will relate more to things happening 'now', than in the past or the future.

Inflections are **Learnt** in **Three Stages**

Cruttenden (1979) identified **three stages** in the acquisition of inflections:

Stage 1 — Inconsistent Usage
A child will use an inflection correctly **some of the time**, but this is because they've learnt the **word**, not the **grammatical rule**, e.g. they might say *I play outside* one day and *I played outside* the next.

Stage 2 — Consistent Usage but sometimes misapplied
For example, applying the regular past tense inflection -*ed* to irregular verbs. A child will say something like *I drinked it*, rather than *I drank it*. This is called an **overgeneralisation** or a '**virtuous error**' — they understand how past tense verbs are formed but **mistakenly apply** the construction to an irregular verb.

Stage 3 — Consistent Usage
This is when children are able to cope with **irregular forms successfully**, e.g. they say *mice* rather than *mouses* and *ran* rather than *runned*.

Children use grammatical rules **Without Being Taught Them**

Children seem to acquire the grammatical rules of language just by being in an environment where language is spoken and where they can **interact with others**:

Berko's (1958) 'Wug' Test

1) Children were shown a picture of a strange creature and told it was a *Wug*. They were then shown a drawing of **two of the creatures** and told 'Now there is another one. There are two of them — there are two...', encouraging the children to complete the sentence. Three-to-four-year-old children said there were **two Wugs**.

2) The test showed that children hadn't used the -*s* because they were **imitating someone**, as they'd **never heard** of a *Wug* before. They'd **automatically** used the **rule** that states -*s* is added to a noun to form a plural.

3) This is called **internalisation** — they'd heard the rule so often that it was second nature to **apply** it to make a plural.

Learning to Ask Questions is a three-stage process

In the first **three** years, children develop the ability to construct **questions**.

> **Stage 1 — around 18 months**
>
> During the two-word stage, children start to use **rising intonation** to indicate a question, e.g. *Sit me?*, or *Go walk?*

> **Stage 2 — between the ages of two and three**
>
> In telegraphic talk, children continue to use rising intonation but now **include *Wh-* words** in the utterances, e.g. *Where tractor?* or *What Mummy doing?* As they continue to develop, they use a wider range of **interrogative pronouns**, such as *why*, *when*, and *how*.

> **Stage 3 — From the age of three upwards**
>
> Children will use what's called a **subject-verb inversion**, e.g. *Can I see it?*, or *Did she break it?*, instead of constructions like *I can see it?* They also use **auxiliary verbs** for the first time, e.g. *What is Mummy doing?*

Oscar the Grouch was never that intimidating before he went into make-up.

Negatives follow a Similar Pattern

At the same time as they start using **interrogatives** (questions), children learn to use **negatives**.

> **Stage 1 — around eighteen months**
>
> Children use *no* or *not* to make things negative, normally at the **beginning of the phrase** rather than at the end, e.g. *no juice*, *not baby's bed*.

> **Stage 2 — between two and three years**
>
> Children start to use *no* and *not* in front of **verbs** too, like *I no want juice* and *I not like teddy's bed*. They also develop the use of **contracted negatives** like *can't* and *don't*, e.g. *I can't drink it* and *I don't like it*. These two forms can sometimes get **mixed up**, e.g. *I can't like it*.

> **Stage 3 — from three years upwards**
>
> Children stop using *no* and *not* in the way they did in stage 1. They **standardise** their use of *can't* and *don't*, and start using other **negative contractions** like *didn't* and *won't*, e.g. *she didn't catch it* and *he won't build it*. The use of *isn't* usually develops **slightly later** (e.g. *Mummy isn't here*).

Practice Questions

Q1 Outline the order in which inflections are acquired. Give examples.
Q2 List Cruttenden's (1979) three stages in the acquisition of inflections.
Q3 What evidence is there to suggest that children use grammatical rules without being taught them?
Q4 What is subject-verb inversion and when do children usually start to use it?
Q5 At what age do children usually start to use contracted negatives?

Essay Question

Q1 Describe how children acquire the grammatical rules of English, with reference to appropriate research.

The examiner won't let you get away with a virtuous error...

Goodness me, they're so demanding — they want the right answers and they want them now. Well, in the exam anyway. But it's better if you get to grips with these pages sooner rather than later. That way, you can get on with the important things in life, like continuing to marvel at the thrilling twists and turns that English Language Acquisition throws at you.

Get your fountain pen out and prime your serious face, cos here's a bit of highly intellectual, slightly dry theory. Yes, I agree that it's rather dull, but get these pages learnt and you'll be on the way to tons of lovely marks.

Behaviourists *argue that* Language *is* Acquired *by* Imitation

Imitation Theory

1) **Skinner (1957)** suggested that language is acquired through **imitation** and **reinforcement**:
   - Children **repeat** what they hear (imitation).
   - Caregivers **reward** a child's efforts with **praise**.
   - They also reinforce what the child says by **repeating** words and phrases back and **correcting mistakes**.
2) This approach says that children learn all the **specific pronunciations** of individual words by copying an adult — therefore in theory it explains an important part of their **phonological development**.

Problems with Imitation

There are some problems with imitation theory:

- Children can construct new sentences they've **never heard before**, so they aren't always directly **imitating**.
- They don't **memorise** thousands of sentences to use later, so their development can't be **exclusively based** on repeating what they've heard their parents or other people saying.
- Imitation can't explain **overgeneralisations**, like *he runned away* (see p. 98). Children **can't copy** these errors because adults don't make them.
- Imitation theory also **can't explain** things like the *fis* phenomenon (see p. 94) — the fact that children can **recognise** a much larger range of words than they are actually able to **use**.

Other people *argue that* Language Acquisition *is* Innate

1) **Chomsky (1965)** argued that a child's ability to acquire language was **inbuilt**. He said that language isn't taught, but it's a **natural development** that occurs when children are **exposed to language**.
2) He suggested that each child has a **Language Acquisition Device (LAD)**, which allows them to take in and **use** the grammatical rules of the language that's spoken where they live.
3) Chomsky's approach seems to explain **how** children end up making overgeneralisations and **why** they acquire inflections in a **certain order** — it's as if the brain is **preprogrammed** to make this happen.
4) Therefore children might learn language quickly because they are **predisposed** to learn it.
5) More evidence for Chomsky's theory is that **all children** pass through the same early stages of language acquisition, before **refining** their range of sounds to their native language (see p. 92-93).
6) There are some **common features** of language known as **linguistic universals**, e.g. every language contains a combination of regular and irregular verbs. This suggests that all speakers acquire language in a similar way, so it supports the idea that children have an **LAD**.
7) One criticism of Chomsky's theory is that the innate approach **underestimates** the **significance** of Skinner's argument that **interaction**, **imitation** and **reinforcement** are important in language development.

Piaget *developed the* Cognitive Approach

The **cognitive approach** focuses on the importance of **mental processes**. **Piaget (1896-1980)** stated that a child needs to have developed certain **mental abilities** before he or she can acquire particular aspects of language:

1) At first a child can't mentally process the concept that something can exist **outside** their **immediate surroundings**. This is called being **egocentric**.
2) By the time they're 18 months old, children realise that things have **object permanence** — they can exist all the time, even if the child can't see them. This coincides with a big increase in vocabulary (see p.96).
3) The child is then mentally better equipped to understand **abstract** concepts like **past**, **present** and **future**.
4) One **criticism** of this approach is that it doesn't explain how some people with **learning difficulties** are still **linguistically fluent**. This suggests that **cognitive** development and **language** development aren't as **closely connected** as the cognitive approach suggests.

Theories of Language Development

Language Development needs Input from Others

The **input approach** argues that in order for language to develop there has to be **linguistic interaction** with **caregivers**.

1) **Bruner (1983)** suggests that there is a **Language Acquisition Support System (LASS)** — a system where caregivers **support** their child's linguistic development in **social situations**.

2) There are clear **patterns** of **interaction** between child and caregiver in **everyday social situations**, like meal times, bath-time and when playing. The caregiver talks to the child and encourages them to talk back by pointing things out and asking questions, e.g. *what's that there, is it a doggy?* As a result of this **linguistic support** the child gradually learns to play a more **active part** in social situations, e.g. asking the caregiver questions.

3) Children who are **deprived** of language early on don't seem able to acquire it easily later. **Lenneberg (1967)** proposed the **Critical Period Hypothesis**, which states that without linguistic interaction **before** ages 5-6, language development is **severely limited**.

4) This view is supported by some rare cases where children **without** any exposure to language in the first five years of life (e.g. cases of extreme **child abuse**) subsequently fail to develop **normal speech**.

Vygotsky presented a Socio-cultural Theory of Language Development

This theory suggests that **social interaction** and experiencing different **social and cultural contexts** are very important for language development. **Vygotsky (1978)** identified two significant factors that contribute to language development — **private speech** and the **Zone of Proximal Development (ZPD)**.

1) **Private Speech** — when a child **talks aloud** to itself. Vygotsky saw this as a major step forward in a child's mental development — this is evidence the child is **thinking for itself**.

2) **The ZPD** — when a child needs a caregiver's help in order to **interact**, e.g. if a doctor asks *Where does it hurt?*, the child might not answer. The caregiver either responds for the child or tries to encourage a response. This gives the child a **model** to apply to **similar situations** in the future when it might respond without help.

This kind of support is known as **scaffolding**. Children require it less and less once they become more able to deal with different social and cultural situations on their own.

Language Acquisition can't be explained by Just One Theory

Unfortunately, there isn't just one model of language acquisition that can **fully explain** how a child learns to speak.

1) Theories of **innate acquisition** and **cognitive developments** do not take into account the role of **interaction** in the development of a child's language.

2) Theories of **imitation** and **reinforcement** can't explain the fact that some features of language apply to **everyone**, and that all babies show similar cooing and babbling features, **regardless** of their native language.

3) The most likely explanation is that language development involves **all** of these different influences to some degree.

Practice Questions

Q1 Outline the behaviourist theory of language acquisition.
Q2 What evidence is there to suggest that all children have an LAD?
Q3 What is object permanence?
Q4 Outline Bruner's theory of the LASS.
Q5 Outline Vygotsky's socio-cultural theory of language development.

Essay Question

Q1 "Children acquire language through imitation and reinforcement." How far do you agree with this statement? Your answer should refer to the benefits and drawbacks of specific linguistic theories.

Surely only boys have LADs...

Welcome, child. Many brave souls have hacked through the Forbidden Forest to reach the mystical land of Kwebegon. And many brave souls have been taken. For it is written in the stars that only one will conquer the dreaded Borsidone Beast and reach the Zone of Proximal Development. Open your mind, and prepare to enter. Just watch your head on the scaffolding...

You might have thought that kids aren't very skilled in the delicate art of social interaction, but actually, tantrums in supermarkets are just their way of interacting with the general public. Well, they've got to practise somewhere.

Caregivers *Talk* to children in a *Particular Way*

1) This kind of language is referred to as **child-directed speech** (CDS), **caretaker speech**, or even **motherese**.

2) The language features of CDS are often **simplified** or **exaggerated** and often have the purpose of **encouraging** a child to **interact** as they're easier to understand.

Child-directed Speech has *Distinctive Linguistic Features*

Phonology and Prosody

1) **Intonation** is exaggerated and words are **stressed** more strongly than they are in adult conversation, e.g. stress on *good* in *What a good girl you are, Annie.* The **pitch** is usually **higher**.

2) Words and phrases are **repeated**, e.g. *Get the ball, Annie, get the ball.*

3) The **pace** is often much **slower**, with **longer pauses** than in adult speech.

Lexis

1) **Vocabulary** is often **simplified**, e.g. instead of saying *banana*, a parent might say *nana* instead.

2) Caregivers use **reduplication** (see p.92) — constructions like *choo-choo, din-din,* or *moo-moo.*

3) They also use **diminutives** — like *birdie, doggie* or *fishy.*

4) A high proportion of words will refer to objects that the child can **see** and **touch** e.g. *Look at the pussy-cat, Annie, it's playing with the ball.*

Grammar

1) **Sentence structures** are simplified, and **function words** (e.g. auxiliary verbs) are often **omitted**. E.g. instead of saying *Annie, shall we go for a walk?*, a caregiver might say *Annie go for walk?*

2) **Proper nouns** (including frequent **repetition** of the child's name) are often used instead of pronouns, e.g. instead of *Are you making a sandcastle?* a parent will say *Is Annie making a sandcastle?* A higher proportion of nouns will be **concrete nouns** (e.g. *cup, apple, bottle*).

3) The **present tense** will be used more than the past tense. The caregiver will talk more about what's **happening 'now'** e.g. *Are you singing?* rather than in the past e.g. *Were you singing yesterday?*

Caregivers *use* *Techniques* to *Encourage Language Development*

1) They **repeat** certain **structures**, e.g. *Annie get the tractor, Annie wash the baby, Annie find the bottle.*

2) They ask lots of **questions**, e.g. *Annie, where's doggie gone?, Have you got a poorly hand?, Is Sally crying, Annie?* This **encourages** the child to **respond**.

3) They use lots of **imperatives**, e.g. *pick up dolly, eat din-dins, drink milk.*

4) Caregivers often **expand** on what the child has said:

> **Mother:** *What you doing, Annie?*
> **Child:** *Playing.*
> **Mother:** *Yes, you're playing with your car.*

5) They also **recast** what the child has said, re-presenting information in a **different way**:

> **Mother:** *What you doing, Annie?*
> **Child:** *Playing with my car.*
> **Mother:** *Yes, that's your car, isn't it?*

No one really knows if CDS *has any* Impact *on Development*

1) Child-directed speech isn't used by parents in **every culture**, but speakers of all cultures grow up to be **fluent**.

2) There's **nothing conclusive** to suggest that CDS does or doesn't work — research has produced conflicting results.

3) It could be that CDS is more about **building a relationship** than about language development in particular.

Children learn how to *Interact* with their *Caregivers*...

Caregivers use **CDS** to **encourage** children to **respond** and teach them about how **dialogue** works.

1) The **early** conversations that children have (at around **age two**) are usually **initiated** and **maintained** by **adults**.

2) They tend to be made up of **short statements** by the child that the **adult** responds to — the child **doesn't** really **respond** to what the adult says. For example:

> **Father:** *Look at the ducks, Annie, can you see the ducks?*
> **Child:** *Quack quack.*
> **Father:** *That's right the ducks go quack quack don't they?*
> **Child:** *In the water.*

3) Children **develop** a lot between the ages of **two** and **four**. They start to understand **turn-taking** and take part in **dialogues**. They start to **understand** the **needs** of the **listener** — they learn to give appropriate **answers** to questions and to **respond** in a way that can **initiate** a **further response** from the other speaker.

4) They also develop more **awareness** of **social factors** in conversations, e.g. they begin to understand when to use **politeness forms** like *please* and *thank you*.

5) They become better at getting someone's **attention**, e.g. they use **adverbs** like *well* to show that they have something to say. They also start to use **people's names** to get their attention.

6) **Starting school** or **nursery** has a big **impact** on **social interaction skills**, as children meet **more people**. They develop more awareness of what **kind** of **language** is **appropriate** in certain **contexts**, e.g. they start to use more **formal** language in the **classroom** compared to the **playground**.

...and with *Other Children*

At around the age of **two** children also start to have **conversations** with **each other**.

1) These **early conversations** are **limited** because at this age the children only have a **lexis** of about **300 words**.

2) They're known as **closed conversations** because there's no **progression** in them. The speakers don't have the **skills** to make **meaningful responses**, so they can't keep the conversation going. The conversations are made up of **short statements**:

> **Child A:** *I got sweeties.*
> **Child B:** *Nice sweeties.*
> **Child A:** *I got big bag.*

As they get **older**, children's use of **lexis** and **grammar** increases, so they're able to have more **complex** conversations.

1) They develop **pragmatic skills** — they learn to use language to **form relationships** with each other, and to try and **get** what they **want**. This can involve **repetition**, e.g. *Can I have the pen now? Can I have the pen now?* and **persuasive tactics**, e.g. *If you don't give me it then I won't be your friend.*

2) They also **imitate** adult speech and develop more **awareness** of the **type** of **language** that's **appropriate** for different **audiences**, e.g. **older** children often use **CDS** when they're talking to **younger** children.

Practice Questions

Q1 List three grammatical features of child-directed speech.

Q2 How do conversations between children and their caregivers change as children get older?

Q3 Why are most two year olds only able to have closed conversations with each other?

Essay Question

Q1 "The main aim of CDS is to encourage the child to respond." To what extent do you agree with this statement?

Does ikkle babba think CDS is annoying? Oo yes he do, yes he do...

When I was at primary school most of our assemblies seemed to be about the story of Louis Braille (the man who invented Braille...). After one such assembly the head asked if anyone had any questions, and Ashley Ross in Year One stuck his hand up and said "My mummy bakes pizzas". Aww, see — knowing the right thing to say in a situation isn't as easy as it sounds...

If you're reading this now then I can pretty much guarantee that you must have been taught how to read at school. And it's a good thing too, cos now you get to read all about how you learnt to read in the first place. Yay.

There are **Different Approaches** to Teaching Children to **Read**

There are **three** major **approaches** to the teaching of **reading**:

1) The phonics approach

- This approach involves looking at **letters** and **letter combinations** in terms of **sounds** (reading **'by ear'**), e.g. *cow* is separated into the phonemes /c/ and /ow/. It means that children can **sound out** unfamiliar words.
- It's **useful** for words like *latch* that are **pronounced** as they're written, but is **less useful** for words like *through*.
- The approach has also been **criticised** because it just **focuses** on **sounds** and **letters**, rather than on the **meanings** of the words.

2) The "look and say" approach

- This is also known as the **whole word** approach. It involves **recognising** whole words by **sight** alone, **rather** than **breaking** them down into **separate phonemes** (reading **'by eye'**).
- It focuses on the **meaning** of words, and teaches children to recognise **common** words like *and*, *see*, *went* etc.
- However, relying on this method requires children to **memorise** a **large number** of words, and **doesn't** give them the **skills** to **work out** the **sound** or **meaning** of **unfamiliar** words.

3) The psycholinguistics approach

- This approach sees reading as a **natural development** that comes from being in an **environment** where books are **read**, **valued** and **available**.
- It's an **active approach** to reading — the **reader** is given **responsibility** for **working out** what a word **means**, rather than just being **told** the meaning.
- When children come across a word they **can't** read, they're encouraged to **work out** the **meaning** by looking at the **rest** of the **sentence** and other **clues** like **illustrations**.
- The idea is to encourage children to **focus on meaning**, rather than just working out **symbols**. It's also designed to make them aware of the **importance** of **context**.
- However, the approach has been **criticised** because it leaves a lot to **chance**.

Teachers tend to use a **Combination** of **Approaches**

Over the past **sixty years**, there's been a lot of **debate** about which method for teaching reading is **best**.

1) Schools tend to use a **combination** of **approaches** rather than just rely on one. This is because some children **respond** better to one method than another.

2) It also ensures that children develop a **range** of **skills**. The **phonics approach** teaches them to recognise **symbols**, while the **look and say** and **psycholinguistics approaches** teach the importance of **meaning** and **context**.

3) It's also really **important** that children **practise** reading **outside** of **school** — some researchers see this as the **most important** factor in **improving** a child's reading ability.

Techniques for **Developing Reading Skills** depend on the **Child's Age**

1) Up to age **five**, caregivers may **read** stories and nursery rhymes to children, and help children enjoy the **physical experience** of books, e.g. turning pages, pointing to letters and saying the sounds out loud.

2) Between **five** and **six**, caregivers / teachers will read them fiction and non-fiction, get them to **break down** words into individual sounds (**phonemes**), and get them to **match sounds** to **letters**.

3) Between six and seven, they'll get children to **read aloud**, set classroom tasks involving speaking, interacting and reading, and encourage them to **talk** about what they've read.

4) Between seven and eight, they may introduce children to **different genres** and provide them with the chance to **discuss** different aspects of what they've read.

Or, here's an idea. How about you TURN YOUR OWN PAGE AND STOP BEING SO LAZY.

Learning to Read

Reading *Develops* in *Stages* as you go through school

Obviously, everyone progresses at different rates, but there are some **general stages** that **most children** pass through.

Pre-school (up to age 5)	• Kids take part in activities that **prepare** them for reading, e.g. playing with bricks, jigsaws, and matching pictures. This helps them distinguish between **different sizes**, **shapes** and **patterns**. In turn this prepares them for identifying **letters** and **combinations of letters**. • They can turn pages in books themselves and verbally **create** their own **stories**. • They begin to identify some **individual letters**, such as the first letter of their name, and also begin to match some **sounds** to letters.
Between five and six years old	• They **increase** the number of **letter-sound** matches that they know. • They realise that in English, letters on a page move from **left** to **right** and **top** to **bottom**. • They begin to **recognise** frequently used words.
Between six and seven years old	• They can read stories they're **familiar** with. • They use a range of **reading strategies** — when they're stuck on a word they may use the context to guess what it is, or sound it out **phonetically**. • They recognise more and more words just **by sight**. • They **break down** words into individual **sounds** to read an unfamiliar word. • They start to read with some **fluency**.
Between seven and eight years old	• They read more **fluently**, and their **vocabulary** continues to increase. • They use reading strategies **accurately** (such as **predicting** what words might come next). • They're better at working through **individual sounds** to read unfamiliar words.

Reading *Skills* carry on *Developing After* you've learnt to read

The learning process **continues** for a long time **after** children are first able to read **fluently**. Up until about the age of **18**, their reading continues to **improve** and their **vocabulary** grows:

> • They become **familiar** with a **wider range** of texts.
> • They **read to learn** — their reading improves enough that they can use texts to find out **information**.
> • They're able to use more **complex** and **varied** texts to find out information **without help**.
> • They read in **different ways** for **different reasons**, e.g. for work and for pleasure.

1) Some children's progress stops here — they're able to read fluently, but they never reach a stage where they can **interpret** what they're reading **critically**.

2) This is often because they **stop reading** apart from when they **have** to.

3) Other children's reading **continues** to **improve**, until they're able to **analyse** and **criticise** what they're reading. This means they can **select** the most **important** points from a text and **develop** their own **opinions** about them.

Practice Questions

Q1 Outline one criticism of the "look and say" approach.

Q2 What does the psycholinguistics approach to teaching reading involve?

Q3 Outline what most children are able to do in terms of reading at a pre-school age.

Q4 How do a child's reading skills continue to improve after the age of 8?

Essay Question

Q1 With reference to the three main approaches to teaching reading, explain why it's often thought to be best to teach a combination of approaches.

Psycholinguistics — not something you'd think would be encouraged...

Seeing the whole process of learning to read set out in a big table like that has made me realise just how much work goes into it. It's amazing to think that at one point I was a little pipsqueak who struggled with the alphabet, and now I'm a fully fledged reader who can understand all the letters and some whole words. My parents are very proud, but they hide it well...

As if learning to read wasn't enough, the poor little mites have to learn to write too, even though they'd probably much rather be having a nice little nap or a biscuit. It hardly seems fair, but it does come in handy I suppose.

Writing *develops in* Stages

1) Children go through **stages** of **development** before they can write and spell entire words. Although they need to be able to **recognise** letters and words before they can write, they seem to learn to write **alongside** learning to read.

2) When young children do **drawings** they're actually starting to learn the **motor skills** (coordination) they'll need for **writing**.

3) As their **motor skills** develop, children are able to learn the **conventions** of written language, e.g. **spelling**, **punctuation** and **layout**.

4) How **quickly** a child learns to write depends on how much **practice** they have, e.g. whether they're given crayons to use before they start school. It also depends on the child's **intelligence**, and how much they've been exposed to **role models** who write.

5) Theorists have **different ideas** about how many stages are involved in learning to write, and how old children are when they go through them.

After eating 74 crayons Gabi's writing had started to suffer.

Barclay (1996) *outlined* 7 Stages *of* Writing Development

Stage 1 **Scribbling**	Kids make random marks on the page, which **aren't related** to letters or words. They're **learning the skill** of keeping hold of a pencil or crayon, which prepares them for writing. They often **talk** about what they're scribbling.	
Stage 2 **Mock Handwriting**	Children practise drawing **shapes** on paper, although it's still not usually possible to work out what the drawing represents. Letter-like forms (**pseudo-letters**) begin to appear in or with drawings as the first sign of **emergent writing** — an attempt to write letters.	
Stage 3 **Mock Letters**	Children produce **random letters**, but there's still no awareness of spacing or of matching **sounds** with **symbols**.	
Stage 4 **Conventional Letters**	Children start matching **sounds** with **symbols** — writing down letters that match the sounds being heard or spoken. Words are unlikely to be spaced out. Children start using **initial consonants** to **represent words**, e.g. *h* for *horse*. The initial letter might be read out as if the **full word** is there on the page.	
Stage 5 **Invented Spelling**	Most words are spelled **phonetically**, though some simple and familiar words are spelled correctly.	they se some horses they ar takeing home a cat I wood lik to be Good.
Stage 6 **Appropriate Spelling**	Sentences become more **complex** as the child becomes more aware of standard spelling patterns. Writing becomes more **legible**.	On Wednesday morning everything seemed the same as usal but I had butterflys in my stomach.
Stage 7 **Correct Spelling**	Most words are spelled **correctly**. Older children have usually started to use joined-up writing, too.	Every animal builds a diffrent type of house, a rabbit dig's itself a burrow deep in the ground.

Learning to Write

Kroll (1981) outlined 4 Stages of Writing Development

James's motor skills were developing, and yet his writing was still appalling.

1) The Preparatory Stage — from 18 months

- Children develop the **motor skills** needed for writing.
- They begin to learn the basics of the **spelling system**.

2) The Consolidation Stage — 6-8 years

- Children **write** in the same way as they **speak**.
- They use lots of **colloquialisms**.
- They use **short declarative statements** and **familiar conjunctions** like "and".
- They won't yet be sure how to **finish** off a sentence.
- They begin to express ideas in the form of **sentences**, though without much punctuation.

3) The Differentiation Stage — age 8 to mid-teens

- Children become aware of the **difference** between the **conventions** of **spoken** and **written** language.
- They begin to understand that there are **different genres**, for example letters and stories.
- They begin to **structure** their work using writing **guides** and **frameworks**.
- They use **more complex grammar** and **sentence structures**.
- **Punctuation** becomes more **accurate** and **consistent**.

> Every child develops at a different rate, so this is just a rough outline of how old they are at each stage.

4) The Integration Stage — mid-teens upwards

- Writing becomes more **accurate**, with a **wider vocabulary** and more **accurate spelling**.
- Children understand that **style** can **change** according to **audience** and **purpose**.
- **Narrative** and **descriptive** skills improve. They write expanded stories, with **developed characters**, a **plot** and a **setting**.
- They develop a **personal writing style**. This continues to develop throughout **adulthood**.

Practice Questions

Q1   How do scribbling and drawing help prepare young children for writing?

Q2   Name two factors that can affect how quickly a child learns to write.

Q3   What is emergent writing?

Q4   According to Barclay (1996), what happens in stage 6 of learning to write?

Q5   According to Kroll (1981), what happens in the consolidation stage?

Q6   According to Kroll (1981), what skills do children develop in the differentiation stage?

Q7   According to Kroll (1981), in which stage do children develop a personal writing style?

Essay Question

Q1   Children go through different stages of development when they learn to write. Outline what happens with reference to one theorist in particular.

One day I woke up and I decided to revise and it was very nice...

There's another stage — the 'learning to write about learning to write' stage. And you reach that stage at the exact age you are today. What a happy coincidence. Anyway, it's the end of the section — hurrah. To celebrate, why not go back to your childhood by getting the squirty cream out the fridge and squirting it straight into your mouth until it inflates like a big toad.

Now have a go at this practice exam question.

Text A is a transcript of an interaction between a three-year-old and her mother.
They are looking at an illustrated story book.

Text B is an extract from the story book.

1. With reference to the texts and knowledge from your study of language acquisition,
   comment on how Ellie is being helped to understand what happens in the story.   *[48 marks]*

Text A — Conversation between Ellie (aged 3 years) and her mother

Ellie:	she's in her bed
Mum:	no look (.) look she's got out of bed now
Ellie:	why
Mum:	well let's see (.) she jumped out of bed and stretched her arms as wide as she could
Ellie:	// ooh
Mum:	can you do a big stretch Ellie (2) that's it (.) ooh <u>very</u> wide (1) and look can you see what colour curtains she's got
Ellie:	curtains
Mum:	yes (.) she's got <u>green</u> curtains like you have in your room (.) hasn't she
Ellie:	there's got (.) I've got green curtains and she's gotted green curtains
Mum:	that's right (.) she's got green curtains (.) clever girl
Ellie:	and she's got water
Mum:	ooh is that the next page (.) yes you're right she's all wet isn't she (.) she's gone to wash her face
Ellie:	wash her in the water
Mum:	in the water (1) she went into the bathroom to wash her face and look (.) <u>splish</u> <u>splash</u> <u>splosh</u> (.) can you say that darling (.) splish
Ellie:	plish
Mum:	splish
Ellie:	and in there there's bubbles in there
Mum:	ooh yes look at all the bubbles in the sink (.) and she's getting all wet isn't she
Ellie:	what is it on the next one
Mum:	okay let's see (.) on the next one (.) can you see what she's doing
Ellie:	she's got her
Mum:	what's that in her hand
Ellie:	she's got her (.) toothbrush
Mum:	<u>very</u> good (.) she's cleaning her toothypegs isn't she
Ellie:	she's bushing them
Mum:	that's right (.) you <u>brush</u> your teeth don't you (1) shall we read it (.) Rosie squeezed out a <u>big dollop</u> of toothpaste and brushed her teeth
Ellie:	I can't see her teeth
Mum:	no but she's got a big smile hasn't she (.) look (.) <u>big wide</u> smile

Transcription Key	
(.)	*Micropause*
(2)	*Pause in seconds*
//	*Interruption / overlap*
<u>underlining</u>	*Emphasis*

Text B — Extract from an illustrated children's story

Rosie jumped out of bed and stretched her arms as wide as she could. She liked to have a big stretch every morning.

Then she went into the bathroom to wash her face. Splish, splash splosh! "Washing your face is fun," thought Rosie.

After she had washed her face, Rosie squeezed out a big dollop of toothpaste and brushed her teeth.

These pages are all about how the words we use change over time. You might have noticed this happening yourself — if you started this book saying 'I will revise,' I bet it's now changed to 'I can't be bothered...'

New Words have been created throughout History

New words are **always** being **created**.

1)   For example, people think that Shakespeare invented over **1700 words**, some of which are still used today, including *assassination*, *courtship* and *submerged*.

2)   In recent years the following new words have been accepted into the Oxford English Dictionary: *fashionista*, *wussy* and *twonk* (a stupid or foolish person).

3)   The **creation** of new words is known as **coinage** and the new words themselves are called **neologisms**.

Hank didn't know it, but he was seconds away from coining 'flame-grilled steak'.

New Words are Created in Different Ways

There are many **different ways** of forming new words. Here are some of the methods:

Borrowing	A simple way to create new words is to 'borrow' a word from **another language**. Many of the words used frequently in everyday language are **borrowings** or **loan words**. For example, *barbecue* comes from **Spanish**, *bungalow* comes from **Hindustani** and *robot* comes from **Czech**. A lot of borrowings relate to **food** or **objects** not traditionally found in the UK, e.g. *spaghetti* from **Italian**.
Scientific Progress	Advances in **medicine**, **science** and **technology** cause new words and phrases to be invented. For example, *in vitro fertilisation* is a term that emerged in the **1970s**.
Affixation	Words can also be created by **affixation**, where **new prefixes** or **suffixes** are added to existing words. Many words in the English language have been created by adding **Latin** or **Greek prefixes** or **suffixes**. For example, the **Greek** word *hyper* is found in the words *hyperactive*, *hypersensitive* and *hypertension*.
Compounding	Sometimes a new word is created by **combining** two separate words to create one word. This is known as **compounding**. For example, *thumb* can be **combined** with *print* to create *thumbprint* and *hand* can be combined with *bag* to create *handbag*.
Blending	**Blending** is when two separate words are actually **merged together**. For example, *netiquette* is a **blend** of *net* and *etiquette*. Similarly, *infotainment* is a blend of *information* and *entertainment* and *satnav* is a blend of *satellite* and *navigation*.
Conversion	New words are also created when an existing word **changes class**. This is known as **conversion**. For example, many words that started off as **nouns** are now also used as **verbs**: *text/to text*, *chair/to chair* (a meeting), *mail/to mail*. Note that the word **doesn't** change its **form** (it looks the same), only its **function** (it does a different job).

New Words can also be created by Different Forms of Shortening

1)   **Clipping** — this is when you drop one or more syllables to create an **abbreviation**. For example, *demo* is often used rather than *demonstration* and, more recently, *rents* rather than *parents*. Abbreviations are a common form of **word creation**.

2)   **Initialism** — this is where the **first letter** of a word **stands for** the word itself. For example, *FBI* takes the first letters of the words in *Federal Bureau of Investigation*, *OTT* takes the first letters of *over the top*, and *FYI* takes the first letters of *for your information*. **Initialisms** are always pronounced **letter by letter**.

3)   **Acronyms** — **initial letters** of words also **combine** to **create** a completely **new word**. For example, *NASA* stands for *National Aeronautics and Space Administration* and is pronounced as a word in itself rather than letter by letter. The acronym *WAGS* refers to the **wives and girlfriends** of footballers.

4)   **Back-formation** — this is a **less frequent** form of word creation. It occurs when a word looks like it has been created by adding a **suffix** to an existing word, but actually, the suffix has been **removed** to create the new term. For example, the noun *baby-sitter* came **before** the verb *baby-sit*, *word-processor* came before *word-process*, *burglar* came before *burgle*, and the verb *enthuse* is a back-formation of *enthusiasm*.

Many New Words come from the Names of People, Places or Things

1) **Words** can also be **derived** from people's **names**. Words that develop in this way are known as **eponyms**. For example, the word *nicotine* comes from **Jean Nicot**, a French ambassador to Portugal in the sixteenth century who sent **tobacco seeds** back to France.

2) **Brand names** are a source of new words too. Two examples (both taken from American English) might be asking for something to be *Xeroxed* rather than *photocopied* or asking for a *Kleenex®* rather than a *tissue*.

3) Sometimes words are derived from a particular **place**. For example the word *limousine* derives from **Limousin** (a French province). This came about because the car's designers thought the shape of the driver's compartment was **similar** to the kind of hoods historically worn by shepherds in that area.

Words can Disappear

1) Just as new words enter the language, old words **disappear**. Words that have become **obsolete** (are no longer used) are known as **archaisms**. For example, these words aren't used any more in modern English: *durst* (dare), *trow* (think).

2) Other words might still be used, but have fallen out of fashion, e.g. *courting* (dating), *wireless* (radio).

"No, grandpa, I'm not courting. I'm just using him for his private jet..."

English Spelling hasn't always been fixed either

The English spelling system (its **orthography**) is notoriously complicated and is actually quite random — although you might expect this from a language that has borrowed words from almost everywhere.

The letters *-ough* are probably the most famous example of a segment that can represent a lot of **different sounds** in spoken English. The spelling of words with *ough* originated in **Middle English**, but probably sounded something like the *-och* part of *loch*. Here are a few **variations**:

through (an 'oo' sound)	*though* (an 'oh' sound)	*tough* ('uff')
cough ('off')	*plough* ('ow')	*hiccough* ('up')

One reason for **idiosyncrasies** like this is that changes in **pronunciation** occurred **during** and **after** standardisation of the spelling system. This meant sounds were lost from spoken English, while their **original historic spellings remained** in written English.

Practice Questions

Q1   What is a neologism? Suggest three ways they can be formed.

Q2   What is affixation? Give an example.

Q3   Explain what back-formation is and give an example.

Essay Question

Q1   Describe the ways in which different forms of shortening can be used to create new words.

All this cramulation is shoodling my thoughtbox...

Personally, I can't think of a Shakespeare play that takes place under water, but he must have had a reason for inventing the word 'submerged.' Maybe Juliet drowned in the first draft of R&J — he was probably right to scrap that idea, bit tacky, don't you think? Anyway, learn how words come and go over time, and pass me the wireless from betwixt those knaves yonder.

Here's an idea — try thinking of this section in life cycle terms. The previous two pages covered the birth and death of words. It's a bit sad, but don't worry — these pages are about the lucky words that manage to get reincarnated...

Semantic Change is when a word's Meaning Changes

1) Words which **remain** part of a language for many years often **change their meaning** over time. This is known as **semantic change**.

2) Language **changes** all the time without you really noticing, e.g. **metaphors** like *surfing the net* are now used without thinking, as are words like *rip* (to copy from a CD), *burn* (to copy files to a CD) and *cut* (a record).

3) **Slang** and **colloquialisms** give **new meanings** to **established words**. For example, the following words are used to **express approval**: *cool, buzzing, safe, mint*.

A word can Develop a more Positive or Negative Meaning

Amelioration

1) Amelioration is when a word develops a more **positive meaning**.

2) For example, *nice* used to mean *foolish*. *Tremendous* used to mean *terrible* but is now used to say something is *very good*. *Mischievous* used to mean *disastrous* but now means *playfully malicious*.

Pejoration

1) Pejoration is when a word **develops** a **negative meaning**.

2) For example, *hussy* used to have the same meaning as *housewife* but now refers to *an impudent woman of loose morals*. *Notorious* used to mean *widely known* but has come to be associated with being **well known** for **doing something bad**.

1) Some words change their meaning **altogether**. For example, *tomboy* used to mean a *rude, boisterous boy* but is now only used to refer to girls who act in what is perceived to be a **boyish way**. *Porridge* used to refer to *soup containing meat and vegetables* but now means *cereal made of oatmeal and milk*. *Bimbo* was originally a term for *fellow* or *chap*. It then took on negative connotations and came to mean *stupid man* before eventually being a term aimed **exclusively** at **women**.

2) Sometimes a word ends up making **less** of an **impact** than it used to. This is known as **weakening**. For example, the word *terrible* used to mean *causing terror* but now it's used to say that something is **very bad**. *Glad* used to mean *bright, shining, joyous* but now it means *pleased*.

The Meaning of a word can get Broader or Narrower

1) A word that has a **specific meaning** can develop a **broader meaning** over time. This process is known as **broadening, generalisation, expansion** or **extension**.

2) For example, the word *bird* used to mean a *young bird* or *fledgling* but now refers to **birds in general**. *Place* used to refer to an *open space in a city, market place, or square* but now means a *portion of space* anywhere. *Arrive* used to be a term that was connected with *landing on shore* after a long voyage. Today, it means to come to the end of any kind of journey, or to **reach a conclusion** (*I have finally arrived at a decision*).

3) A word that has a general meaning can develop a **narrower meaning**. This process is called **narrowing, specialisation** or **restriction**. For example, the word *meat* used to mean *food* in general but now specifically refers to *animal flesh*. *Girl* was a term used to refer to a *young person* generally and *liquor* used to mean *liquid* but now refers to *alcoholic drink* specifically. You still see the old meaning of *liquor* in a cooking context, e.g. you cook something then *pour off the liquor*.

4) Words can go though **multiple semantic changes**, e.g. *silly*:

Silly:	*blessed > innocent > pitiable > weak > foolish*

Who are you calling 'girl'?

Political Correctness *can Cause Semantic Change*

1) In the last thirty years, **political correctness** has had a major impact on how language is used. Its purpose has been to **remove** words and phrases that have **negative connotations** from the language.

2) For example, *old people* are referred to as *senior citizens*, and *disabled people* as *people with disabilities*. The term *half-caste* is no longer used for people who are *mixed race*.

3) **Trivialising suffixes** such as *–ess* and *–ette* are **no longer used** in many cases. The word *actor*, for example, now refers to either a **male or female performer** and the word *actress* is gradually becoming **redundant**.

4) Many people feel these types of **semantic change** are **positive** and that they remove negative connotations from the language. However, some people feel it's gone a bit too far when the changes begin to **obscure meaning**, e.g. using the job title *sanitation consultant* instead of *toilet cleaner*.

Figurative Expressions *give New Meanings to Old Words*

METAPHOR

1) Metaphors describe things as if they were actually **something else**.

2) For example, the following phrases were originally associated with the sea, but are now used metaphorically: *plain sailing*, *high and dry*, *clear the decks*.

METONYMY

1) Metonymy is when we use a word **associated** with an **object** instead of the object's actual name.

2) For example, *cash* used to mean *money box* but over time it came to mean the **money itself**.

IDIOM

1) Idioms are **sayings** that don't make sense if you **literally interpret** the meanings of the words.

2) E.g. you **can't tell** from the words alone that *it's raining cats and dogs* means *it's raining very heavily*.

3) Idioms **don't appear** out of **nowhere**. They usually have some **factual**, **literary** or **historical** basis.

4) For example, the expression *to have a chip on your shoulder* comes from nineteenth century America. A young man would challenge others to a fight by inviting them to knock a wood-chip off his shoulder.

EUPHEMISM

1) Euphemism is the use of **alternative** words or phrases to **avoid offending** someone or to make something **appear less unpleasant**.

2) E.g. there are lots of euphemisms for **death**, like *kicking the bucket*, *pushing up daisies*, or *popping your clogs*.

CLICHÉ

1) If idioms are used a lot, they may become **clichés** — **overused phrases** which fail to excite the imagination.

2) The **business world** has many **clichés**, such as *pushing the envelope* and *blue-sky thinking*.

Practice Questions

Q1 Explain the terms amelioration, pejoration and weakening, giving an example for each one.

Q2 What do narrowing and broadening mean?

Q3 How do metaphor, metonymy and euphemism contribute to semantic change?

Essay Question

Q1 Giving examples, discuss the impact that political correctness has had on semantic change.

Where do words go if they want to get narrower? Word Watchers...

It's all fun and games, this, isn't it? If you don't know what kind of figurative expression that last sentence is, go back and read these two pages all over again. Twice. As for me, I'm off to invent myself a new job title. Maybe I could be a 'Learning Aid Perfectioning Operative,' a 'Revision Expert' or, as someone has just kindly suggested, an 'office monkey.' Nice.

Just as you thought it might be safe to nod off on your desk for a few minutes and have a little dribble, here's some grammar to slap you round the face and rouse you from your lovely slumber. It's a hard life, isn't it...

The way words are **Formed** is **Always Changing**

Here are some of the biggest grammatical changes that happened to **Late Modern English** — English since 1700:

Verbs

1) The **past tense** of some **irregular verbs** used to be formed differently — over time the **stem vowels** have changed, e.g. the verb *spake* has become *spoke* in PDE (Present Day English).
2) **Auxiliary verbs** (e.g. *do*) started to be used more in Late Modern English (English from 1700). This had an effect on **word order** (see below).

Adjectives

1) **Comparative** and **superlative** inflections (i.e. *greater* and *greatest*) exist in PDE as they did before. However, in the **nineteenth century** superlatives like *properest* were also **grammatically acceptable**. In PDE you'd use *most proper* instead.
2) The two ways of forming comparatives and superlatives could also be **combined**, e.g. you could use **double comparatives** like *more cleverer*. In PDE it's enough to use *more clever* or *cleverer*.

Nouns

1) The way that nouns are used in sentences has changed less than other word classes, although they were **capitalised** more frequently until the 18th century (see p.118).
2) One change is that the **definite article** is now used less often with certain nouns, e.g. constructions like *the Russian* to mean Russians in general, and *the Sciatica* (back pain) would now be replaced with *Russians* and *sciatica*.

Syntax used to be more **Complex**

Since 1700, there's been a trend towards **sentences** being **shorter** and **syntax** has become **less complicated**.

Sentences used to contain a lot more **subordinate clauses**. For example, there are **three** subordinate clauses in this sentence (shown with square brackets) from an 1886 novel by Thomas Hardy:

What was really peculiar, [however,] [in this couple's progress,] [and would have attracted the attention of any casual observer otherwise disposed to overlook them,] was the perfect silence they preserved.

PDE tends to use **simpler punctuation** — there are **fewer commas** and **semicolons**. This makes it seem **less formal**.

Word Order has also **Changed**

Use of **auxiliary verbs** (like *do, have, be*) has **increased**. This has had an impact on **word order**.

Interrogatives

1) Interrogatives didn't always include auxiliary verbs. In Early Modern English (from around 1500-1700) they were formed with the **verb** at the **start**, so the order was **verb-subject-object** (V-S-O). You might still see this in **Late Modern English** texts:

V	S	O
[Spake]	[you] with	[him]?

2) In PDE, interrogatives are often formed using an **auxiliary verb**, and the **subject** and **main verb** are **inverted** from the old construction to S-V-O. Auxiliary verbs like *do* are now used at the **start** of the question:

Auxiliary	S	V	O
[Did]	[you]	[speak] with	[him]?

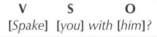 *Questions are also often formed with wh-words (see p. 15).*

Negative Constructions

1) In PDE, the negative *not* is placed **before** the verb rather than after it.
2) A '**dummy auxiliary**' is used (an auxiliary verb like *do* that isn't really necessary for the meaning of the phrase to be understood).
3) For example, phrases like *I do not deny it* have **replaced** older constructions like *I deny it not*.

Contractions *have gone* **In** *and* **Out** *of* **Fashion**

1) By the **early 18th century**, **contractions** had become very common in written and spoken English.
2) This was partly because they were often used in **poetry** to make sure that words fit the **metre** of the verse. It was also because **printers** contracted words to make them fit on the line. This meant that the use of contractions was **inconsistent**, often within the same printed text.

- Contractions that are still used in PDE were common in the early 18th century e.g. *can't, would've, she'll*.
- Others were also used, e.g. *'twas* (it was), *o'er* (over), *e'en* (even).
- **Proclitic** contractions are used less in PDE. This is when the contracted part of the word is at the beginning, e.g. *'tis*. In PDE there are more **enclitic** contractions, where the contracted part of the word comes at the end, e.g. *it's*.
- **Past participles** used to be contracted, to show that the final syllable wasn't pronounced, e.g. *disturb'd, defer'd*.

3) However, **18th century** writers like **Jonathan Swift** complained that contractions were 'corrupting' English — they were **inelegant**, and would make the language very difficult for future generations to understand.
4) This **backlash** against contractions led to them going **out of fashion**. By the **19th century** they were much less common. For example, this is an extract from a letter written in 1866 by the Victorian writer Wilkie Collins (words that would have probably been contracted in the 18th century are underlined):
   I am unfortunately already engaged to dinner on Sunday — or I should have been delighted to dine...
5) Contractions then started to be used more frequently in the second half of the **20th century**. It's normal to see them used in **printed texts** (like this one), although you don't always see them in very **formal** texts.

Double Negatives *used to be* **Common** *in English*

1) Today, **double negatives** such as *I don't want nothing* are considered **non-standard**.
2) The authors of 18th century **prescriptive grammar books** (see p.120) tried to standardise and 'improve' English. They decided that double negatives were 'incorrect' and shouldn't be used.
3) The grammarian Robert Lowth used **mathematical logic** to argue that double negatives weren't acceptable: *"Two negatives in English destroy one another, or are equivalent to an affirmative,"* i.e. they make a **positive**.

The **Function** *of* **Words** *can change over time*

1) As people use more and more **new technology** like mobile phones and the Internet, the **function** of some words associated with it has changed — **nouns** like *text*, email and Facebook® have become **verbs**.
2) Some **adjectives** are now used instead of **adverbs**, e.g. *I'm good* instead of *I'm well*. This is an American usage that has become common in British English.
3) In **Standard English**, the adverb *well* is used with **past participles**, e.g. *the meal was well cooked*. In contemporary English it's also common to see *well* as an intensifying adverb before an **adjective**, e.g. *that was well good*.
4) *Innit* used to be a shortened version of the **tag question** *isn't it?* In **urban slang** it's become interchangeable with a **variety** of other tag questions too, e.g. *we can do that tomorrow innit?* where *innit* means *can't we?*
5) In the 1990s the **intensifying adverb** *so* started to be used with not, e.g. *I'm so not ready for this*.

Practice Questions

Q1 Give an example of how word order has changed since 1700.
Q2 Give three examples of grammatical change since 1900.

Essay Question

Q1 Describe the main features of grammatical change in English since 1700.

I've just had the most horrible cold — it was a superlative infection...

You'd think that the fact that grammar is constantly changing would make it a bit more exciting. Poof! There goes the complex syntax — vanished forever. Bang! Here's the all-new dummy auxiliary. It promises so much, and yet in reality it's about as interesting as fourteen rice cakes and a kilogram of houmous. Tastier, but no more inspiring.

Phonology is the study of sounds in a language. Phonological changes affect the pronunciation of individual sounds, which can help explain how and why certain sounds are acquired or lost over time.

Pronunciation *is Always Changing*

1) The most **significant shift** in pronunciation occurred between 1400 and 1600. During this period the **long vowels** of Middle English changed a lot. This transition is called the **Great Vowel Shift**.

2) Between **1700** and **1900**, the long a vowel sound in words such as *path* (pronounced *parth*) came to be used in **southern parts** of Britain. Before this it would have been pronounced in its **shorter form**, as it is in **Northern** and **Midlands** accents.

3) In Present Day English (**PDE**), the **schwa** ([ə]), is a **generic vowel sound** we use instead of **fully pronouncing** the vowel. It's become more common in **everyday speech** than it used to be, even in **RP** (Received Pronunciation — see p.117). For example, we tend to say *uhbout* rather than **a**-bout, and *balunce* rather than *balance*.

4) **Consonants** have also changed. For example, before the nineteenth century, *-ing* was generally pronounced *in*, (as it is in many regional accents today), even by the **middle** and **upper** classes.

5) Today, some speakers **replace** the *th* sound with *f* (saying *fink* rather than *think*, or *vem* rather than *them*). This is a feature of **Estuary English** (see p. 117) called **th-fronting**.

Intonation Patterns *have also changed over time*

1) A specific change in intonation since the early 1990s is **uptalk** or **upspeak**. Usually, intonation **rises** when people ask a question. With uptalk, intonation rises when you're **making a statement**.

2) The following sentences demonstrate how uptalk might come across in conversation:

> I was going to town? And I saw this man? He was acting really strange? Then he came up to me? Asked me for a cigarette?

3) At first uptalk was a feature of **teenage speech**, but it's now found in a **wider range** of age groups.

4) One theory is that it's been picked up from **Australian intonation patterns** that are heard in soaps like *Neighbours* and *Home and Away*.

5) There are different theories about people's **reasons** for using it. Some linguists say it's used because speakers don't want to sound **aggressive** or too sure of themselves. Others claim that it's only used when speakers are telling someone **new information**.

Pronunciation *changes for* Lots *of Reasons*

1) **Social factors** can affect pronunciation — people often change the way they talk depending on the **context** and who they're talking to.

2) Your pronunciation probably changes when you're being formally **interviewed**, compared to when you're talking with **friends**, e.g. you might be more **careful** about pronouncing *h*s in words like <u>how</u> and <u>have</u>. This is known as **upward convergence** — making everyday language sound closer to **RP**:

> A study in Norwich by **Trudgill (1983)** showed that women were more likely to speak closer to RP when they knew their language was being observed.

3) **American English** has also affected British English pronunciation. For example, the traditional British English pronunciation of *harass* stresses the **first syllable** (*harass*), but in PDE people might stress the **second syllable** (*harass*), as in American English.

4) The **media** can influence pronunciation. The BBC has a **Pronunciation Unit** which guides broadcasters on how to pronounce words. This is to make sure that the presenters are **consistent**, but **viewers** then often **copy** the pronunciation of **unfamiliar** or **foreign** words, and they become seen as the **standard** pronunciation.

5) **Aitchison (1991)** suggests that phonological change is a **process**. First, the accent of one group differs from that of another. The second group is **influenced** by the pronunciation of the first group, a **new accent** emerges and the process continues.

Received Pronunciation *has changed significantly*

1) **Received Pronunciation (RP)** was seen as the standard English accent and is sometimes called the **Queen's** English. It's a **prestige** accent — it's associated with a good standing in **society** and with being **well-educated**.

2) The emergence of RP in the **twentieth century** also caused **regional accents** to be seen as socially inferior.

Stephen only bought the book so Maureen would stop RPing on about her crossword.

3) RP was adopted as the **official accent of the BBC** in 1922, because they thought it was the accent that everyone would be able to **understand**. This added to its **prestige value** — as all the news and public broadcasts were in RP, it became the accent of **authority**. This is why RP is also sometimes called **BBC English**.

4) From the late **1950s onwards**, RP changed quite significantly. For example, in RP before the 1960s the word *hand* was pronounced more like *hend*, *often* was pronounced more like *awften* and *tissue* was pronounced as *tisyu*.

5) In the 1960s, with **working-class** teenagers going to **university** in larger numbers and the emergence of **celebrities** who spoke with **regional accents**, RP lost some of its desirability. Emerging pop stars, actors and artists had regional accents (e.g. Paul McCartney, Mick Jagger), and young speakers wanted to **imitate** them.

6) Today, RP has been **toned down** and is rarely heard. For example, broadcasters will use **Standard English** when they are speaking, but might have a **regional accent** rather than RP.

New Accents *have emerged*

Nowadays very **few** people actually use **RP** in its 'original' form. Even the Queen's accent has changed a bit from when she was first crowned over 50 years ago.

Estuary English

1) Some linguists claim that **RP** is being replaced as the most 'acceptable' English accent by **Estuary English**. This is an **accent** that has roots in the speech found around the **Thames Estuary** area in **London**.

2) It contains many similar features to the **Cockney** accent, e.g. dropping *h*s at the beginning of words (pronouncing *hit* like *it*), and pronouncing *th* like *f* (so *tooth* becomes *toof*). For example, estuary speakers will use a **glottal stop** instead of *t*, so *bottle* is pronounced *bo-ul*. They'll pronounce *tune* as *choon* rather than *tyune*, *wall* as *waw* and *north as norf*.

3) It's used by a lot of people in the **entertainment industry**, as it's seen as a **commercially acceptable** accent.

4) Because of the **influence** of the **media**, Estuary English is becoming quite common **outside** London. You can't necessarily tell where someone's from if they use Estuary English — it's become a **widespread accent**, probably a result of people **copying** the speech of **radio** and **TV presenters**.

Practice Questions

Q1 What is the *schwa*? Give an example of when it's heard.

Q2 What is Received Pronunciation?

Q3 What is Estuary English? Give three examples of how an Estuary English speaker's pronunciation would differ from that of an RP speaker.

Essay Question

Q1 Discuss some of the reasons why English pronunciation has changed.

So there are vese free pieces of string, right...

And they're trying to get into a bar. But the door policy is 'strictly no pieces of string allowed'. So one piece of string says to his mates, "Leave this to me lads, I'll get us in". He folds his arms, ruffles up his hair and walks to the door. The bouncers see him and ask, "Hang on, aren't you a piece of string?" And he says, "No, I'm a frayed knot." Phonology — always hilarious.

As if looking at words wasn't enough, graphology involves things like layout, typeface (what you might normally call 'font') and handwriting. It's about how the visual features of a text can have an impact on the overall meaning.

The **Appearance** of **Letters** has **Changed** over **Time**

Texts written hundreds of years ago look very **different** from modern day texts. This is partly because the way that some of the **letters** are written has changed.

1) From the **17th century** onwards the letter *s* was often written as *ſ* (like an *f* without the cross-bar), e.g. *ſit* instead of *sit*. This was based on the **handwriting style** of the period, and it appeared like this in **printed texts** until the early **19th century**, so you might see it in texts from that period. It wasn't written as *ſ* if it was at the end of a word though, and was often written alongside an *s* if a word contained a double *s*, e.g. *claſses*.

2) Until the **18th century** more words began with **capital letters** than they do in Present Day English. Words were capitalised if they were at the start of a sentence or if they were proper nouns (as in PDE). However, **abstract nouns** and any other word that the writer wanted to **emphasise** could also be capitalised.

Typefaces have also changed:

1) Up to the middle of the twentieth century, **serif** typefaces were usually used. They have a fine 'stroke' attached to the tops and bottoms of letters.

2) From the mid-twentieth century onwards **sans-serif typefaces** (ones **without serifs**) became fashionable.

3) Typefaces with serifs tend to seem **traditional**, while sans-serif typefaces look more **modern**.

4) Modern **printed material** has a wider range of typefaces than in the past. Print advertising, newspapers, leaflets, posters, and books will use different fonts for **different purposes**.

5) For example, *The Sun* newspaper mainly uses a **sans-serif** typeface for **headlines**, and **serif** typefaces for **articles**. It also uses a wide **variety** of **typefaces** in the headlines on its entertainment and gossip pages to attract attention and make the pages **visually stimulating**.

Newspaper Layout has *Changed*

Newspaper designs have **changed** a lot in the last 100 years.

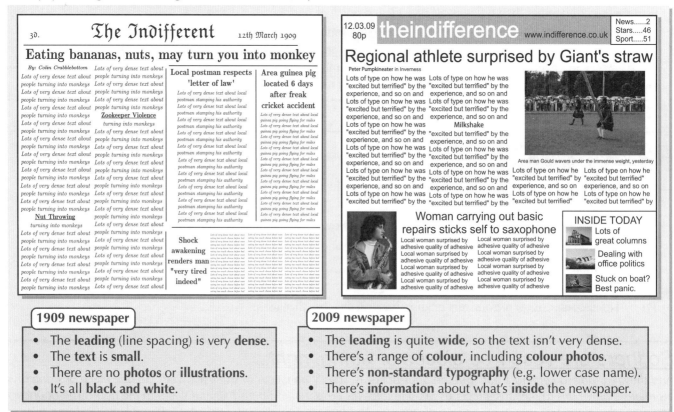

1909 newspaper
- The **leading** (line spacing) is very **dense**.
- The **text** is **small**.
- There are no **photos** or **illustrations**.
- It's all **black and white**.

2009 newspaper
- The **leading** is quite **wide**, so the text isn't very dense.
- There's a range of **colour**, including **colour photos**.
- There's **non-standard typography** (e.g. lower case name).
- There's **information** about what's **inside** the newspaper.

Magazine Layout has also Changed

1) Modern magazines are very different from those of the eighteenth century.

2) In the past, the front page of a men's magazine, e.g. **The Gentleman's Magazine (1736)**, consisted of a **decorative illustration** at the top of the page, a title and then two **dense** blocks of print, black on white.

3) In contrast, the cover of a **modern** men's magazine such as *FHM* has a full page **glossy photograph** in the background. This is **overlaid** with print, indicating the main features to be found inside the magazine. The print has different **font types**, **colours**, and some of the text is presented in unconventional angles and styles.

The editors were less than impressed with Paul's choice of 'long legged stunner'.

The graphology of Modern Books is Varied

1) The earliest books often had **two columns** to a page, justified text and large margins for making notes. Modern books, like novels and textbooks, tend to have **one column** of print.

2) However, modern books can show a great deal of **variety** in terms of **layout**, **typeface** and **colour**. Non-fiction books in particular often show a lot of **innovation** and **creativity** with **colour** and **graphics**.

3) In children's books you might see blocks of print at **unusual angles**, and different **shapes** of text boxes (e.g. circles or speech bubbles). There's often a variety of **font colours** and **background colours**, and sometimes text **superimposed** on **background images**.

Electronic Media has changed the appearance of Written Communication

1) **Electronic media** allows writers and publishers to be more **creative** with graphology.

2) Web developers can use different **layouts**, **typefaces** and **colours** without having to think about printing costs. Web pages tend to contain **small chunks** of text broken up with **headings**, **subheadings** and **links** because this is **easier to read** on screen.

3) Web pages can also incorporate **animated text** and **images**. **Audio** is also used as part of **interactive videos**, **games** and **adverts**.

4) **Word-processing software** has given ordinary people access to loads of different **typefaces** and styles. You can **choose** which style to use depending on the **purpose** of the writing, for example:

> This is Times New Roman PS   This is Litterbox ICG

5) You'd use these typefaces to create **different effects**. For example, you might use Times New Roman PS if you were writing a serious newspaper article, and Litterbox ICG in a text for children.

6) **Mobile phones** have also had an impact on **graphology**. People can send photos and videos along with small amounts of text, which often contains features like abbreviations, numbers and emoticons.

Practice Questions

Q1 What is graphology?

Q2 Outline three ways in which the graphology of newspapers has changed over the last 100 years.

Q3 How do books today differ from the first printed books in terms of typeface and layout?

Essay Question

Q1 Describe the impact of electronic media on the graphology of the English language.

Just remember to label your axes...

X and Y — along the corridor and up the stairs. That's pretty much all the maths I remember — something to do with people living in houses made of graphs I think. It all sounds hideously impractical. The squares on that graph paper are too small even for a box room, let alone an open plan kitchen-diner. Still, mathematicians aren't exactly known for their logic, are they...

The biggest thing to happen to Late Modern English (1700-present) was that it became much more standardised. However, the standardisation process had actually started centuries earlier, so you need a bit of background first.

The **Printing Press** helped to **Standardise English**

1) In 1476, **William Caxton** established the first **printing press**. It was an important step towards **standardisation**. Producing **identical copies** of a text meant that everyone was reading the **same** thing, written the same way.

2) However, it was pretty tricky for Caxton. Words were often spelled **differently** according to **dialect** or the **personal choice** of the writer, so he had to **decide** which **spellings** to use.

3) He chose the type of English being used in the **courts**, the **universities** (particularly Cambridge) and in **London** at the time.

4) This dialect was already associated with **political authority**, **learning** and **commerce**. Using it in printed books gave it a feeling of **permanence** and **prestige**.

5) English became **standardised** to a certain extent, but there was still a lot of **variation** in printed texts.

6) In the **18th century** the '**state**' of the language became a great concern for some writers and grammarians. They worried that because English wasn't governed by a strict set of rules, it was **decaying**. **Dictionaries** and **grammar books** telling people how to use English 'properly' were published and became very **popular**.

The first **Dictionaries** had a strong influence on **Standardising Spelling**

One of the most important publications in the history of English was Samuel Johnson's *A Dictionary of the English Language (1755)*, which contained about 40,000 words.

1) **Johnson's** *Dictionary* laid down rules for the **spelling** and **meanings** of words. It wasn't the first English dictionary, but it was definitely the **biggest** at the time.

2) Johnson backed up his definitions with **quotes** from 'the best writers', e.g. Shakespeare and Milton. He also provided the **etymology** of words (how they entered the language). Other English dictionaries have since used the **same method**, e.g. the OED (see p.129). This shows how **influential** Johnson's dictionary was.

3) He said that his aim was to **record** the language — that he wanted 'not to **form**, but **register**' English.

4) However, he also stated that he wanted to **tame** the language because he felt that it was **out of control**. This is a more **prescriptivist view** (see below).

5) The dictionary was so important because it helped **standardise spelling** and **meaning**. If someone needed to know the meaning of a word or how to spell it, the dictionary could be used as a standard **reference point**.

Prescriptive Books had a major impact on **Grammar**

Prescriptivism is an **attitude** towards language that assumes there are a set of 'correct' **linguistic rules** that English should follow (see p.128).

1) Although **grammar books** had existed since the 16th century, they became really **popular** in the **18th century**, when they were written to lay down **rules** about language and **prescribe** the **correct usage**.

2) For example, a rule that's still taught today is that *whom* should be used when *who* is the **object** of the sentence:

'Incorrect'	'Correct'
Who did you see today?	**Whom** did you see today?

3) 18th century **grammarians** were also **proscriptivists** — they outlined rules on the types of language people **shouldn't** use (while **prescriptivism** involves stating what types of language people **should** use). For example, one **proscriptive rule** states that sentences **shouldn't end** with a **preposition**, e.g. the sentence *where do you come from?* should be *from where do you come?*

4) A lot of these rules were **invented** by 18th century grammarians like **Robert Lowth**, who wrote *A Short Introduction to English Grammar (1762)*. Some were imposed on English from **Latin** or **Ancient Greek**, because these were seen as **superior languages** — they weren't spoken any more, so they couldn't 'decay' like English could.

The **Lexis** continued to **Grow**

1) The expansion of the **British Empire** led to words being **borrowed** from the countries that came under British rule. For example, these **loan words** came from **India**: *bangle* (1787), *dinghy* (1810) and *thug* (1810).

2) During the Late Modern period, advances in **science** and **medicine** led to the invention of new words like: *centigrade* (1812), *biology* (1819), *laryngitis* (1822), *antibiotic* (1894), *chemotherapy* (1907), *penicillin* (1929), *quark* (1964) and *bulimia* (1976).

3) **New inventions** brought more **new words and phrases** into the dictionary such as *typewriter* (1868), *motor car* (1895), *radio* (1907), *video game* (1973) and *podcasting* (2008).

4) **Social**, **cultural** and **political developments** have contributed to the **lexis** (vocabulary), e.g. *hippie* (1965), *airhead* (1972), *grunge* (1980s), and *credit crunch* (2000s).

5) New words also emerged through **international conflict** and **war** — *Blighty* (to refer to Britain, 1914-18), *blitz* (1939), and *kamikaze* (1945).

Accents and **Dialects** changed in the **Twentieth Century**

Improved **communication** and increased **mobility** in the Late Modern period (from 1700 onwards) meant that people were exposed to a **wide range** of accents and dialects for the **first time**.

COMMUNICATION

- Radio, films and television have affected regional pronunciation.
- For example, **Estuary English** (see p.117) is a relatively new accent that is **spreading**, partly because it's used by a lot of people on **TV** and the **radio**. It originated in south-east England and London, but some people think it's **influenced speakers** as far away as Glasgow and Manchester.
- **International** soap operas (e.g. Neighbours) may have affected **younger speakers'** accents, too.
- Inventions like the **telephone** have meant that people from **different regions** can communicate much more easily.

Misinterpreting "Push here for change", Jim imprisoned six innocent people.

MOBILITY

- The invention of the **railway** and **cars** meant that people began to **travel** more around Britain. This means that **regional dialects** aren't as **self-contained**, so they're becoming '**diluted**'.
- **Very strong accents** have tended to get **softer**, so people from different regions can understand each other better than they could.
- **International travel** has also affected English. **Non-native** speakers from different countries use Standard English or American English to **communicate** with each other and with **native** English speakers (see p.123-124).

Practice Questions

Q1 What influence did Johnson's dictionary have on spelling?

Q2 Give three examples of how grammarians became more prescriptivist in the Late Modern period.

Q3 Which factors contributed to the expansion of vocabulary during the Late Modern period? Give examples.

Q4 Explain how and why regional accents and dialects have changed since 1700.

Essay Question

Q1 Discuss how advances in transport, technology, science and medicine affected English in the Late Modern Period.

Prescriptive English — for standard eyes only...

You might remember a Blackadder episode where Johnson turns up with his dictionary. You might also remember Blackadder throwing in some words like 'pericombobulation', as if they were real words that Johnson had overlooked. Think that's funny? Just imagine what a pain it would be if you'd spent years on the dictionary only to find you'd forgotten to include "knitting".

The last few pages have covered the ways that language can change, but unfortunately it's never really down to just one single reason. These two pages bring all the different causes together, making them 24 carat essay gold.

Language change can be **Internal** or **External**

1) **External** language change is a result of **outside influences** on a group of speakers. For example, English has been influenced by things like **invasions**, **immigration** and the **media**.

2) **Internal change** happens because of a need for **simplification** and **ease of articulation**. For example, **inflections** like -*eth* may have died out because the meaning was still clear when they weren't used, so they gradually became **unnecessary**.

Phonological Change tends to make *Pronunciation Easier*

Omission and **assimilation** are **trends** of phonological change that make things easier to pronounce.

Omission

1) Omission is when sounds are gradually **lost** from the language, because speakers **stop pronouncing** them.

2) For example, in about the last fifty years, **RP** speakers have dropped the *y* sound in words like *tune*, which used to be pronounced *tyune*. It now sounds more like *choon*.

Assimilation

1) Assimilation is where one sound in a word is affected by an **adjacent sound** to produce a new pronunciation, e.g. some people pronounce the word *sandwich* as *samwich*.

2) Assimilation also occurs across **word boundaries**, e.g. *What do you want / whatju want* or *Get it? / geddit?*

Standardisation caused a lot of *Change*

SPELLING

1) The first major development was **Caxton's printing press (1476)**. It helped to establish the medieval **East Midlands dialect** as the 'standard', as well as making texts more **readily available** to people.

2) However, there was still quite a lot of variation with spelling for the next few centuries, and it wasn't until the eighteenth century that spelling began to look fully standardised. **Johnson's *A Dictionary of the English Language*** (see p.120) laid a firm foundation for the spelling system we have today.

GRAMMAR

1) People tried to standardise grammar in the eighteenth century. A number of scholars published books **prescribing** how English should be **constructed**, e.g. **Robert Lowth's *A Short Introduction to English Grammar* (1762)** (see p.128).

2) These ideas have influenced what people consider to be 'good' English. This has meant that there's **less variety** in Standard English.

PHONOLOGY

1) Teaching a standardised form of **pronunciation** was a key feature of private school education. The main person behind this was the actor and educator **Thomas Sheridan** in the **mid-eighteenth century**.

2) He believed there was a **correct** way to speak and that this could be acquired through **elocution** lessons.

3) Like the other prescriptivists, Sheridan published books, including *A General Dictionary of the English Language* in **1780**, which outlined how to pronounce words 'properly'.

Technology has influenced language change

1) **Industrialisation** in the eighteenth and nineteenth centuries introduced new words and phrases relating to labour, such as *productivity*, *shift work*, and *clocking-on*.

2) **Scientific advancement**, **new inventions** and **brand names** have resulted in new words entering the language (e.g. *spacesuit, microwave, PC, chatroom, MSN®, email, download, hard drive, web page*).

It took Margaret a while to get the hang of phonetic spelling.

Causes of Language Change

Other Languages have Influenced English language change

A lot of language change has been brought about by the **influence** of **foreign languages**, especially because of **loan words** (**borrowings**). The table below shows just **some** of the languages that have influenced English over the centuries.

Period	Influence	Examples
8th-11th centuries — invasions from other countries.	Scandinavian	*skirt, cog, skip*
	French	*accompany, department, tax*
16th-17th centuries — words brought into English from Latin and Greek by writers.	Latin	*benefit, temperature, the prefixes sub and trans*
	Greek	*catastrophe, pneumonia,* the affixes *auto and pan*
18th-19th centuries — words borrowed from colonised countries during the expansion of the British Empire.	Malay	*amok*
	Hindi	*shampoo*
20th century — immigration to the UK.	Cantonese	*wok*

American English has had a Big Impact

1) In the 20th century, **America** developed into a **superpower**. Its **political**, **economic** and **cultural influence** has maintained the importance of **English** as a **world language**.

2) **American English** can be accessed all over the world, especially because of the influence of **music**, **films** and **TV**. American **brand names** are **internationally recognised** due to the influence of **advertising**.

3) **Standard American English** has a few specific lexical, grammatical and orthographical (spelling) differences from **Standard English**. For example:

Lexis		American Grammar	Orthography	
American	**British**		**American**	**British**
trash	rubbish	• More frequent use of the **subjunctive**, e.g. *I wish I were taller* instead of *I wish I was taller*.	meter	metre
sidewalk	pavement	• Omission of *on* in reference to days of the week, e.g. *see you Tuesday* instead of *see you on Tuesday*.	color	colour
soccer	football	• Noun phrases ordered differently, e.g. *a half hour* instead of *half an hour*.	organize	organise
gas	petrol		gray	grey

Practice Questions

Q1   What's the difference between internal and external language change?
Q2   Explain the terms omission and assimilation in the context of language change.
Q3   What have been the major factors in the standardisation of English?
Q4   What impact have science and technology had on the language we use today?
Q5   Why has American English been such an influence on Present Day English? How do they differ?

Essay Question

Q1   Describe how standardisation, technology, and the influence of other languages have contributed to language change.

Learning all this stuff might seem like a bit of omission...

But if you like, I'll give you a-ssimilation of how it should be done. See that section on standardisation? Read it. Then cover it up. There are two points on spelling, two on grammar and three on phonology. Write them down... did you get them all right? Excellent. Well done. But 'tis only a fraction of this double page spread, so eyes down and look in for the rest...

I knew you would turn to this page today. Now look closer, and I will reveal the terrifying truth about what English will be like in the future. But first, you must cross my palm with silver... No? Well, it was worth a try I suppose.

English has an Uncertain Future

1) English has the **fourth highest** number of **native speakers** in the world.
2) More people speak it as a **second language** than any other language, and this number is **growing** all the time.
3) With so many people speaking English, there are **various possibilities** for how the language will change in the **future**.

English might become more Uniform

1) It's necessary for **international trade** to have a **lingua franca** (a language that people from different countries can all understand). English has taken this role.
2) As well as this, some **countries** (such as Nigeria) that weren't originally English-speaking have adopted English as their **official language**. They feel that it's necessary to have a **standardised language** that **everybody** in the country can **understand**. This has happened especially in countries that have a lot of different **tribal languages**.
3) This shows a **trend** towards **uniformity**, and it suggests that eventually some other languages may **die out**.

> 1) **American English** may become the **global standard** (the variety of English spoken by everyone in the world). It's already the **dominant** form, and the number of English speakers is **increasing**. People want to learn American English because it's the language of **world trade** and has global **prestige** and **authority**.
> 2) American English is also **growing** because of the global presence of American **films**, **music** and **brands** (see p.123). As more people in less economically developed countries gain access to **TV** and the **internet**, they'll have **more exposure** to American English, so they'll be more likely to use it.
> 3) As the **importance** of American English grows, other varieties might **lose status** and gradually die out. This is called **dialect levelling**.
> 4) **Differences** between world **varieties** of English are **decreasing**. It's possible that one day this will lead to the emergence of a **World Standard English** — one that becomes the **official international language** of business and takes the place of all other varieties.

Technology might help make English more Uniform

1) English has been established as the language of **scientific** and **technological advancement** for a long time, so it's been an important language for **foreign scientists** and **academics** to learn.
2) The **internet** has spread English even further. It's been estimated that **90%** of computers connected to the internet are in **English-speaking** countries. Because of this, around **80%** of the **information** stored on computers **worldwide** is in **English**.
3) Technology has already had a dramatic impact on English usage. Computer software usually uses **American spelling**, such as *programs* and *fav<u>o</u>rites*. This is helping to establish American English as a **global standard**.

Janet was thrilled. Finally she could combine her two loves — technology and uniforms.

4) Computers are **changing** English in other ways too, for example:

> • **Spell check** programmes mean people don't need to know how to spell unusual words **correctly**. This could lead to less emphasis being put on **teaching spelling** at **school**, because it isn't considered necessary.
> • **Web addresses** don't contain **capital letters**, so they might gradually **die out** in **other written texts**.
> • **Punctuation** isn't needed when you look something up on a **search engine**, so some marks might **die out**.

5) As **internet access** grows around the world, more people will have access to this **electronic variety** of English, so it could end up being the **World Standard English** that everyone uses.

English might become more Diverse

1) Another possibility is that different **varieties** of English around the world could develop into **separate languages**, e.g. American English would be completely different from Indian English. This is what happened to **Latin**, which was once spoken across a lot of **Europe**, but then **split** into **romance languages** like **Italian**, **French** and **Spanish**.

2) These separate varieties of English could then become a way of displaying **national identity** and **independence**. People might see it as a way of **rejecting cultural imperialism** from countries like America and Britain.

3) As the varieties became more different from each other, **localised national standard Englishes** might emerge, e.g. a particular form of Indian English. These forms of the standard would then become the **official language** of the country, rather than Standard English or Standard American English.

4) As well as this, **America's** economic, political and cultural **dominance** might be **challenged** by countries like **China** or **India** in the future. If this happens, then American English might not be the most useful or powerful language to learn any more.

Technology might make English more Diverse

1) English isn't the only language of the internet. As more people in **less economically developed countries** gain **internet access**, English might stop **dominating** the web. As **online translation software** improves, people won't have to be able to speak English to look at British or American websites. As well as this, there are already lots of versions of American and British websites and search engines in **other languages**.

2) Countries like **India** and **China** are likely to have much more of an impact on **science** and **technology** in the future. This could mean that languages like **Mandarin Chinese** become more important to learn than English.

> If you're writing an essay about the impact of technology on the future of English, you can make it more balanced by discussing both the arguments for technology making English more diverse, and the arguments for technology making English more uniform on p.122.

Bidialectism means speaking Two Dialects

1) Another thing that could happen in the future is that people will be able to **switch** from one **dialect** of English to the **standard**, depending on the **context** and **purpose**. Switching between two dialects is **bidialectism**.

2) This scenario imagines the possibility that **standard** forms of English will become more **uniform**, while **regional** and **social** varieties will become more **diverse**. People will have to learn the **standard** form for **formal** situations and for communicating with people from **other countries**.

3) This is **already happening** to a certain extent. For example, a Nigerian business executive might use a **regional** form of Nigerian English when speaking **informally** with **local** customers, but use a more standard English or American form with **international** customers.

Practice Questions

Q1 What is a lingua franca?

Q2 What factors might help American English become the global standard?

Q3 How might the internet lead to greater uniformity in English?

Q4 What is bidialectism?

Essay Question

Q1 'The strength of English as a world language is set to grow and grow.' How far do you agree with this statement?

In the future we won't need English — we'll just read each other's minds...

Oh, English. Just like Pocahontas, you must choose your path. One may be steady, like the river. The other may be rapid and exciting, like the river... This isn't really working out. Perhaps Pocahontas wasn't the best comparison to use. Basically what I'm trying to say is that no one knows where English is going in the future, so just learn the different arguments and move on.

Here are some exam-style questions, with sources like the ones you'll get in the real paper.

> Text A is from *The First Book of Manners* (1856), a guide to polite behaviour for young people.
> Text B is taken from a page of a modern website, www.growingkids.co.uk, which offers advice to parents about their children.
>
> 1. With reference to both texts, comment on what they show about changes in written language over time.
>
> *[48 marks]*

Text A — from *The First Book of Manners* (1856), by Felix Urban

When the hour for meals draws nigh, take care to be ready, properly dressed and washed, so as not to be behind time; it is a breach of manners to keep others waiting.

Shew no unbecoming haste to sit down; but take your place as you are desired. Wait until a blessing has been asked: the head of the family (or a clergyman, when present) usually does this; not unfrequently, however, the youngest present is called upon: should it be your duty, perform it reverently, with a due feeling of devotion, remembering that it is the offering up of a solemn prayer to Almighty God.

It is not proper to sit either so close to the table as to touch it with the body, nor too far back; the right distance is that at which the wrists can rest naturally upon the table's edge.

Sit upright, not throwing yourself back, nor yet sitting upon the edge of the chair. To place the elbows on the table, is a most unmannerly act. When a table-napkin is put for you, unfold it, and place it securely before you upon your knees.

You will find the knife and spoon at your right hand, and the fork at your left; they are to be so used.

It is unmannerly to ask to be helped before others, or to shew signs of impatience by moving about the plate or the body; such behaviour may be ascribed to greediness. Await your turn; be assured you will not be forgotten.

Text B — from www.growingkids.co.uk/TableManners.html

If a child has an assigned seat, it is easy for him/her to get into the routine of eating at the table from the moment they sit down. When comfortable and calm, encourage children old enough to eat at the table to:

· Scoot their chair in so that they can easily reach the table without having to rest their elbows on it.
· Put their napkins in their laps, not tucked into their shirts.
· Understand that their plate is in the middle, forks are to the left and knives/spoons are to the right.
· Know that their glass is up to the right of their plate.

Chow Down

When it's time to eat, even the most mild mannered of children can turn into ravenous monsters! Ask your children to:

· Politely request the dish they would like to spoon onto their plate (if you have not already served them).
· Serve food onto their plates using the serving utensils provided, not their own utensils.
· Serve only one helping of food at a time. Assure your children there will be seconds if they so desire.
· Give each foodstuff a separate space on the plate. Piling a plate with a mountain of food is a recipe for frustrations!

Chew and Chat

Some table manners have survived for centuries with good reason. Remind your kids:

· Not to chew with their mouths open. No one wants to see what's in their mouths.
· Not to talk while eating. Again, no one wants to see what's in their mouths.
· If they need to remove something from their mouth (such as a pit or a bone), remove it the same way they ate it. If they ate fish from a fork and discovered a bone, have them remove it with their fork...

No matter how crazy mealtime can get in your house, a few basic table manners will serve you (and your kids!) well. Find out which rules work for you, and which you are willing to bend every now and then.

Text C is a letter written in 1819 by Lord Byron, to a woman he was in love with.
Text D is a letter written in 1972 by an engineer working in Saudi Arabia to his wife.

2. With reference to both texts, write about what they show about the development of language over time.

[48 marks]

Text C — a letter to the Countess Teresa Guiccioli (1819), by Lord Byron

My dearest Teresa-

I have read this book in your garden; - my love, you were absent, or else I could not have read it. It is a favorite book of yours, and the writer was a friend of mine. You will not understand these English words, and *others* will not understand them, - which is the reason I have not scrawled them in Italian. But you will recognize the handwriting of him who passionately loves you, and you will divine that, over a book which was yours, he could only think of love. In that word, beautiful in all languages, but most so in yours - *Amor mio* - is comprised my existence here and hereafter. I feel I exist here, and I fear that I shall exist hereafter, - as to *what* purpose you will decide; my destiny rests with you, and you are a woman, seventeen years of age, and two out of a convent. I wish that you had stayed there, with all my heart, - or, at least, that I had never met you in your married state.

But all this is too late. I love you, and you love me, - at least, you *say so*, and *act* as if you *did* so, which last is a great consolation in all events. But I more than love you, and cannot cease to love you.

Think of me, sometimes, when the Alps and the ocean divide us, - but they never will, unless you *wish* it.

B.

Text D — a letter written from a husband to his wife (1972)

Dearest Julia,

　　　I arrived here in Riyadh on Monday evening after the most awful flight. I should be feeling really happy and excited, I suppose, but I am already missing you. Back in England, the thought of being separated from you for three months didn't seem so bad but now just the thought of being without you *even for a week* makes me feel desolate.

I suppose I'm just feeling a bit homesick, jetlagged and, dare I admit it, even a bit lonely. Yes, that's *me* talking, the person who always says he likes his own company!

I've met a few people so far and they seem really nice. I start work tomorrow – Saturday – so I expect that I won't feel so bad once I get stuck in to things. All I know is that already I can't wait till March when I'll be back home with you in our nice little house that has a garden and trees and rain! Yes *rain*, can you believe it?

I know you'll be thinking I'm a terrible wimp but I do hope you're missing me the same. Give my love to all the family and tell them I'm fine (even though I'm not!).

Will write again soon.

All my love
Toby x

*If there's one subject that's likely to cause a row down at the annual linguists' convention then it's language change.
More people have got more bees in more bonnets over this than anything else. Time to get stuck in...*

Attitudes *towards* Language Change *can be* Prescriptivist *or* Descriptivist

There are **two** main approaches to language change:

Prescriptivism

1)   Prescriptivism involves stating a **set** of **rules** that people should follow in order to use language '**properly**' (**prescribing** what the language **should be like**).

2)   Prescriptivists believe that language should be **written** and **spoken** in a certain way — in English this means using **Standard English** and **RP** (see p.117). Other **varieties** of English are seen as **incorrect** and **inferior**.

3)   Prescriptivists argue that it's **essential** to stick to the rules of the **standard** form, so that everyone can **understand** each other.

4)   The prescriptivist view is that language **decays** as it **changes**, and the only way to stop **standards falling** further is to try and **stop linguistic change**.

Descriptivism

1)   Descriptivism involves **describing** how language is actually **used**.

2)   Descriptivists **don't** say that aspects of language are '**correct**' or '**incorrect**'. They believe that different **varieties** of English should all be **valued equally**.

3)   The idea is that language **change** is **inevitable**, so it's a **waste of time** to try and **stop** it. Instead, descriptivists record **how** and **why** change occurs, rather than assuming all change is bad.

4)   Some descriptivists see **language change** as **progress** — they believe that English is becoming more **accurate** and **efficient**. E.g. they'd say that Old English inflections were lost because they no longer served a purpose.

5)   Other descriptivists, like **David Crystal**, argue that language change is **neither** progress nor decay, as all languages **change** in **different** ways (e.g. some languages gain inflections).

Prescriptivist Attitudes *have been around for a* Long Time

1)   In the second half of the eighteenth century there was a sudden flourishing of **grammar books** that outlined what the **rules** of grammar should be. The most influential was Robert Lowth's *A Short Introduction to English Grammar (1762)*. He argued that some constructions were grammatically **wrong**, e.g. split infinitives:

> THE SPLIT INFINITIVE
> *   The infinitive (*to* + *verb*) should not be split by an **adverb**. The most famous example is *to boldly go*, from *STAR TREK™*.
> *   Lowth argued that the construction *to* + *verb* is a **complete grammatical unit** and that's how it should remain.
> *   However, the **meaning** isn't affected whether you say *to boldly go* or *to go boldly*, so **descriptivists** would argue that it's a **pointless** rule.

He was going to split an awful lot more than an infinitive if he didn't get up quick-smart.

2)   Other prescriptivist texts have been more flexible about certain grammar rules, e.g. Henry Fowler's *A Dictionary of Modern English Usage (1926)*. Fowler argued against some of Lowth's rules, because he thought that constructions should be used if they **sounded comfortable**, e.g. ending a sentence with a preposition:

Fowler would argue that:	*That depends on what they are hit <u>with</u>*
sounds much better than:	*That depends on <u>with</u> what they are hit*

3)   However, many people still argue that certain rules **shouldn't** be **broken**, even though they **don't** affect the **meaning** of a sentence. For example, people often complain about constructions like *different <u>to</u>* and *different <u>than</u>*. They claim it should be *different <u>from</u>* because that's what you'd say in **Latin**, even though it's not the way that most English speakers say it.

Descriptivism has become much more Popular in Recent Times

1) *The Oxford English Dictionary* (OED) was first published in the early **20th century**.

2) The editors of the dictionary were **descriptivists** — they stated in the **preface** that their **aim** was to **record** the language as it was, **not** to **prescribe** rules. Lots of other modern dictionaries have the same aim.

3) However, most people look words up in the dictionary to **make sure** they get a **meaning** or **spelling** 'right'. This shows that most people think of dictionaries as **prescriptive rule books**, not just records of the language.

> Many linguists are completely **against** prescriptivism. In the 1980s **Milroy and Milroy** argued that language change is **inevitable** and shouldn't be fought against. They also argued **against** the **high status** of **Standard English**. They claimed that fears about **falling standards** meant that people are often **discriminated** against, e.g. by employers, if they **don't** follow the **arbitrary** rules that were set out by grammarians in the **18th century**.

4) However, **Cameron (1995)** argued that prescriptivism **shouldn't** be **discounted** as just people being **fussy** or **pedantic** about something that doesn't really matter.

5) She's a **descriptivist**, but argues that **prescriptivism** shows that people realise that **language** is an important **social tool** and **care** about how it's used.

6) She also argues that **fear** about **language change** often **symbolises** fear about **social problems** — people worry that **declining** standards of **language** mirror **declining** standards in **behaviour** and **education**.

7) This means that people **focus** on **language change** because they want to **make sense** of **bigger problems** in **society**. She argues that this should be used to **start** a **debate** about what **attitudes** towards language change **symbolise**, rather than just being discounted as an **illogical belief**.

There are Different ways to Study Language Change

These tips should be handy if you want to base your language investigation on language change.

You can use different **methodologies** to **study** language change. You could look at:

Lexis
New words are constantly being **added** to the language. You could focus on **borrowings** from **other languages** or the **impact** of **technology**. To do this you could look at the **etymology** (origin) of new words in the **OED**.

Grammar
For example, you could look at how **syntax** has become a lot **less complex** since the **19th century**. You could do this by **comparing** the syntax in a page of a **Dickens novel** with the syntax in a page of a **contemporary** one.

Phonology
For example, you could analyse how **accents** have **changed** in **broadcasting** by looking at how **newsreaders** spoke in the **1950s** compared to **today**. You could **transcribe** recordings from the different periods and **analyse** how their **pronunciation** has changed, using the **phonetic alphabet** (see p.154).

Practice Questions

Q1 What is the difference between the prescriptive and descriptive approaches to language change?

Q2 What was the purpose of 18th century grammar books and dictionaries?

Q3 Outline one method you could use to study language change.

Essay Question

Q1 "Something must be done to halt the rapid decline in standards of English."

How far do you agree with this statement? Refer to prescriptivist and descriptivist views in your answer.

Some of these prescriptivists have got a real attitude problem...

...I mean, really, fancy telling people that the way they use language is wrong. Except, of course, everyone does it all the time. So maybe we're all prescriptivists at heart... Anyway, enough thinking, just try and force this into your brain — prescriptivism lays down rules about how the language should be, and descriptivism describes how it actually is. The clue's in the name really.

The thing you have to remember about English is that everyone who speaks it seems to have an opinion about it.
Fortunately a lot of people have quite similar opinions, otherwise you'd be in for a very long night...

People have **Different Attitudes** *towards* **Standard English**

1) As one variety of the language became standardised (p.120-121), other varieties became seen as **less prestigious**.

2) **Standard English** is a **social dialect**. It's usually associated with **educated**, **middle** and **upper class** people. It's the way that you're taught to use English at school, and the language of **formal speech** and **writing**.

3) **Regional dialects** were associated with the **uneducated** and the **lower classes**, so it was seen as important to be able to use English '**properly**' if you wanted to be successful.

- Prescriptivists see **Standard English** as the '**correct**' or '**pure**' form of the language.
- Other varieties are sometimes thought to be '**corruptions**' of it.
- There's a view that if you use another dialect, you're not using English '**properly**'.

- However, **descriptivists** argue that all varieties of English should be **valued equally**.
- There's **no reason** why Standard English should be seen as better than any other dialect.
- They claim that people shouldn't be considered **uneducated** if they **don't** use Standard English.

4) Whether it's **appropriate** to use Standard English depends on the **mode** and **context**. You'd expect a **formal text** to be **written** in Standard English, but you wouldn't necessarily expect people in an **informal** setting to **speak** to each other using Standard English.

People Have **Different Attitudes** *towards* **Accents** *and* **Dialects**

Someone's **accent** or **dialect** is often a good indication of **where they're from**. But it can also influence attitudes about a speaker's **social background** and **education**.

1) Some people **assume** that people who use **regional dialects** are **poorly educated** or **lower class**.

2) On the other hand, **regional varieties** of English are often associated with being **down-to-earth** and **modest**, e.g. because regional accents are seen as being more **accessible** to audiences, they are used more in voice overs in adverts (to **sell things**) and by presenters (on **national** as well as **local** radio or television stations).

1) **Workman (2008)** studied people's **perceptions** of different **accents**. Participants listened to recordings of different accents while they looked at photos of people.

2) It was found that participants rated the **intelligence** of the people in the photos differently, depending on which accent they thought they had.

3) **Yorkshire** accents were rated as sounding the **most intelligent**. When a recording of a **Birmingham** accent was played, the people in the photos were rated as being much **less intelligent**. Obviously this **isn't** actually **true**, but it shows how strong the **stereotypes** about different accents can be.

People have **Different Attitudes** *towards* **Slang**

Slang is sometimes seen as **low level**, **vulgar** language, which shouldn't be used in **writing** or in **formal situations**.

1) Some people think that if you use slang you're **undermining standards** by not using the language '**properly**'. They assume that people who use lots of slang are lower class and uneducated.

2) Slang is seen as the language of **informal speech**, so it's considered **inappropriate** to use it in a **formal context**, e.g. you'd lose marks if you wrote an essay using slang words and phrases.

3) This is because slang has a reputation for being **rebellious** and **subversive**, so it isn't formally accepted as a variety of English. Some people worry that it doesn't follow the 'proper' **spelling** and **grammar rules** of **Standard English**.

4) However, most slang words and phrases **do** follow the rules of Standard English — they're just more flexible.

5) People who are interested in slang argue that it's an **intelligent** and **creative** variety of language, which **changes** and **develops** very quickly. It also serves an important purpose in **social contexts** — people use it to **identify** themselves as part of a **group**.

There's **Debate** about **Regional Varieties** and **Slang** in **Education**

People have different attitudes towards the role of **standard** and **vernacular** varieties of English.

1) Linguists like **Milroy and Milroy** (1985) have argued that it's **not fair** to correct children for using **non-standard** varieties of English.

2) Children who use regional varieties of English can end up **struggling** at **school** because **Standard English** is **unfamiliar** to them. Because regional dialects are linked to **social class**, it's often **working class** children who are put at an immediate **disadvantage** because they're told that the language they use is **wrong**.

3) The Milroys argued that all varieties of English should be **valued equally** and children **shouldn't** be **discouraged** from using non-standard English.

"Henry VIII were a proper
mardy bum..."

1) However, people such as **John Honey** (1997) argue that children **should** be taught **Standard English** at school, because this is the only way to make sure that all children have **equal opportunities**.

2) Because Standard English is the **prestigious** form of the language, children will be **disadvantaged** if they **don't** learn how to use it.

3) For example, they might miss out on **job opportunities** because they fill in applications using non-standard spelling. Employers might assume that they're unintelligent, and not give them the job. Therefore, it's important to teach all children the **writing skills** they need to succeed.

4) This viewpoint sees non-standard varieties as **barriers** to **universal communication**. Non-standard varieties are appropriate for informal speech, but **Standard English** should always be **favoured** because it ensures that **everyone** will be able to **understand** each other. This is called **bidialectism** — children end up using **two dialects**.

These tips should be handy if you want to base your language investigation on variation.

There are **Different** Ways to **Study Language Variation**

Different **methodologies** are used to **study** language variation, depending on the linguistic features you're focusing on:

Lexis
For example, you could look at poetry written in **dialects** and focus on **regional vocabulary**. You could also record **informal speech** and look at the amount of **slang** used by people of different ages.

Phonology
Phonemic transcriptions (p.154) from recordings of people with different **accents** are the best way to study different phonological features. They are compared and contrasted, highlighting **distinctive features** in particular accents.

Grammar
For example, researchers might compare transcriptions of the speech of a **Standard English** speaker with someone with a **regional dialect**. A good place to start looking is the **verb forms**, e.g. whether a speaker says *the dog wants fed* or *the dog wants feeding*.

Practice Questions

Q1 Name a mode and context that the use of Standard English might be associated with.

Q2 Outline the negative associations that some people might have with regional varieties of English.

Q3 Outline the two different viewpoints on the use of slang.

Q4 What did Milroy and Milroy argue about the role of Standard English in education?

Q5 Why do some people feel that it would be unfair not to teach children how to use Standard English?

Essay Question

Q1 Discuss whether non-standard varieties of English should have the same status as Standard English.

Never make up your mind about someone based on their accent...

Those poor Brummies, always getting a hard time about their accent. Personally, I think it's a lovely accent — and it doesn't seem to have done Cat Deeley's career any harm, or Jasper Carrott's, or Adrian Chiles'... Anyway, you need to know what other people think about language variation, whether you agree with them or think it's a load of twaddle.

'Writing about language issues' can sound tricky, but it doesn't have to be. It's really just about looking at how people feel about language, how important it is in society, and how it's symbolic for lots of other things. See — easy...

Language Issues aren't only for Linguists

1) Language issues are **frequently debated** in wider society.

2) Regional and national **media** — TV, radio, newspapers, magazines and the Internet — often conduct debates about the 'state of language' today. They discuss how it's **developing** and **changing** (for better or for worse).

3) Debates amongst linguists are sometimes brought to the **general public's attention** in this way.

4) While you might think that not many people are that bothered about how they and others **speak** or **write**, lots of non-specialist readers and writers care about **how** language is used. They think it reflects on the **individual** and on **society** as a whole, and they care **strongly enough** to join in the debate with their **own thoughts** or **examples**.

Some people complain that Language is Declining

Editorials in newspapers and magazines often have their say about the **state of language** today. They often link changes in language to a sense of **decline** rather than **development**. Some also link what they see as the deterioration of language with the **state of society** in general.

1) Writing for a non-specialist audience means writers can get their point across in lots of different ways.

2) If you look at how these texts work according to **linguistic frameworks**, you'll have a better understanding of how to put one together **yourself**. This sample magazine editorial is about **language change**:

> "It's apparent that the English language in its purest form, having enriched itself with borrowings and loans from the world's most progressive and intellectual cultures, has peaked. Worst of all, and to our horror, it is now receding. From the summits of Johnson and Lowth, English has tumbled almost toward the Neanderthal — a series of (albeit now electronic) monosyllabic grunts and minimalisms that reek of laziness rather than meaningful or worthy contributions to a formerly rich tapestry. The biggest culprit — "text message speak", has no place in linguistic debate, unless we realise that *pmsl* means not so much *piss myself laughing* as *please murder some language*."

Semantics

- The author specifically aims to create a **pessimistic atmosphere** by using terms with very **negative associations** like *receding, tumbled, horror, reek, laziness, culprit, murder*.

- The author also **juxtaposes** an idealised form of English (*peaked,* Johnson's and Lowth's *summits*), with a **physical fall** or **collapse** (*tumbled*), and a **lack of civilisation** (*Neanderthal*).

- Constructing a **different meaning** to *pmsl* also aims to make fun of the number of abbreviations that are used in informal English but maintains a serious undertone by using the term *murder*. The author's aim is to make the readers feel as if the English language is in **danger**, and it's their **responsibility** to stop the changes.

Grammar

- **Superlative adjectives** like *biggest, purest, most progressive* and *worst* give the text an air of **authority** and make it (both the text and the situation of English) seem much more **serious**.

- **Declarative sentences** e.g. *It's apparent that the English language... has peaked* also make the writing sound **authoritative** and mean that the points made in the text seem **definite** and **unquestionable**.

- Using **collective address** e.g. *unless we realise* directly **involves** the reader in taking responsibility for the problems the author identifies.

Lexis

- The lexis is mostly **non-specialist terminology** — the author doesn't use any linguistic phrases, and even **sensationalises** the writing by describing current English as *Neanderthal* and **exaggerating** everyone's emails and text messages into *grunts and minimalisms*.

- The lexis creates **oppositions** between the *meaningful* and *worthy... rich tapestry* of English *in its purest form*, and **informal varieties** of English, using *culprit* and *murder* to highlight the author's judgement that non-standard English like the kind used in text messages has *no place in linguistic debate*.

Some writers *Embrace Language Change*

Not everyone has the same feelings about language issues. Writing about something you support or agree with sometimes requires a **different approach** from when you're criticising or complaining.

> "If English had been to school it would've been the small kid in first year that matured into the playground bully — always pushing French in puddles and stealing Latin's dinner money. But it is dismissive of teachers' discipline, and has never been fully tamed by its many adoring students. The English language is a living organism, assuming myriad forms, rebuffing invasions (both military and prescriptive), constantly changing and developing. It is at once beyond control and our one pervasive constant — our identity. Shouldn't we be celebrating it for the unique world force it has now become?"

The **tone** and **style** of this piece of writing are different from the one on p.132, because of the following techniques:

Personification

Writing that aims to highlight the good things about language change and variation often tries to give English a **personality** and make it appear **alive**. The aim is to make the reader feel like the language can't be **controlled** by prescriptivism, and that is exactly what makes it so great. Attributing the **qualities** needed to *rebuff* invasions also makes English seem **superior** to other languages.

Metaphor

The author places the concept of a 'living' English language into a **familiar human situation** — using a humorous metaphor of a school playground. This communicates the writer's message in a way that **non-specialists** can easily understand.

Rhetorical Questions

The rhetorical question at the end **leads** the reader into **agreeing** with the writer's opinion, by suggesting that there is no other possible logical answer.

Non-specialist Books on Language are Popular

Non-linguists are now quite **well informed** about language. This has resulted in lots of different opinions — everyone's got their **own view** on what constitutes 'good' or 'bad' English and whether they accept or understand certain phrases.

1) It's not only **textbooks** that discuss the various aspects of English.
2) **Linguists** write non-specialist titles, like David Crystal's *By Hook or by Crook: A Journey in Search of English* (2007) and *Txting: The Gr8 Db8* (2008), which are both very descriptive.
3) There are also books like the *How to talk proper in Liverpool: Lern Yersel' Scouse* or *Larn Yersel' Geordie* series, which are examples of **light-hearted** popular titles that document **regional variations**. There are also plenty of books about the differences between men and women in terms of **language and gender** too.
4) **Journalists / broadcasters** — who aren't necessarily experts on linguistics — sometimes write about language too, for example Melvyn Bragg's *The Adventure of English* (2003).

Practice Questions

Q1 How does the general public become involved in debates about language change?
Q2 What devices could be used to make ideas about language accessible to a non-specialist reader?
Q3 Apart from textbooks or revision guides, what sort of texts about English are available to a non-specialist reader?

Essay Question

Q1 Discuss the different styles you could adopt to get your views about English language across to a reader in a persuasive article.

Writing about language issues can give you writing about language issues...

My problem with it is the sheer wastefulness of the operation. It seems such a shame to use up so many precious words just writing about other words. They should be out there living the dream in marriage proposals, song lyrics and great political speeches, not cooped up in stuffy essays and newspaper articles. They'll probably run out one day, then we'll be sorry.

Here are some exam-style questions, with sources like the ones you'll get in the real paper.

Text A is from the Preface to Samuel Johnson's *A Dictionary of the English Language* (1755).
Text B is from the linguist Jean Aitchison's book *The language web* (1997).

1. Comment on Johnson's and Aitchison's ideas using information from your language change studies.
   Discuss the way these two texts use language to communicate their ideas about language change.

[48 marks]

Text A — from the Preface to *A Dictionary of the English Language* (1755), by Samuel Johnson

I have, notwithstanding this discouragement, attempted a dictionary of the *English* language, which, while it was employed in the cultivation of every species of literature, has itself been hitherto neglected, suffered to spread, under the direction of chance, into wild exuberance, resigned to the tyranny of time and fashion, and exposed to the corruptions of ignorance, and caprices of innovation.

When I took the first survey of my undertaking, I found our speech copious without order, and energetick without rules: wherever I turned my view, there was perplexity to be disentangled, and confusion to be regulated; choice was to be made out of boundless variety, without any established principle of selection; adulterations were to be detected, without a settled test of purity; and modes of expression to be rejected or received, without the suffrages of any writers of classical reputation or acknowledged authority.

Having therefore no assistance but from general grammar, I applied myself to the perusal of our writers; and noting whatever might be of use to ascertain or illustrate any word or phrase, accumulated in time the materials of a dictionary, which, by degrees, I reduced to method, establishing to myself, in the progress of the work, such rules as experience and analogy suggested to me; experience, which practice and observation were continually increasing; and analogy, which, though in some words obscure, was evident in others.

In adjusting the ORTHOGRAPHY, which has been to this time unsettled and fortuitous, I found it necessary to distinguish those irregularities that are inherent in our tongue, and perhaps coeval with it, from others which the ignorance or negligence of later writers has produced. Every language has its anomalies, which, though inconvenient, and in themselves once unnecessary, must be tolerated among the imperfections of human things, and which require only to be registered; that they may not be increased, and ascertained, that they may not be confounded: but every language has likewise its improprieties and absurdities, which it is the duty of the lexicographer to correct or proscribe.

As language was at its beginning merely oral, all words of necessary or common use were spoken before they were written; and while they were unfixed by any visible signs, must have been spoken with great diversity, as we now observe those who cannot read catch sounds imperfectly, and utter them negligently. When this wild and barbarous jargon was first reduced to an alphabet, every penman endeavoured to express, as he could, the sounds which he was accustomed to pronounce or to receive, and vitiated in writing such words as were already vitiated in speech.

exuberance — unrestrained enthusiasm
caprice — unpredictable action, whim
fortuitous — happening by chance
coeval — contemporary, happening at the same time
vitiated — corrupted

Text B — from *The language web* (1997), by Jean Aitchison

Naturally, language changes all the time. This is a fact of life. In the fourteenth century, Geoffrey Chaucer noted that *in forme of speche is chaunge* 'language changes' (see figure I.I), and the same is true today. But change is one thing. Decay is another. Is our language really changing for the worse, as some people argue?

Of course not. Over a hundred years ago, linguists — those who work on linguistics, the study of language — realised that different styles of language suit different occasions, but that no part of language is ever deformed or bad. People who dispute this are like cranks who argue that the world is flat. Yet flat-earth views about language are still widespread. As the Swiss linguist Ferdinand de Saussure said over seventy-five years ago: 'No other subject has spawned more absurd ideas, more prejudices, more illusions or more myths.' Things have not changed very much since then.

On inspection, the web of worries surrounding change turns out to be largely traditional, somewhat like the worries each new generation of parents has about its offspring. Laments about language go back for centuries.

A fourteenth-century monk complained that the English practise *strange wlaffyng, chytering, harryng, and garryng grisbittyng* 'strange stammering, chattering, snarling and grating tooth-gnashing'. And the complaints continued. 'Tongues, like governments, have a natural tendency to degeneration', wrote the lexicographer Samuel Johnson, in the preface to his famous *Dictionary of the English language* published in 1755.

Eighteenth-century worries are perhaps understandable. Around 1700, the seemingly fixed grammar of Latin aroused great admiration, at a time when English itself was in a fairly fluid state. Many people hoped to lay down similar firm precepts for English, and assumed that somebody, somewhere, knew what 'correct English' was. Jonathan Swift wrote a famous letter to the Lord Treasurer in 1712 urging the formation of an academy to regulate language use. He complained that 'many gross improprieties' could be found in the language of 'even the best authors'. But 'correct English' was as hard to define then as it is now. In practice upper- and middle-class speech was often praised as 'good', artificially supplemented by precepts from logic and imitations of various Latin usages.

*For one of your pieces of coursework you'll have to produce a **language investigation**.*
This involves exploring and analysing language data using a variety of methods. Bet you can't wait...

You need to find a **Suitable Topic**

You need to have some idea about what **aspect** of **language** you want to study.

1) Think about your choice of topic so that you don't end up wasting time or getting stuck. This is probably the **most important** point of all — think ahead and be **realistic**. You'll need to produce **enough work** to satisfy the unit's requirements, but you don't want to choose too **wide-ranging** a task or one that ends up being **too demanding** and **impossible to complete**. Your teacher can help you with this.

This section gives you some general advice about how to carry out an investigation. You should still check the details with your teacher, in case they change.

2) It's best to pick something that really **interests you**. If you know the subject well, you should be able to work out whether it will offer enough **scope**, and if you'll be able to get **enough suitable information**.

3) Make sure you choose a topic where the data you need will be **accessible**. If you can't find **enough information** about your topic, then you're bound to struggle.

4) Your investigation should be **1750-2500** words long, excluding data and appendices.

Different Types of **Investigation** look at different **Aspects** of language

1) Being able to identify **different types** of language investigation and applying them to the area you're thinking of studying will help you to **narrow down** your topic.

2) It can also **highlight potential problems** (e.g. if your method is going to give you enough suitable information about your topic) before you get started.

3) This list of different investigation types should help you focus on a more specific area for your study.

Language Based	An investigation that looks at a **particular type of language** in order to determine something about its distinctive features.
	For example: *Looking at regional variations in English by recording people from different parts of the country reading or speaking, and analysing these examples.*

Function Based	An investigation that focuses on the **use of language**, and how one type of language achieves a particular effect.
	For example: *The specific language techniques used in political speeches to persuade, convince or influence an audience so that they end up sharing the point of view of the speaker.*

Attitudes Based	An investigation that focuses on **reactions** and **responses** to a particular type of language.
	For example: *You could look at how people across different age groups feel about the language of teenagers, or their attitudes to slang words etc. You'd have to identify specific groups to talk to in relation to this though.*

User Based	An investigation focusing on the **people** who use a particular type of language — how they use it and how it affects them and those around them.
	For example: *The jargon or sociolect used by people in a particular trade or profession, or in relation to a hobby or an area of personal interest.*

You might find it *Easier* to stick to something you've *Already Studied*

Here are a few things that you'll have covered at **AS** or **A2** that you could investigate (but you don't have to — you can pick other topics). Make sure you **discuss** your **topic** with your **teacher** before you start.

LANGUAGE ACQUISITION	LANGUAGE IN SOCIAL CONTEXTS	LANGUAGE CHANGE
For example:	**For example:**	**For example:**
What role does the caregiver play in language development? Is there an order in which children acquire features of language?	How are regional dialects perceived in schools? Do men and women use language differently?	How has a particular grammatical feature of English changed over time? How do people express their attitudes towards language change?

Think about *How* you're going to *Investigate Your Topic*

There are 3 main ways you can set up your investigation. You can suggest a **theory** (hypothesis) that you want to prove or discredit, set yourself a **specific question** to answer, or go for a **study** based on discussing a certain area and its features.

1) **Hypothesis** based topics

- A hypothesis is a statement that proposes a **possible explanation** for some issue but doesn't offer proof, e.g: *If language changes through generations, then there will be identifiable language differences across three generations of the same family.*
- A hypothesis-based investigation tests the hypothesis by collecting data, and then by **evaluating** the **results**.

2) **Question** based topics

- Questions can be based on something you've **observed** about the way language functions, or how it's used, that can then be **explored** in more detail.
- Any question that you set yourself should be clear and make it **obvious** what you plan to look at, e.g: *To what extent is the language of children's television adapted to assist or influence their linguistic development?*

3) **Descriptive** topics

- A descriptive language investigation focuses on **comparing** and **evaluating** data without trying to prove a point or investigate a theory. Instead of analysing results, you **comment** on the **linguistic features** in your data, e.g. you might look at how verbs have changed over time, and discuss why this might have happened.

Think about how you'll *Get Your Information*

1) The **methodology** is the approach you use to **obtain your information**. It needs to be carefully planned in advance, because in your write-up you need to **describe** and **analyse** the process in detail and comment on what worked well — as well as what didn't.

2) These are the methodologies you might use for the types of topic listed above:
- For a **hypothesis based topic** you might **record** and **transcribe** samples of speech in order to prove a theory about certain speakers.
- For a **question based topic** you might look at **different types** of language and suggest which is most **effective** for its purpose.
- For a **descriptive topic** you might look back at the archives of selected newspapers to **compare** and **evaluate** the style of writing and presentation methods between old examples and up-to-date ones.

A seriously flawed methodology for studying the language of birds was about to teach Terry a very unpleasant lesson.

Time to pic a topic...

This stuff can all seem a bit daunting — you want to choose something vaguely interesting that isn't going to require shed loads of extra work, but isn't too easy either. Tricky. But it's not impossible. Just find a topic that isn't going to completely bore your brains out, and once you get stuck into it you'll soon become an enthusiastic linguist. That's the idea, anyway...

There are plenty of ways to collect data — but you need to make sure that your collection method gives you the best chance of getting what you need. If that happens to include the use of a sharp stick or forcing people to watch Noel Edmonds on TV for 6 hours, then so be it. Just kidding. Don't do that.

You should collect *Primary* and *Secondary Language Data*

Data is the **raw material** that you'll be collecting so that you've got something to write about in your investigation. There are **two types** you should look at:

1) **Primary Language Data** — data that can be obtained directly. For example — recordings of spoken language, samples of written language, lists of words used in conversation or in writing, examples of slang or dialect, and features of pronunciation.

2) **Secondary Language Data** — data from other sources that can tell you about language. For example — other people's research findings or newspaper articles about attitudes towards language. You should use it to support your argument, either by agreeing with it, or explaining why you think it's wrong.

There are *Different Types* of *Primary Data*

You'll collect **different types** of data depending on what you're studying. Use these terms in your coursework to describe the kind of data you've got and impress whoever marks it.

1 Comparative and Contrastive Data

This is when you study **two or more types** of data and **analyse** the **similarities** and **differences** between them. For example, you might compare and contrast the language of text messages with the language of emails.

2 Longitudinal Data

This is when data from **one source** is gathered over a period of **time** so that comparisons or contrasts can be made. For example, you might compare the language of news coverage from the past with news coverage from today.

You can use *Different Methods* to collect your data

1) Collecting Spoken Language Data

There are various different ways in which spoken language data can be collected.

- **Note-taking** — making notes as people are speaking.
- **Preparing a questionnaire on language use**. You can give a questionnaire to someone to fill in, or conduct an interview with them and fill in the answers yourself. You need to plan the questionnaire so that the person's answers demonstrate or discuss whatever feature of spoken language you've chosen to investigate.
- **Tape-recordings** — these could be of conversations between two people, or of a single person reading, speaking about a particular experience, or explaining their opinions on an issue. However, if you record someone without their knowledge, then you're **legally obliged** to obtain their **permission** afterwards, otherwise you can't use their responses as part of your investigation.

Collecting spoken language data is a **time-consuming** business. You might also have to transcribe recordings (in case you need a hard copy, or want to do a phonemic analysis). Doing this can be **useful** and will look really impressive, but you shouldn't spend loads of time doing it at the **expense** of the **other parts** of your investigation.

2) Collecting Written Language Data

Written language data is just any **written text**, e.g. fiction, media texts, emails. In theory, collecting written language data should be easier than collecting spoken language data, as long as it's fairly **concise** and **relevant** to your topic.

3) Combining Spoken and Written Language Data

You could also choose to analyse some of the **differences** between spoken and written language, either in everyday use or in language acquisition. For example, if you're looking at how children begin to develop their language skills, you could **record** their conversations and get **samples** of their writing/drawings.

Questionnaires need to be Carefully Designed

1) First of all, you need to have a **clear idea** of what you want to gain from your questions. It may be better to avoid questions that only have a 'yes' or 'no' response (known as **closed questions**) if you're looking for evidence of linguistic **features** or **opinions** on language.

2) You could ask **open questions** that will encourage people to talk for a while, e.g. asking them for their **opinion**, encouraging them to talk about themselves or getting them to tell **anecdotes** or **stories**.

3) You need to decide **who to ask** in order to get the information you want — this will be your **sample**. You need to make sure that participants fit into the group that your research question has specified (e.g. differences between **male** and **female teenagers**), and design your questions so **everyone can answer them effectively**.

You have to do some Planning before conducting an Interview

There are a number of decisions to make **before** you start:

1) **Who** are you going to interview — just **one person**, or a number of people so that you end up with a wider **range** of responses (but potentially more work)?

2) Are you going to **record** the interview, in which case you'll need to **transcribe** it later, or are you going along with just a notebook for **note-taking**?

3) Are you going to conduct your interview **face-to-face**, over the **phone**, or in some other way, for example via the **Internet**?

You'll also need to decide whether to ask for facts or opinions, or a combination of the two.

There are Problems with studying People

Whatever type of investigation and methodology you choose, collecting data from **other people** can be a bit tricky.

1) If they've been told exactly what the study is about, some participants can end up doing what **they think** the researcher wants them to, rather than **acting normally**.

2) Experimental situations aren't the most **normal experiences** at the best of times (it's pretty hard to just ignore a **camera** or a **microphone**, for example).

3) This is called the **observer's paradox** — the researcher can affect participants' reactions just by being present or making people aware they're being watched.

4) On the other hand, **not telling** participants what they should expect to experience can be **extremely unethical** — they have a right to be briefed on what the investigation is all about in case they're uncomfortable with the study.

The reaction to the 'language and the law investigation' was largely unfavourable.

Some Methods are better suited to certain Investigations

Language Based Investigation	You could collect **spoken** or **written** language data, or both. **Transcriptions**, particularly phonemic transcriptions, give you lots of **detail** but can be very **time-consuming**.
Function Based Investigation	For this type of investigation you'll need to use a **variety of sources**, so you can make **comparisons** between them.
Attitudes Based Investigation	This is the most likely type of investigation for using **secondary language data** (p.138), as it's all about how people respond to the use of language in a particular **context**.
User Based Investigation	This type of investigation could use **various methods** of data collection. It could focus on spoken or written language in a **particular context**, or on a **combination** of the two.

You'll get the most natural responses if you ask about data-day stuff...

... like holidays, or biscuits, or walking the dog. You need to make sure your participants (if you've got any) are at ease, so they'll act naturally and not just say what they think you want them to. That's what the observer's paradox is all about — influencing your own results just by being in the same room. When are they going to invent that invisibility cloak...

When you've collected all the data you need, it's time to decide how you're going to present it in the context of your investigation. Serving suggestions include a nice salad garnish, or maybe a slice of lemon...

Be **Selective** with **Written Data**

1) If you're using **long pieces** of written data (like newspaper or magazine articles), then pick out some **shorter extracts** that **support** the point you're making. This saves you from having to do a detailed linguistic analysis of a huge amount of text, and should mean that the points you make are more **focused** on the topic.

2) Use **footnotes** (see p.146) to draw attention to **specific linguistic features** in the text that **back up** the point you're making.

Spoken Data has to be Transcribed

1) Transcribing conversations is **tricky** — you'll probably need to listen to your recordings closely quite a **few times** before you write up your **final version**.

2) It's also quite **time-consuming**, so if you've recorded an **interview** or **conversation** as part of your data collection, you don't need to **transcribe** the whole thing. However, you do need to make sure that the extracts you choose are **relevant** to your investigation and that you **reproduce** what was said **accurately**.

3) Your data might include things like **pauses**, **repetitions** and **emphasis**. You should represent these features and include an **appendix** or **key** so the reader knows what it all means.

For example:

If you decide to look at differences in language because of **gender**, you could **record** a **conversation** between a **mixed group** of students at school or college.

This short **sample conversation** shows the things you could focus on when transcribing spoken language:

This extract is of an unsupervised conversation between 2 male students (1M and 2M) and 2 female students (1F and 2F), all aged 18. They have been asked to talk about 'holidays'.

1F: can't wait for mine (.) I haven't been away in <u>ages</u>

2F: I know (1) it'll be (.) just be <u>so</u> nice to be away

1M: // where you two going then

2F: er (.) France (1) like somewhere in the south I think

1M: // cool   // okay

1F: // the Dordogne

2F: it's well nice

2M: the <u>where</u> (1) what I've never heard of it

1M: that's because (.) because you're an idiot

2M: just because you're going camping in your garden

Don't use punctuation in your transcript — it isn't articulated, so it shouldn't be included. Use pauses or emphasis instead.

Key

(.) or (1) = *micropause or pause (number of seconds)*

// = *overlapping speech / interruptions*

<u>xxx</u> = *underlining — emphasis by speaker*

The transcript above includes the following features to make it as **clear** and **accurate** as possible:

- Identifies each speaker **individually** (1M, 2M, 1F and 2F) and gives the **context** of the conversation.
- Uses a **consistent symbol** to denote overlapping speech and interruptions (//).
- Underlines words that were **emphasised** by the speakers in the conversation.
- Uses **micropauses** and **numbers** to show **pauses** in the conversation e.g. (.) and (1).
- Lists all the features in a **key**.

If you're investigating **slang** or **dialect**, then you might want to include a **phonemic transcription** (see p.154-155). If you're looking at **intonation** or **stress** you could use **extra symbols** to highlight the differences. If you do decide to do this, remember that although it can be really impressive, producing a very detailed transcription can take **absolutely ages**.

You need to **Base Your Analysis** on a **Linguistic Framework**

You don't have to present **all the data** you've collected in your analysis — select specific parts of the data to **focus on** instead. Make sure you choose the parts that are **most relevant** to the subject of your investigation, and the bits that will make your discussion as clear and focused on the topic as possible.

1) Before you start analysing the data, try to group it into **categories**. You might decide to place some items of data from different sources together to illustrate some **similarities** and **differences**. This will help you when you're making **comparisons**, and it might work better than going through each piece of data systematically from beginning to end.

2) Next you'll need to decide what kind of **framework** you're going to use for your analysis:
   - **Lexis** — words and phrases.
   - **Semantics** — the meaning of words.
   - **Grammar** — structural relationships.
   - **Phonology** — sounds and how they're produced.
   - **Pragmatics** — social conventions of language and its implied meanings.
   - **Graphology** — the physical appearance of language.
   - **Discourse** — how texts are structured and made cohesive.

See p.2 for more on language frameworks.

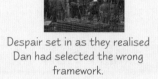

Despair set in as they realised Dan had selected the wrong framework.

3) The framework you choose should be the one that you feel will **best demonstrate** the points you're trying to make. You should try to keep to whichever one you choose, although topics do inevitably **overlap**.

Make sure you choose the **Right Framework**

It's important to choose a **relevant** framework to work with when you're analysing data. For example, it'd be pretty stupid to look at the graphology of a conversation. Here are a few suggestions:

Comparing written data — if you're comparing language use over a period of time you may be focusing on **lexis** or **grammar**. A function or user-based topic might focus on **pragmatics**, **discourse** or **graphology** too.

Comparing spoken data — a **phonological** framework would be an obvious choice for a topic focusing on slang or dialect, but you could use **lexical** or **grammatical** frameworks too.

Comparing spoken data to written data — for language in everyday use, the question of **formality** versus **informality** is likely to come up, so you'll probably choose a **lexical** or **grammatical** framework. A topic on language development in the early years of childhood might also focus on lexis and grammar — you'd be looking for comparisons between **rates of development** of spoken and written language in those years.

Draw Conclusions from your Analysis

1) Ideally, you want to conclude your investigation by showing that you've found out **something new** and **worthwhile** that can be proved by the **evidence** you've presented.

2) You should **broaden** out your analysis to look at **other factors** that could have **influenced** the data. For example, you should consider the impact of **contextual factors**, like where a conversation took place, or the historical context a text was produced in.

3) There may be things you have to **leave open** because you can't fully prove them — e.g. with a hypothesis based topic you might find evidence that suggests a particular trend without providing **comprehensive proof**.

4) Your conclusions should always be **related** to your **evidence**, but they don't have to agree with your **original predictions**, or with any secondary sources you've looked at. The most important thing is that you **justify** what you say by showing how it's **supported** by your data.

Transcription might take ages, but it's worth sticking with it...

Do you think Rebecca Adlington invented swimming overnight? No — it took her years. The same goes for Lewis Hamilton and cars. Don't even get me started on how many rubbish breakfasts I had before I finally came up with the concept of putting milk on cereal. The point here, of course, is that it's worth it in the end. A thorough analysis will be too.

Now for the important part — producing a write-up of your investigation. Otherwise, it doesn't really exist...
There's a pretty standard layout for all of this, so it's not too tricky. Just be methodical and work through the sections.

Start by **Explaining** your **Work (Introduction)**

1) First of all, you need to **explain your reasons** for choosing a particular area of study, including any advice or guidance from **other sources** that helped you towards this decision.

> Zimmerman and West's (1975) dominance model suggests that male speakers are responsible for 96% of interruptions in male-female conversations. As this research is now over 30 years old, I wish to investigate whether the model they proposed still applies to today's mixed-gender conversations.

2) Then you'll need to explain what **type** of **investigation** you've chosen, and whether it's hypothesis based, question based or descriptive — give **reasons** for these decisions too. You could also include some information about the data you've collected.

> This investigation will therefore deal with the following hypothesis: female students in mixed-gender conversations will compete with male speakers to dominate a conversation by non-supportive interruptions, not following rules of turn-taking, prolonging their own turns with non-verbal fillers, and instigating changes in conversation topic.

3) Finally you'll need to outline the **aims of your investigation** — what you set out to **discover** and **achieve**.

Explain **How** You **Collected** your **Data (Methodology)**

1) In this section you'll need to explain how you **obtained your data**, and what **decisions** you made as part of the process. For example, whether your data is **written**, **spoken** or a **combination of the two**, and why this is.

> The data for this investigation comes from a series of unsupervised conversations between male and female students. In order to investigate the effect of gender on these conversations, the participants were informed that they would be recorded, and given the neutral topic "holidays" to discuss.

2) You should then explain how you **designed your investigation**, together with the **techniques** you used in your research and the **language frameworks** you chose. You should explain why these techniques were **appropriate**, and outline any **problems** you encountered while you were collecting your data.

> As this investigation deals with how male and female participants respond to each other, the principle framework that will inform the discussion is that of pragmatics — how the conventions of spoken language are respected, followed or broken according to the gender of different speakers.

Present your **Findings** clearly **(Analysis)**

1) This should be one of the **largest sections** of your investigation. You need to give a **detailed** and **systematic** **analysis** and **interpretation** of the data you've collected.

2) To make this section easier to follow (and write), divide it into **subsections**, with **relevant subheadings** to show how it all fits together.

3) Most of your results will be presented as a **discussion**, but you can also include **charts or diagrams** to support your points — they make the analysis **clearer** and more **systematic**.

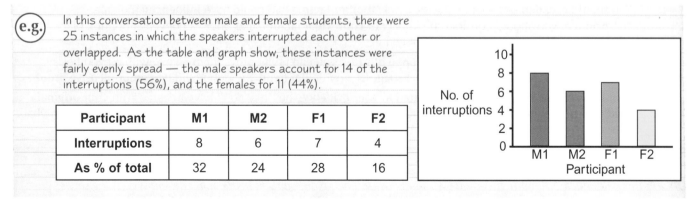
> In this conversation between male and female students, there were 25 instances in which the speakers interrupted each other or overlapped. As the table and graph show, these instances were fairly evenly spread — the male speakers account for 14 of the interruptions (56%), and the females for 11 (44%).

Participant	M1	M2	F1	F2
Interruptions	8	6	7	4
As % of total	32	24	28	16

Bring your **Results** and **Analysis Together (Conclusion)**

1) In your conclusion you should explain what you've been able to **work out** from your **analysis**. You should refer back to the **aims** in your introduction section and say if they've been met, and what you've found out.

 This investigation tested the hypothesis that female speakers are as dominant as males in mixed-gender conversations. The evidence suggests that due to a similar frequency of non-supportive interruptions, topic shifting and disregarding turn-taking, female speakers are more similar to males than Zimmerman and West's dominance model suggests.

2) Whichever form of investigation you choose, you'll need to say if your **expectations** were met or not. If your findings aren't what you expect, **don't be afraid to admit it** — you can **discuss** why this might be the case, and you'll still get plenty of **credit**.

3) The point of this investigation is to reveal something **new** or of **interest**. However, in **relative terms**, your sample size and resources won't be **very big**, so be careful about boldly claiming that you've worked out everything there is to know about female conversational habits (for example).

 The evidence I have produced suggests that female speakers are just as likely as males to dominate conversations. This may reflect how gender roles in conversation are changing, and may mean that Zimmerman and West's (1975) dominance theory can be updated. However this is a very small sample so it is clear more research is needed.

4) If you can see a **potential** for **further study**, the end of your conclusion is a good place to suggest it.

Explain whether you could **Improve** your **Investigation (Evaluation)**

1) When you're evaluating your own work, **be honest** about the success of your investigation. Try and deal with some (if not all) of the following questions:
   - Was the process of **data collection** easier or harder than you anticipated?
   - How **effective** was your chosen method of **analysis**?
   - Did you find you had **sufficient data** for your results to be **significant**?
   - Did the information you came up with offer opportunities for **further research**?

 I tried to avoid the observer's paradox in this investigation by giving the participants a conversation topic and some written instructions rather than being present in the room. However the presence of the recording equipment may have affected the participants' conduct and made them feel more self-conscious than they would normally.

2) It's never particularly easy to criticise your own work, but you should try to **evaluate** the whole process — it looks really good if you can say what worked well and what you would improve if you did the investigation again.

Reference your **Sources** in the **Bibliography**

There's loads more on bibliographies on p.147.

1) The **bibliography** is where you **acknowledge** every **secondary source** you've used. It's basically a big list of books and articles etc. that goes at the **end** of your investigation.

2) The easiest way to do it is to **keep a note** of every secondary source you use in relation to your investigation **as you go along**. Then you won't have to scrabble back through it all when you've finished.

You have to provide **Copies** of your **Original Data (Appendices)**

1) At the very end of your investigation, include any **extra information** that supports it, or that might be helpful to someone reading it. This could include **copies of questionnaires**, **transcripts of spoken data**, and **copies of written data**.

2) You should only include **primary research material** here — data that you've **collected yourself** during the course of your investigation.

"Ah, I see the problem here — you don't seem to have included your appendix."

Writing up is all very well, but make sure you write everything down too...

In fact, why is it called writing up? Just goes to show you can't trust the English language to make any sense whatsoever. On that revolutionary note, it's now your job to take a deep breath and start writing about your investigation (another 'write' preposition there). Remember — be thorough, methodical and accurate and the 'marks for' column will stack up just fine.

For your other piece of coursework, you have to write an informative media text that's based on the broad subject focus of your language investigation. It should be 750-1000 words, and it should be aimed at a non-specialist audience.

You have to write an **Informative Media Text**

1) Your media text should be on the **same topic** as your **language investigation**. However, because it's for a different audience, you need to **re-present** the topic so that it's accessible to **non-specialists**.

2) What you write **doesn't** have to **reflect** what you found in your **language investigation**. This means it doesn't matter which order you do the tasks in.

3) Here are some examples of the type of text you could write.

- Newspaper editorial
- Magazine article
- Article for an online publication

- Blog
- Script for a radio or TV programme or podcast

Make sure you discuss your idea with your teacher before you start.

Make sure you **Research** your chosen **Genre**

1) You should do some **background reading** in the genre you choose, to give you tips on the appropriate **style** and **tone** to use.

2) Think about the **purpose** of your text too. It has to be **informative**, but it could have other purposes too, e.g. a magazine article could be written to **entertain** and **persuade** as well as **inform**.

3) Here are some general hints on the **structures** and **conventions** of a few different media texts:

1) *Tabloid Newspapers* use *Different* language from *Broadsheets*

If you're writing a newspaper article, you should think about whether it's for a **tabloid** or a **broadsheet** newspaper, as this will affect your **language choices**.

1) **Tabloid newspapers** are ones like *The Sun* and *The News of the World*. They tend to be written in an **informal register** and make their viewpoint very clear. They use quite **straightforward language**, which often contains features of **spoken English** like **slang** and **contractions**.

2) Tabloids have **less space** than **broadsheets**, so writers need to get the story across in as **few words** as **possible**. They also rely more on **grabbing** the reader's **attention** and **entertaining** them.

3) **Broadsheets** are newspapers such as *The Guardian* and *The Daily Telegraph*. They're aimed at **professional**, mostly **middle class readers**, so the **register** is more **formal** and articles tend to be **longer** (see p.14).

2) Some *Online Texts* are *Less Formal* than *Printed* ones

Online texts can have different **purposes** and be written for different **audiences**. For example, an article that appeared on a newspaper's website, or one for people interested in linguistics, would probably be more **formal** than a **blog**.

1) A **weblog** (or **blog** for short) is a website which allows internet users to **publish** their writing online. These sites are usually **unregulated**, so the content is decided by the writer.

2) Many blogs take the form of **diaries** or **editorials**. They can be written **anonymously**, allowing writers to express views that they might otherwise keep to themselves. The language used can be forthright and confrontational.

3) More professional blogs use Standard English to mimic newspaper editorials and make them **accessible** to a wide audience. However, many bloggers use the **slang** and **shorthand** they'd use in a text message or email. It's probably best to stick mostly to **Standard English** if you write a blog for your media text.

3) *Scripted Language* is *Written to be Spoken*

You should bear these points in mind if you write a **radio** or **TV script**.

1) Because these texts are designed to be **spoken**, you could include some hints to the speaker on how it should be **performed**. For example, it could contain **prosodic features** like **pauses** and **emphasis** (you could use underlining, italics or capital letters for this).

2) If it's TV then you could include some **visual directions**, e.g. suggestions for how the performer should move.

You need to **Research Other People's Ideas**

1) As well as looking at texts in your chosen genre, you should read other texts to see **what else has been said** about the topic you're covering.

2) These should be the same kinds of **secondary language data** (see p.138) that you use in the **language investigation**. This could include things written for specialists, like books written by **linguists**. It could also include texts for **non-specialists**, e.g. newspaper articles written for much **wider audiences**. You could use the bibliography from a textbook or journal article to find some good sources.

> **Secondary sources**
> - Textbooks
> - Academic journals
> - Newspaper and magazine articles
> - Television or radio broadcasts
> - Web pages

3) It's a good idea to read some sources that show people's **attitudes** towards the aspect of language you're studying. Doing this can help you decide which **angle** to approach your coursework from, as well as providing you with material to **support** the points you make.

4) Remember that secondary sources can be useful even if you **disagree** with what they're saying. You can bring them up in your text and then explain why you think these views are wrong.

5) Using secondary sources can get you loads of marks. You need to show that you can **evaluate** and **synthesise** (bring together) ideas from different texts. Don't feel like it's cheating to include other people's ideas (as long as they've been properly acknowledged) — it shows you have the **skills** to **understand** the **main points** from a text and **use** them in a way that **fits** your **argument**.

Don't Plagiarise

1) It's good to use secondary sources in your text, but what you mustn't do is take words or ideas from other sources and pass them off as your own. This is **plagiarism**, and you can **fail** if you're caught doing it.

2) To avoid this you have to **acknowledge** any work that isn't your own, and credit where you got your ideas from.

3) You should reference everything you've read in your **footnotes** and **bibliography** (see p.146-147). This can be quite time-consuming, but it's **absolutely essential**. The best way to do it is to make a **detailed note** of everything you read as you do it, then you can put it all together in your bibliography once you've finished. This will save you going back through all your secondary sources at the end.

Aim your text at a **Non-Specialist Audience**

One of the ways you can show that you've really understood the secondary sources you've read is by **re-wording** the information to suit a **different audience**. The exam board calls this **re-presentation**.

1) When you **re-present** information, it shows that you've understood all the texts you've studied. It's a way of proving that you can draw out the **most important ideas**, decide what's **relevant** to your **new audience**, and **deliver** it in a way that they'll **understand**.

2) Because you've studied the topic you're re-presenting, you're a **specialist**. But you have to write for a **non-specialist audience**, which means you should think about which technical terms you can use, and how much you'll need to explain to make sure they understand. Remember that your text should show off your **writing** and **editorial skills**, as well as your **subject knowledge**.

3) Usually you'll be re-presenting material to a **different audience** from the one your secondary sources were written for. For example, if you've been studying child language acquisition, you might read some **studies** on how children learn to read. But if you're then **re-presenting** this information for an article in a parenting magazine, you **wouldn't** include all the **specialist detail** and **terminology** you'd read. Instead, you'd give a much more **simple, user-friendly overview**.

MORE coursework???...

It seems a bit cheeky to make you do this as well as a language investigation, but that's exam boards for you. Mischievous little rascals they are. Why, only the other day one sneaked up behind me and poured a bucket of water over my head. I wouldn't have minded but I was actually in an exam at the time and it was a bit off-putting. Made the ink run and everything.

It's important that you acknowledge your sources in both pieces of coursework. It's dull, but at least it's straightforward — there's a very specific way of doing it. Luckily for you, it's on these two pages. I wouldn't leave you hanging.

Include All your References

1) You have to include **references** in your investigation. It means that anyone reading or assessing your work can use the **same sources** as you have, and can check where you got your information from.

2) Referencing also provides **evidence** of the sources that you've consulted to widen your own **knowledge** and formulate your **hypothesis / research question**.

3) You have to include a list to show that you're not **plagiarising** — copying other people's work and/or ideas without **due acknowledgement** (see p.145).

4) References let you **illustrate specific points**, and provide **support** for the arguments you're putting forward (or discrediting).

Make sure you Understand the Terminology

1) **Citations** and **footnotes** are the two main forms of *references*. They refer the reader to a **source** or **piece of information** that isn't in the **main body** of your text. If it's a citation, the information is highlighted **briefly** in the **same sentence**. If it's a footnote, the information is at the **foot of the page**.

2) A **bibliography** is the section at the end of the work where all the references are **drawn together** and listed in full. All sources **need to be acknowledged**, even if you don't specifically refer to them. Anything you've read as part of your investigation needs to go in the bibliography.

You can make Citations in the Middle of your Writing

1) Citations **refer briefly** to a reference source in the **main body** of your writing.

2) If the citation mentions the **author's name**, you should include the **year** that the work was **published** in brackets.

> This model was found to be suitable at higher levels and was adopted by Alexander (1973).

3) If you do include a citation, you'll need to mention the source **again** at the **end** (in the bibliography, see p.147), giving the **full details**.

Footnotes allow you to Add Extra Information

1) Another way to make references is to use **footnotes**[1], where you place small numbers in the text that lead the reader to the **corresponding number** at the bottom of the page or at the end of the text.

2) Footnote references can refer to **any kind of source** — books, magazines, websites etc. They can also give **extra information** about the point you're trying to make[2].

3) The best thing to do is to keep footnotes **short and sweet**. Long or complicated footnotes take the reader's attention **away** from the main body of your writing and mean they might **lose** the flow of your argument completely.

They were furious that the footnote held no useful information whatsoever.

---

[1] Just like this one. What a fine example.

[2] Keep footnotes in order — the first one on a page is 1, the second is 2, and so on. On the next page you go back to 1.

Bibliographies Reference all your sources In Full

Here's a **sample** of what your bibliography might look like. This example uses the **Harvard Referencing system**. However, there are lots of other systems for referencing, so **check** with your teacher exactly which one you'll be expected to use for your coursework. Whatever style you use, keep all the entries in **alphabetical order**.

Crystal, D. (1995) *The Cambridge Encyclopedia of the English Language*. Cambridge: Cambridge University Press p. 364.

Manches, A. (2008) *Language and Gender — TESOL Talk from Nottingham 07/08*. http://portal.lsri.nottingham.ac.uk/SiteDirectory/TTfN0708/Lists/Posts/Post.aspx?ID=21. Accessed 15/01/2009.

Zimmerman, D. and West, C. (1975) 'Sex roles, interruptions and silences in conversation', in Thorne, B. and Henley, N. [eds] *Language and Sex: Difference and Dominance*. Rowley, Massachusetts: Newbury House pp. 105-29.

Each type of source has to be Referenced in a Certain Way

① Published Books

e.g. Crystal, D. (1995) *The Cambridge Encyclopedia of the English Language*. Cambridge: Cambridge University Press p. 364.

1) All the **published books** that you consulted during the course of your investigation **should be acknowledged**.
2) The correct way of doing this (in the **Harvard** system) is by giving the **name** of the author(s) first — their **surname** followed by the **first letter** of their first name (e.g. Crystal, D. above).
3) Follow the author's name with these details, in this order — **date** of publication, book **title** (in italics), the **city** it was published in and the **publisher**.
4) If you've only used a **section or certain pages** of the book, list these at the **end** of the reference (see above).
5) The bibliography should be arranged in **alphabetical order**, according to the first letter of the author's **surname**.

② Contributions in Other Books / Articles in Magazines or Journals

e.g. Zimmerman, D. and West, C. (1975) 'Sex roles, interruptions and silences in conversation', in Thorne, B. and Henley, N. [eds] *Language and Sex: Difference and Dominance*. Rowley, Massachusetts: Newbury House pp. 105-29.

1) You credit the **author and date** of the article first. Include the **title** of the article in **inverted commas**, and then put the details of the **book, magazine** or **journal** in which it appears, in the same way as you would reference any other published book.
2) If you're referencing a magazine or journal, you'll need to include the **volume** and **issue number** (if applicable) **after the title** of the publication itself (e.g. *Journal of Applied Linguistics,* Volume 3, Number 2, pp. 422-436).
3) The general order for referencing **articles** is — **author, date, article title, title of journal** (italics), **volume number, part number, page numbers**. If an article appears in a published book you need to include the **publisher's details**.

③ Websites / Online Resources

e.g. Manches, A. (2008) *Language and Gender — TESOL Talk from Nottingham 07/08*. http://portal.lsri.nottingham.ac.uk/SiteDirectory/TTfN0708/Lists/Posts/Post.aspx?ID=21. Accessed 15/01/2009.

1) If you need to acknowledge a source from **the Internet**, then you have to bear in mind that this material can be **updated** and could have changed **after** you looked at it.
2) You need to give the **URL** (the website's address) so that your source can be **traced**. You can find it in the **address bar** of your web browser. If you're using a lot of websites, make sure you **keep notes** of the addresses.
3) You should reference the **entire address**, starting with *http://*, as above, and put the **date** you looked at the site.
4) On the other hand, if you've consulted a **digital version of a printed publication** (lots of journals etc. are available online), then you should reference these in the **same way** as you would if it was a printed text.

The only source I ever need is ketchup...

Why is it that there's never quite enough in those little pots you get? Why do they do that? If you're not going to provide enough ketchup, then serve fewer chips. Or, shock horror, provide more ketchup, and still serve fewer chips. You'd best learn all this stuff about referencing by the way, before I really go off on one about inverse chip-condiment correlations.

For your A2 exam, you'll need to understand and apply language frameworks, know how to analyse different types of discourse, organise your answers, write clearly and precisely, and join in on a jolly old language debate along the way. If that's all sounding a bit too much like hard work, then read these exam tips to get you started.

Make sure you know your **Language Frameworks**

Language frameworks can be thought of as **headings** to help you to **structure** your **analysis**. You need to be able to **identify them** in different kinds of texts and explain how the features are used to **create meaning**. So here they are:

Language Frameworks

- **Lexis** (vocabulary)
- **Semantics** (the meanings that words convey)
- **Grammar** (word classes, syntax and morphology)
- **Phonology** (sounds)
- **Pragmatics** (social conventions surrounding language use)
- **Graphology** (the visual appearance and arrangement of the text)
- **Discourse** (how sections of language are developed and structured)

Have a look at section 1 in the AS part of this book to recap on the language frameworks in more detail, and for specific linguistic terminology.

1) You need to refer to as many of these as possible, as long as they're **appropriate** to the text and the question.

2) Remember to always give examples from the text to support your point, e.g. *Speaker A uses a formal 'title plus surname' address form to address speaker B: 'Mrs Biggs'.*

3) It **doesn't matter** whether you use **single** or **double quotation marks** when you're quoting from the text, as long as you're **consistent**.

4) Don't just be descriptive. You have to relate the frameworks to **purpose** and **meaning**, e.g. *The adjective 'unique' is persuasive, suggesting that the product is special.*

| purpose | meaning |

Think about how you're going to **Approach** the **Questions**

All of the exam questions you get will be based around **data**. You might have to write about **written texts**, **spoken material** or **tables** of **data**. When you first open the paper, think about the points on this checklist:

1) Read the **questions** so you know what kind of things to look out for in the texts. Read the texts **quickly** to get a feel for what they're about, then read them again **more carefully** and make brief notes in an essay plan.

2) The best way to prepare is to **underline key features** in the texts you're given.

3) For **written** texts, identify genre, register, likely audience and purpose.

4) For **spoken** texts, identify context, role of participants, register and pragmatics.

5) Find **examples** of the language frameworks — be selective and **link** linguistic features to purpose and meaning.

6) Look for features that **link** the texts (e.g. power, gender, occupation, technology, etc.).

Bear in mind the different **Assessment Objectives**

Assessment objectives are the **criteria** the examiners use to mark your exam answers (and coursework). The number of different AO marks you can get depends on the task.

AO1	You get AO1 marks for using **linguistic terminology** correctly and writing **accurately** and **effectively**.
AO2	You get AO2 marks for showing knowledge of **linguistic approaches**, and showing that you understand issues related to the construction and analysis of **meaning** in spoken and written language.
AO3	You get AO3 marks for analysing and evaluating the influence of **context** on the language used, showing understanding of the **key constituents** of language.
AO4	You get AO4 marks for using linguistic concepts to show **expertise** and **creativity** in your **own writing**.

Think about how to *Organise Your Answers*

These are **general guidelines** for how to best cover everything in your answers — if you're asked about something **specific**, you'll have to **tailor** what you say to the particular areas the question asks you to focus on.

Written Discourse	Spoken Discourse
Write a **couple of paragraphs** on: Genre, purpose, register, mode, likely audience.	Write a **couple of paragraphs** on: Context, function, participants.
Write in **more detail** about: **Lexis** (e.g. lexical fields, figurative language) **Grammar** (e.g. word classes — nouns, adverbs etc.) **Discourse structure** (e.g. beginning, development, end) **Phonology** (e.g. alliteration, assonance, repetition) **Graphology** (e.g layout, fonts, images)	Write in **more detail** about: **Non-fluency features** (e.g. pauses, false starts, fillers) **Non-verbal aspects of speech** (e.g. stress) **Pragmatics** (conversational theory) **Phonology** (e.g. pronunciation features) **Lexis**, **grammar** and **discourse structure**.

The A2 exam is *Synoptic*

1) The paper you sit for A2 is **synoptic** — it tests you on the subject as a **whole**.

2) This means that you need to **build on** what you've learnt from **AS**, to show a **broader understanding** of the subject, and recognise when it's **appropriate** to use which bits of information.

3) This is especially the case with your use of **linguistic terminology**. You'll need to be really **familiar** with **specific linguistic terms**, because you're expected to **build** on everything you learnt from AS.

4) All of the questions you'll get will be based on **data**. You need to stay **focused** on this, but use it as a **springboard** for discussing **wider points** about topics you've covered in the rest of the course.

Make sure you know the *Difference* between *Comment* and *Discussion*

1) If you're asked to **comment** on a text, you need to look at the language in **detail**. You'll have to **identify** and **explain** the **key components**.

2) You do this using the **language frameworks** — e.g. you can analyse a text **specifically** in terms of lexis or phonology, or you can do a **broader** analysis where you look at all the relevant frameworks.

3) If you're asked to **discuss** the **issues** in a text, you have to make **judgements** about it. For example, you might comment on the **ideas** that a text raises about a **language debate**, like the superiority of Standard English. You can bring in ideas from **experts** if they help the point you're making.

"Then Little Red Riding Hood addressed the wolf using the second person pronoun..."

4) You should analyse specific ideas in the text, using **quotations**. You should then bring in evidence to **support** these ideas, as well as **contrasting points of view**.

It's *Important* to write *Clearly* and *Precisely*

The points you make need to be as **precise** as possible. There's no need to use **big words** for the sake of it, but it's really important that you use **linguistic terms** appropriately.

1) Spend a few minutes jotting down a **plan** so your answer has some **structure**. Your writing should be **fluent**, so **don't** use **bullet points** in your essay.

2) Write in **paragraphs** and make sure that each paragraph has a clear focus. For example, you might do separate paragraphs on lexis and grammar. **Short sentences** and **paragraphs** are better than long rambling ones.

3) Always use **quotations** and **examples** to **back up** your points. **Short quotations** are better than long ones, and it's good to **weave** them into sentences rather than present them as big separate chunks.

*The A2 exam is **Unit 3**, **Developing Language**. (It's possible that the information here could change, so make sure you check the details with your teacher, and read the instructions on the paper carefully on the day.)*

The exam has Two Sections

The exam lasts **two and a half hours** and is split into **two sections**. You need to answer **one** question from **each section**. You should spend **half an hour** reading and preparing the sources, and an **hour** answering **each question**.

Section A — Language Acquisition *[48 marks]*

1) You'll have a choice of **two questions**, each based on a selection of **data**. The data could be things like transcripts of spoken language, or texts written by or for children. It will be based on child language acquisition from **birth** to **eleven years old**.

2) Your answer should **analyse** the children's language development shown in the data. For example, you might analyse the language of two three-year-old children playing.

Section B — Language Change *[48 marks]*

1) For section B you also have a choice of **two questions**, each based on a selection of **data**. The data will be taken from the **Late Modern Period** (from **1700**) to the **present day**.

2) The texts will show evidence of **historical** and **contemporary change** to English, so you need to **analyse** changes in lexis, semantics, grammar, orthography, graphology and discourse structure.

3) You may also have to **discuss** what they show about **issues** like attitudes to language change, the impact of standardisation and how social and political forces can lead to language change.

Here's an Example Question and Answer to give you some tips:

3   **Text E** is from an article called *Observations in Gardening for January* which appeared in *Gentleman's Magazine* (1731).
      Text F is from a website that gives gardening advice: www.allotment.org (2008).
      •   Describe and comment on what these texts show about language change over time.

The texts you'll get in the real exam will be longer than this.

Text E

Lop and top Trees, cut your Coppice and Hedge Rows; in open weather remove and plant Trees and Vines, lay up your Borders, uncover the Roots of Such Trees as require it, putting Soil under them, also prune Vines and Trees, nail and trim wall Fruits, cleanse Trees from Moss and Succors; gather Cions for grafts about the latter end of this month before the Bud sprouts which stick in the ground for some time, because they will take the better for being kept some time from the Tree, graft them the beginning of next month.

Text F

We all know not to plant when it's too wet or too cold, but when we have had a few good days its very difficult to resist popping in a seed or two. How can we be a little more certain whether or not it's ok to start sowing? Well one sure test is the "**baby water test**". Yes, place your elbow in the soil and if it's too cold you will soon know it. Just like baby's bath water your elbow makes a great tester to check if the soil is suitable or not. Your fingers and hands are just not suitable for either task.

Text E has some eighteenth century orthographical features, for example the capitalisation of proper nouns: 'Vines and Trees'. The syntax is complex and contains lots of subordinate clauses. Lexical change can be seen in the division of the now compound noun 'hedgerows' into two separate words: 'Hedge Rows'. → *Good use of language frameworks*

Identifies similarities in the texts → Both texts address the reader directly with the second person pronoun 'you'. This draws readers in and makes them more likely to take the advice. Text F also uses the plural pronoun 'we', to make readers feel included, and uses interrogatives: 'How can we be a little more certain whether or not it's ok to start sowing?'. → *Makes direct contrasts between the two texts*

Discusses the effect of certain language features → Text F has a less formal tone than Text E. It uses features of spoken language, for example the informal present participle 'popping'. The syntax is less complex — there are fewer subordinate clauses and sentences are shorter. It's also less authoritative than Text E — there is only one imperative ('place your elbow...') compared to numerous ones in Text E (e.g. 'nail and trim'). It's typical of the period Text E was written in that it sounds more authoritative than friendly....

This answer covers **lexis** and **grammar** well. There is effective use of **linguistic terminology**, particularly when discussing **grammar**. There's **good comparison** between the two texts. **Quotations** are used to support most points, and the examples are **well-integrated** into the main body of the answer. Some parts of the answer, e.g. the point about complex syntax, need to be **supported** by **quotations** from the text. The essay should go on to discuss other language frameworks, such as semantics and discourse structure. This is only a partial answer, but the essay would get about **39 marks** out of **48** if it kept up this standard all the way through.

This answer section gives you some tips about what to include when you have a go at the sample exam questions at the end of sections 1 to 3. We haven't written complete essays (everyone writes essays differently), but these points are suggestions for the things you should include in your answers.

Section 1 — Language Acquisition
Pages 108-109

1 The question asks you to comment on the texts in terms of language acquisition and discuss how the child is being helped to understand what happens in the story. Here are some points you could include in your answer:

Text A — conversation between Ellie and her mother

- In text A, Ellie's mother is making sure that Ellie understands the story. Ellie's mother is the main contributor, which is to be expected, as early conversations are usually initiated and maintained by adults. Ellie's contributions to the conversation are mainly short statements that her mother responds to.

- The mother uses direct questions (e.g. *what's that in her hand*) and imperatives (e.g. *look*). She also uses tag questions: *you brush your teeth don't you*, and addresses Ellie directly. These devices are used to encourage Ellie to respond. She gives positive feedback to encourage pragmatic development and make sure that Ellie keeps giving answers, e.g. *very good*. The mother also maintains the conversation by repeating what Ellie says, e.g. *ooh yes look at all the bubbles*. These are all features of child-directed speech. Ellie's comments are expanded by her mother to further encourage her development: the utterance *and she's got water* is expanded to *yes you're right she's all wet isn't she (.) she's gone to wash her face.*

- The mother uses the story as something to base a dialogue on — she uses it to prompt discussion, rather than just reading it out in full. This is probably partly because Ellie is too young to be able to follow the words properly.

- Ellie doesn't always respond to what her mother says. She points out things that she finds interesting, and her mother follows her lead and then brings the conversation back to the topic. This shows that Ellie is still learning how to take part in a dialogue, which is typical for a 3-year-old. She is able to take turns most of the time though, and seems to understand adjacency pairs. For example, when her mother asks the question: *what's that in her hand*, Ellie replies: *she's got her (.) toothbrush.*

- Ellie's speech is typical of a 3-year-old's. She's able to use some full sentences, e.g. *I can't see her teeth.* She can also ask questions using *wh-* words and auxiliary verbs: *what is it on the next one.* She shows some inconsistent usage of inflections, e.g. using *got* and *gotted*. She also has difficulty pronouncing consonant clusters. This is cluster reduction, e.g. she says *plish* instead of *splish* because it's easier.

Text B — extract from an illustrated children's story

- The story is child-focused — it's based on a topic that a young child could recognise and relate to. It's also about simple actions and concrete things that the child could see and touch, e.g. a toothbrush.

- The sentences in the extract are simple — they're mostly short, single clauses, e.g. *She liked to have a big stretch every morning.* The coordinating conjunction *and* is used, which children usually become familiar with quite quickly and tend to find easy to use.

- Most of the words are monosyllabic, e.g. *jumped out of bed.* This makes them easier for a child to understand and pronounce. There's a lot of repetition, e.g. the verb *to wash* is used three times. This gives children a chance to become familiar with a word, rather than being confused by lots of synonyms.

- The story also contains some phonological devices, which make the language more interesting. For example, onomatopoeia is used to describe Rosie washing her face: *Splish, splash, splosh!* This mimics the kind of child-directed speech that Ellie's mother uses. It lends itself to the exaggerated intonation that lots of adults use when they talk to children — Ellie's mother emphasises these words, as well as the words *big dollop*. Phonological features also encourage interaction, as the child can join in and enjoy making unusual sounds.

Section 2 — Language Change
Pages 126-127

1 The question asks you to analyse both texts in terms of what they show about the changes in written language over time. Here are some points you could make in your answer:

Text A — from *The First Book of Manners*

- The syntax in this text is quite complex, which is typical of English from the Victorian period. It contains a lot of subordinate clauses: *should it be your duty, perform it reverently, with a due feeling of devotion.* The opening sentence appears archaic to a modern reader because it begins with a subordinate clause and is in the passive: *When the hour for meals draws nigh.* However, because this was written for children, the language isn't as complex as a text written for adults from the same period. Most of the clauses are quite straightforward, even though the sentences are long: *You will find the knife and spoon at your right hand...*

- The lexis is also formal compared with Present Day English. It contains more Latinate words than text B, e.g. *ascribed*, *unmannerly*. There is also nineteenth century spelling, e.g. *Shew* (in modern texts it would be *show*) and *unfrequently* (instead of *infrequently*).

- The text is quite heavily punctuated and semi-colons are frequently used, whereas in more modern texts they are quite unusual, e.g. the writer uses one in *shew no*

unbecoming haste to sit down; but take your place...
Placing a semi-colon before a coordinating conjunction is rare in modern texts.

- By addressing the reader directly using the second person pronoun *you* and possessive pronoun *your*, the writer creates a sense of a formal lecture. It's as if the reader is being directly spoken to by the writer. If it had been in the third person then the writer would seem more detached.

- The writer assumes the role of an expert, using imperatives like *Sit upright* to instruct the reader. He is very prescriptive about the way the reader should act, for example, the use of the modal verb *will* in *You will find the knife and spoon* creates an authoritative and definite tone.

- The text aims to educate the reader about a strict hierarchy — there is a *head of the family* or *clergyman* in charge, and the *youngest present* is expected to perform their duties *reverently*.

Text B — from a website for parents

- This text is an extract from a twentieth century website giving advice to parents about how to get their children to conduct themselves at mealtimes.

- As in text A the writer addresses the reader directly using *you* and *your*: *Find out which rules work for you.* They also use imperatives like *serve*, *give*, and *assure* to come across as knowledgeable and authoritative.

- The writer uses direct statements to persuade the reader into accepting a shared understanding of proper behaviour (*No one wants to see what's in their mouths*).

- The lexis in text B is not as formal as it is in the nineteenth century text (it includes informal terms like *kids* and adjectives like *crazy*) and includes exclamatory sentences: *piling a plate with a mountain of food is a recipe for frustrations!*). This is intended to show the process as having an element of entertainment and fun about it, as well as making it seem like the writer is using the voice of experience. The text contains metaphor (*ravenous monsters*), which makes it more entertaining and informal. This effect is emphasised by the use of phonological features, e.g. assonance in *Chow Down* and alliteration in *Chew and Chat*.

- The sentences in the text are of varying complexity. The writer uses conditional clauses to pre-empt how the children in question might behave, e.g. *If they need to remove something from their mouth*, which also suggests they've experienced the same thing. It puts them at the same level as the reader, rather than dictating strict rules like the author of text A.

- The punctuation of the text reflects the relative unpopularity of semi-colons in modern written English compared to the Victorian English in text A. The writer in text B uses commas, full stops and colons.

- Rather than being in linked paragraphs like text A, this text is broken down into sections with individual headings, and uses bullet points to make lists. This is

intended to make it easier for the reader to digest the information as it's in smaller, manageable blocks. This is typical of the layout of web-based texts, and shows a more modern, informal style than text A.

2   This question also asks you to comment on how the language in each of the texts reflects the development of language over time. Here are a few things you could discuss in your answer:

Text C — a letter by Byron (1819)

- Text C has a very personal, intimate tone, and includes terms of endearment like *my love*, and *dearest Teresa*, suggesting that the purpose of the letter is to convey Byron's affection. The personal nature of the text is intensified by the frequent use of the personal pronouns *I*, *me* and *you*.

- The letter mainly uses the simple present tense, which also intensifies the sentiments contained in it. There is a sense of immediacy to Byron's writing, e.g. *I feel, I love, I wish that*. This makes the reader feel as if they're being spoken to directly.

- There isn't much archaic lexis in the letter, other than the use of *hereafter*, which is a compound that isn't often used in English any more. The lexis is occasionally complex, e.g. *comprised*, *cease*, but is generally the same as you would expect from any personal letter written in Standard English for a known audience.

- However one common feature of older texts is that they have quite complicated syntax, making them seem much more formal than modern texts. For example, this letter contains several coordinate or subordinate clauses in one sentence, e.g. the sentence that begins *But you will recognize....*

- Byron also uses a shorter sentence to conclude the letter and some shorter clauses towards the end of it. The final sentence, which begins with an imperative: *Think of me*, has a very direct impact and ensures the letter stays in the reader's mind.

Text D — a letter from 1972

- This text seems less emotive than text C, despite also having a very personal tone. It's similar to text C in that it also uses the second person pronoun *you* to directly address the reader.

- The letter is in a different style from text C. It engages with the reader in a familiar, conversational manner without any of the wild or intense declarations of love or feelings that mark Byron's letter.

- The lexis is not quite as formal as Byron's, and has some quite informal turns of phrase like the noun phrase *terrible wimp* and the colloquial verb phrase *stuck in to*. A lot of the lexis is in the lexical field of travel, e.g. adjectives like *jetlagged*. This shows the impact of technology on Present Day English, as this word wouldn't have been available to Byron in the early nineteenth century.

- The writing is conversational and regularly self-referential (e.g. *yes, that's me talking*). It maintains its informal style with contractions like *I've, I'm, can't* and *till*. This marks it out as a Present Day English text, as contractions were used much less in the nineteenth century. It also contains ellipsis: *will write again soon*.

- Text D is similar to text C in its ending — the writer also uses imperatives to make the sentiments more direct (*Give my love, tell them I'm fine*).

Section 3 — Attitudes towards Language
Pages 134-135

3   This question asks you to discuss the ideas contained in the two texts using your knowledge of language change, and to comment on the type of language used. Here are some points you could pick out to talk about in your answer:

Text A — from the Preface to Johnson's Dictionary

- Johnson's ideas about language change were based upon the fact that he thought English needed to be recorded, regulated and controlled. He recognises how important the role of language was in the *cultivation* of literature, but then says that as the language grew it became *neglected* and corrupted by people not using it properly (*ignorance*), and the unpredictable ways that people created new phrases (*caprices of innovation*).

- This shows that Johnson was a prescriptivist — his aim was to create an *established principle* by which words or phrases used in English could be *rejected or received*.

- Johnson recognises that there's a difference between distinguishing the *irregularities that are inherent* in English from the features that have come about through *ignorance or negligence*. This shows some agreement with text B, as there's an acceptance that languages always change and will never be completely consistent,

- However, text A differs from text B because Johnson makes value judgements about which features are *improprieties* and *absurdities* that he feels it is his *duty... to correct or proscribe*.

- The language of this text is typical of eighteenth century English. The sentences are long and the syntax is complex — there are lots of subordinate clauses separated by commas and semi-colons. The lexis is formal and there are a lot of Latinate words, e.g. *perplexity*, *tyranny*. There is also some archaic spelling, e.g. *energetick*.

Text B — from *The language web*, by Jean Aitchison

- In contrast to Johnson, Aitchison is in favour of describing linguistic change, rather than trying to regulate it. She states that *Naturally, language changes all the time*, and contrasts this descriptive approach with the more extreme attitude that change represents *decay*.

- Aitchison makes her feelings about the linguists who identify aspects of language as *deformed or bad* pretty clear, comparing them with out of touch *cranks who argue that the world is flat*. This suggests that she thinks prescriptivism is archaic compared to the descriptive approach of the majority of modern linguists.

- She attributes the concerns other people have about language change being a bad thing to *traditional* feelings. She argues that it's a stage that each generation seems to pass through as they become worried about protecting the conventions of language that they learned as they grew up.

- Aitchison also highlights how the notion of *correct* English was often related to how the members of the *upper- and middle-class* would speak, as well as the influence of Latin. She mentions how Latin was prestigious at the time of the first prescriptivists, due to its fixed grammar. There is evidence for this view in text A — Johnson talks about *writers of classical reputation or acknowledged authority*, showing how the idea behind prescriptive attitudes was to copy what was seen as a rigid model of language that guaranteed prestige.

- Aitchison's language is generally quite informal, and she tries to balance both sides of the argument by giving the history and motivations behind prescriptive views. However she disagrees with them through direct statements like '*correct English' was as hard to define then as it is now*, and by asking rhetorical questions, e.g. *Is our language really changing for the worse, as some people argue?*

One last thing that it's useful to understand. You'll be given this information in your exam, but if you read it now you'll be familiar with it on the day. It'll also be handy if you want to include a phonemic transcription in your coursework.

Phonemic Symbols *express the* Sounds *of the language*

Here is a list of the phonemic symbols that represent the **basic sounds** of the English language. You don't have to memorise them, but you should be **familiar** with the ones that are likely to be different across **regional accents** — mainly the **vowels**. This list gives you examples of the sounds of English as they would be pronounced in **RP**.

Consonants of English

/f/ = **f**riend, tou**gh**	/ʃ/ = **sh**ape, bru**sh**	/b/ = **b**id, ro**b**	/n/ = me**n**, **sn**ake
/v/ = **v**enue, **v**illain, ha**ve**	/ʒ/ = lei**s**ure, vi**s**ion	/d/ = ba**d**, **d**eman**d**	/ŋ/ = ha**ng**er, lo**ng**
/θ/ = **th**ink, **th**rough	/h/ = **h**aunt, **h**it, be**h**ind	/g/ = ba**g**, **g**ain	/l/ = **l**arge, be**ll**
/ð/ = ei**th**er, **th**em, **th**ough	/p/ = **p**ot, ti**p**, s**p**at	/tʃ/ = **ch**ur**ch**, hun**ch**	/j/ = **y**ou, **y**acht
/s/ = **s**ell, do**ts**, cro**ss**es	/t/ = **t**op, pi**t**, s**t**ep	/dʒ/ = **j**ud**g**e, **g**in, **j**ack	/w/ = **w**hat, **o**nce, s**w**itch
/z/ = **z**oo, dog**s**, squee**z**e	/k/ = **k**ick, **c**ope, s**c**rew	/m/ = **m**iddle, s**m**ell	/r/ = **r**oad, d**r**y

Short vowels of English	**Long vowels of English**	**Diphthongs of English**	
/ɪ/ = t**i**p, b**u**sy, h**i**ss	/iː/ = sh**ee**p, h**ea**t	/eɪ/ = gr**ea**t, d**ay**	/əʊ/ = b**oa**t, h**o**me
/e/ = sh**e**d, **a**ny	/ɑː/ = c**ar**, b**al**m	/aɪ/ = fl**y**, br**igh**t	/ɪə/ = h**ere**, n**ear**
/æ/ = c**a**t, h**a**d, b**a**nk	/ɜː/ = b**ir**d, h**ear**d	/ɔɪ/ = b**oy**, n**oi**se	/eə/ = st**are**, **air**
/ɒ/ = w**a**nt, r**o**bot	/ɔː/ = p**or**t, t**al**k	/aʊ/ = c**ow**, h**ou**se, g**ow**n	/ʊə/ = m**ore**, p**oor**
/ʌ/ = c**u**p, s**o**n, bl**oo**d	/uː/ = f**oo**d, shr**ew**d		
/ʊ/ = w**oo**d, p**u**t, b**oo**k			
/ə/ = **a**bout, bal**a**nce			

Don't panic — you don't have to transcribe anything, OR learn all these symbols off by heart. You'll get a copy of the symbols in the exam paper, so you can use them in your answers if it's appropriate. You could also use them in your coursework.

There are different types of Vowel Sound *in* English

There are three **distinct types** of vowel sound in English — short vowels, long vowels and diphthongs (two vowels in one).

> *bin* /bɪn/, *ban* /bæn/ and *bun* /bʌn/ are examples of **short vowel sounds**.
> *bean* /biːn/, *barn* /bɑːn/ and *burn* /bɜːn/ are examples of **long vowel sounds**.

Two vowel sounds can also be **fused together**, to form a **diphthong**.

> *bite* /baɪt/, *bait* /beɪt/ and *boat* /bəʊt/ are examples of **diphthongs**.

Phonemic symbols provide a valuable way of demonstrating the **differences in sound** — something that you can't necessarily show by the way the **words** are **spelled** — think of *read* /riːd/ and *read* /red/.

You can use phonemic symbols in Language Analysis

The standard practice when you're including a phonemic transcription is to start it on a **new line** so it can be read easily, leaving spaces **between the words** as in normal writing.

To give you an idea, this is how the definition of phonetics from p.24 would look in transcription:

> *Phonetics is the study of how speech sounds are made and received*
> fənetɪks ɪz ðə stʌdi ɒv haʊ spiːtʃ saʊndz ɑː meɪd ænd rɪsiːvd

And this is how part of the definition of phonology would look:

> *Phonology is the study of the sound systems of languages*
> fənɒlədʒi ɪz ðə stʌdi ɒv ðə saʊnd sɪstəmz ɒv læŋgwɪdʒɪz

Phonetics *shows the* Differences *between* Accents

Here's a sentence as an example:

> *How are you feeling today?*

A phonemic transcription of this sentence in **Received Pronunciation** (RP) would look like this:

> haʊ ɑ ju: fiːlɪŋ tədeɪ

However, the same sentence spoken in a **Scottish accent** would appear like this:

> hɒʊ er ju fiːlɪn tɪde: ⟵

A **Geordie accent** would be different again:

> hu: ɔ ju: fiːlɪn tɪdɪə ⟵

And so would a **West Country accent**:

> aʊ ɑːr ju fiːlɪŋ tədeɪ ⟵

Today, Gemma was feeling how she always felt — funky.

> You wouldn't be able to see the different pronunciation in a transcription that used **regular spelling**.

Phonemic Symbols *can identify* Specific Features *of* Pronunciation

If you're using a phonemic transcription in some analysis, you can record specific **linguistic features** very accurately. This is especially useful if you're looking at **accent** and **dialect**. Here are a couple of examples:

Glottal Stops — e.g. in the word *matter*

- The 't' sound in *matter* often **isn't articulated** with the tongue.
- Instead the speaker will use what is known as a **glottal stop**. This is technically a movement of the **vocal chords** that mainly (in English) acts as a **substitute** for the non-pronunciation of the 't'.
- The glottal stop is shown in phonemic transcriptions by a symbol that looks a bit like a **question mark** /ʔ/. So *matter* would look like this in transcription: /mæʔɒ/

Elision — e.g. in the phrase *Alright mate?*

- This greeting is likely to be said **quickly**, and this will result in **elision** (see p.25).
- Some sounds will be **left out altogether**, even though they're included when the phrase is spelled out.
- A phonemic transcription of what is actually spoken might look like this: /ɒwɔɪmaɪʔ/

Practice Questions

Q1 What are the three distinct types of vowel sound in English?

Q2 What is a diphthong?

Q3 What is a glottal stop?

Essay Question

Q1 Explain, with examples, why a phonemic transcription is more useful in highlighting the differences between regional accents than a direct transcription of a conversation or interview.

It's a shame no one coined 'diphthong' as an insult first...

Can you imagine if you were able to call someone a 'massive diphthong'? That would be brilliant. It's a real shame that it's a very technical term for two vowel sounds realised as one. Anyway, I'm sure you'll get over it. Phonemic symbols are really useful for highlighting the differences between regional speakers — so it's pretty handy to be familiar with them, at least.

abstract noun A **noun** that refers to a concept, state, quality or emotion.

accent The distinctive way a speaker from a particular region pronounces words.

acronym A new word made from the initial letters of all the words in a name or **phrase**, e.g NASA.

active voice When the **subject** of the sentence is directly performing the **verb** e.g. *Steve burst the bubble*.

adjacency pair Dialogue that follows a set pattern, e.g. when speakers greet each other.

adjective A class of words that can appear before (attributive) or after (predicative) a **noun** to describe it, e.g. *pretty*.

adverb A class of words that modify **verbs** according to time, place, manner, frequency, duration or degree. They can also sometimes modify nouns and adjectives too.

affixation The process of adding an affix before (**prefix**) or after (**suffix**) an existing word to change either its meaning or grammatical function.

alliteration When two or more words close to each other in a **phrase** begin with the same sound, e.g. *down in the dumps*.

allusion When a text or speaker refers to a saying, idea, etc. outside the text or conversation.

amelioration When a word develops a more positive meaning over time.

anaphoric reference When a word, usually a pronoun, refers back to something or someone that has already been mentioned, e.g. *Barrie can't come because he's ill*.

antithesis Type of **rhetorical language** where contrasting ideas or words are balanced against each other, e.g. *it's just too good from Green, and just too bad for the goalkeeper*.

antonyms Words with opposite meanings.

archaism An old-fashioned word or phrase that isn't used in Present Day English, e.g. *forsooth*.

article A kind of **determiner** that shows if the reference to a **noun** is general (*a / an*) or specific (*the*).

aspect A **verb's** aspect shows whether the action it refers to is already completed, or if it is still taking place.

assimilation When sounds next to each other in a spoken word or **sentence** are pronounced in a different way from normal to make them easier to say.

assonance When the main vowel sounds of two or more words that are close together in a text are similar or the same, e.g. *low smoky holes*.

audience A person or group of people that read, view or listen to a text or performance. A writer or speaker can aim to appeal to a certain type of audience by using specific literary techniques and language choices.

auxiliary verbs Verbs used before the **main verb** in a sentence to give extra information about it, e.g. *I have seen him*.

babbling The production of short vowel / consonant combinations by a baby acquiring language.

back-channelling A kind of **feedback** in spoken language that supports the person speaking and shows that what is being said is understood.

back-formation In word formation, back-formation occurs when it looks like a **suffix** has been added to an existing base form to create a new word, but in fact the suffix has been removed to create a new term e.g. the **verb** *enthuse* was formed from the **noun** *enthusiast*.

behaviourism A theory of language acquisition that suggests children learn language through a process of imitation and reinforcement.

bidialectism The ability of speakers to switch between two **dialect** forms, the most common being between **Standard English** and a speaker's regional variety.

blending When parts of two words are combined to make a new one, e.g. *netizen*.

borrowing When words from one language fall into common usage in another as a result of contact.

broadening When a word that has quite a specific meaning becomes more general over time (also called generalisation, expansion or extension).

cataphora A reference in a text to something that follows in later **phrases** or **sentences**, e.g. *These are the directions...*

characterisation The way that a writer conveys information about a character relating to their appearance, speech, etc.

child-directed speech (CDS) The way that caregivers talk to children — usually in simplified and / or exaggerated language.

clause The simplest meaningful unit of a **sentence**.

cliché A expression that has lost its novelty value due to being overused.

clipping When a shortened version of a word becomes a word in its own right, e.g. *demo, phone*.

cluster reduction When a child only pronounces one consonant from a consonant cluster, e.g. saying *pay* instead of *play*.

cognitive theory A theory of language acquisition that suggests children need to have developed certain mental abilities before they can acquire language.

cohesion The linking of ideas in texts to ensure the text makes sense.

coining The general term for creating new words.

collective noun A **noun** that refers to a group of people, animals or things, e.g. *team*.

collocation Words that commonly appear together in order, in specific lexical units, e.g. *done and dusted*.

colloquialism An informal word or phrase that wouldn't normally be used in formal written English, e.g. *How's it going, mate?*

common noun A **noun** that refers to a class of things or a concept. Every noun is a common noun except those that refer to unique things, e.g. the names of particular people or places.

comparative An **adjective** that makes a degree of comparison, normally by adding an *-er* **suffix**, e.g. *faster*.

complement A word or **phrase** that gives more information about the **subject** or **object** in a sentence, e.g. *the boy is actually a cow*.

compound A new word created by combining two or more existing words, e.g. *skyscraper*.

concrete noun A **noun** that refers to things you can physically touch or see, e.g. *chair*.

conjunction A linking word that connects **phrases** and **clauses** to each other to form **sentences**, e.g. *but*.

connotation The associations that are made with a particular word.

context The circumstances that surround a word, **phrase** or text, e.g. time and place produced, intended audience.

contraction A word that's formed by shortening and combining two or more words, e.g. *can't, might've*.

conversion When a word becomes part of a different **word class** in addition to its original sense (e.g. *text* is now both a **noun** and a **verb**).

cooing The earliest sounds children are able to make as they experiment with moving their lips and tongue.

coordinate clause An independent **clause** that's linked to another independent **clause** in the same **sentence**.

coordinating conjunction A linking word like *and, but* and *or* that connects independent phrases and **clauses** to each other, e.g. *He was handsome and she was jolly.*

count noun A **noun** that can be preceded by a number and counted, e.g. *one book, two books* etc.

Critical Period Hypothesis A theory popularised by Lenneberg (1967), which states that if a child does not have any linguistic interaction before the ages of 5-6, their language development will be severely limited.

declarative sentence A **sentence** that makes a statement to give information, e.g. *she enjoyed her scampi.*

deixis A reference to something outside of the text or conversation (e.g. location, time) that can't be understood unless you know the **context**.

deletion When a child misses out consonants in words, e.g. saying *sto* instead of *stop*.

demonstrative Words that refer to specific objects that only those involved in the discourse can see. They can be **pronouns**, e.g. *I like this*, or **adjectives**, e.g. *I like this bike.*

denotation The literal meaning of a word.

descriptivism The attitude that no use of language is incorrect and that variation should be acknowledged and recorded rather than corrected.

determiner A word that goes before a **noun** to show possession or number (e.g. *his, two*).

dialect The distinctive **lexis**, **grammar** and pronunciation of a person's spoken English, usually affected by the region they're from and their social background.

dialect levelling A process of **language contact** where differences between **dialects** in proximity to each other are gradually lost.

dialogue Any exchange between two or more characters or speakers.

difference model Tannen's (1990) theory about gender and conversation which states that men and women have different objectives when they interact.

diphthong Two vowel sounds that are joined together to form one sound, e.g. the *a* in *late* is a diphthong as it starts with an /e/ phoneme and finishes on an /ɪ/.

discourse An extended piece of written or spoken language.

dominance model Zimmerman and West's (1975) theory that gender differences in conersations reflect male dominance in society.

double comparative Using an **adjective** that makes a degree of comparison, normally by adding an *-er* **suffix**, with the word *more*, e.g. *more faster*.

double negative When negatives are used twice in a phrase, e.g. *I didn't do nothing*.

egocentric The early mental state of a child in which they can only understand things existing in relation to themselves, i.e. things they can see or touch, etc.

elision When sounds or **syllables** are left out in speech to make pronunciation easier and quicker. They end up sounding like they're slurred together, e.g. *d'ya* instead of *do you*.

ellipsis When part of a grammatical structure is left out of the **sentence** without affecting the meaning.

Estuary English An **accent** that was originally from the Thames Estuary area in London but is now heard outside the area and may be replacing **RP** as the country's most widespread form.

euphemism A word or phrase that is used as a substitute for harsher or more unpleasant sounding words or concepts.

exclamative A **sentence** that has an expressive function and ends with an exclamation mark.

exophoric reference Referring to something outside a text, e.g. *that* tree over *there*.

feedback Verbal and **non-verbal** signs that a person is listening to a speaker.

figurative language Language that is used in a non-literal way to create images and form comparisons, e.g. metaphor and simile.

filler A sound produced by speakers to keep a conversation going and avoid silence, e.g. *mm*.

fricative A group of consonant sounds in English produced by forcing air through a restricted passage (e.g. between the lips or teeth). Some of the English fricatives are *th* sounds, *f*, *v*, *s*, *z*, *j* sounds, and *sh* sounds.

generic term A **marked term** that is used to refer to men and women, e.g. *chairman*.

genre A group of texts with a particular form or purpose, e.g. letters, poems, adverts.

glottal stop A sound produced when the vocal cords interrupt the flow of air, often to replace a /t/ sound (e.g. *water* becomes *wa-uh*).

grammar The system of rules that governs how **words**, **clauses** and **sentences** are put together.

grapheme The smallest unit of writing that can create contrasts in meaning, e.g. individual letters or symbols.

graphology The study of the appearance of a text, how it looks on the page and how the layout helps to get the meaning across.

head word A word that has the same grammatical function as the **phrase** that has been built around it, e.g. in a noun phrase, the head word is a **noun**.

hedging Word choices that show uncertainty in conversations, e.g. *probably*, *maybe*.

holophrase In language acquisition, a single word that expresses a complete idea, e.g. *ball*, which could mean the child wants it, or has found it, etc. Caregivers need contextual clues to interpret holophrases.

hyperbole When exaggeration is used for effect.

hypernym A general word that is a term for many **hyponyms**, e.g. *vehicle* is a hypernym of *car*, *bus*, *lorry*, etc.

hyponym A word that refers to a specific type of a **hypernym**, e.g. *car*, *bus*, *lorry* are hyponyms of *vehicle*.

ideology A set of ideas and beliefs.

idiolect An individual's **accent** and **dialect** features, which are a result of their personal upbringing and experiences.

idiom A saying that doesn't make sense if interpreted literally but is understood because it's commonly used e.g. *I could eat a horse*.

imagery Describing something in a way that creates a picture of it in the mind of an audience.

imperative A **sentence** that gives orders, advice or directions. It starts with a **main verb** and doesn't have a **subject**.

implication When a meaning is suggested, rather than explicitly described.

infinitive The base form of a **verb**, preceded by *to*, e.g. *to sing*.

inflection An **affix** that is attached to a base word and gives extra information about it, e.g. its tense or person.

initialism Where the first letter of a word stands for the word itself as part of an abbreviation e.g. *FBI* (for Federal Bureau of Investigation). Initialisms are always pronounced letter by letter.

internalisation When a child learning language starts to apply one of the language's rules consistently, even to words they've never seen before.

interrogative A sentence or utterance that asks a question.

intertextuality When a text makes reference to another existing text for effect.

intonation The pitch of a speaker's voice, e.g. rising intonation shows it's a question.

jargon **1**. The chattering sounds that babies make before they start using proper words. It sounds like a made-up language.
2. Specialist words that are used by a particular social or occupational group that may not be understood by a non-member.

juxtaposition Positioning words, ideas or images next to each other in a text to create certain effects.

language acquisition device (LAD) The innate ability of children acquiring language to take in and use the grammatical rules of the language they hear, according to Chomsky (1965).

language acquisition support system (LASS) The system of support from caregivers to children that helps them to acquire language and become sociable, according to Bruner (1983).

language contact Occurs when speakers of different languages or varieties of the same language interact for prolonged periods.

Late Modern English The more **standardised** form of the English language, used from around 1700.

lexical asymmetry When two words that appear to be direct opposites of each other actually have different connotations, e.g. *to father* means to conceive a child, *to mother* means to look after it.

lexical field A group of words that relate to the same topic, e.g. *hotel* and *destination* are in the lexical field of travel.

lexis A general term for the words of a language.

liaison When a consonant is pronounced between words or **syllables** to make them run together.

lingua franca A language used for communication between speakers who don't have the same native language.

loan words Words that are taken from other languages.

main verb A word that identifies the action of a **sentence**.

management speak A way of communicating in the workplace designed to sound up-to-date and formal, but usually overly complex.

marked term A word that reveals a person's gender, e.g. *mistress, postman*.

mass noun A **noun** that can't be counted and doesn't have a plural, e.g. *information*.

metaphor Words or phrases that describe something as if it was actually something else, e.g. *the heart of the matter*.

metonymy Using a part of something, or one of its attributes, to describe the whole thing, e.g. *the press* to refer to journalists and the news industry.

modal auxiliary verbs Verbs that give more information about the **main verb**, but can't occur as main verbs themselves, e.g. *can, will*.

mode A way of classifying texts, e.g. written or spoken or a combination of the two.

modifier A word, usually an **adjective** or **adverb**, that changes (modifies) the meaning of a **head word**.

monologue The utterances of one speaker or performer to an audience.

monosyllabic Words with only one **syllable**.

morpheme The individual meaningful units that make up words (although they can't always stand alone).

morphology The study of the internal structure of words.

multimodal text A text that involves elements of different **modes**, e.g. text messages are a mixture of written and spoken language.

narrative voice The point of view a text is written from, e.g. a first person narrator tells the story from their personal point of view.

narrowing When a word that has a general meaning becomes more specific over time (also called specialisation or restriction).

negatives Words like *not* and *no*, that turn positive statements into negative ones, e.g. *I'm not here tomorrow*.

neologisms New words that enter a language.

non-fluency features Features that interrupt the flow of talk, e.g. hesitation, repetition, **fillers**, interruption and overlap.

non-verbal communication Any method of communication that isn't words, e.g. gestures, facial expressions, body language and tone of voice.

noun A word used as the name of a person, place, thing or concept.

object The part of the **sentence** that the **verb** acts upon, e.g. in *I broke a plate*, the plate is the object and ends up *broken*.

omission When sounds are left out from words. If a lot of speakers do this over a prolonged period of time, the sound can end up being lost altogether.

onomatopoeia A word that sounds like the noise it's describing, e.g. *buzz*.

orthography The writing system of a language — how the language is represented through symbols (letters) and spelling.

overextension When a child acquiring language uses a word too generally to refer to different but related things, e.g. calling everything with four legs a *dog*.

oxymoron A phrase that brings two conflicting ideas together, e.g. *bittersweet*.

parallelism The repetition of structural features in a sentence or throughout a text, e.g. repeated use of the past tense in a sentence — *he came home, ran up the stairs and jumped in the bath*.

parentheses Another word for brackets.

parody Subverting traditional expectations of a text's features to produce humour or satire.

passive voice When the **object** of the verb is described first, rather than the **subject** (e.g. *the bubble* was burst by Steve).

pejoration When a word develops a more negative meaning over time.

personification When an object, concept or situation is given human qualities.

phatic language Expressions that have a social function rather than expressing serious meaning, e.g *hello*.

phoneme The smallest unit of sound.

phonemic contraction When a baby stops making certain sounds, and just makes the sounds it hears from the language its caregivers use. This happens at about 10 months.

phonemic expansion When a baby starts to make lots of different sounds in the babbling stage. This occurs before **phonemic contraction**.

phonetics The study of how speech sounds are made and received.

phonology The study of the sound systems of languages, in particular the patterns of sounds.

phrase A meaningful unit of language built around a **head word**.

plosive A consonant sound in English produced by completely stopping the flow of air from the lungs and then releasing it. English plosives include *p*, *b*, *t*, *d*, *k*, and *g*.

politeness strategy A way of phrasing something to avoid causing offence, e.g. apologising or being evasive.

political correctness Avoiding using language or ideas that might be offensive about members of a particular group (e.g. ethnic, gender, or age groups).

polysyllabic Words with more than one **syllable**.

post-modifiers Words that come after the **head word** in a **phrase** and tell you something about it.

pragmatics The study of how language functions in social situations.

pre-modifiers Words used before the head word of a **phrase** (often **determiner** + **adjective**) that tell you something about it.

prefix An **affix** that comes before the base form, e.g. *unfortunate*.

preposition A word that defines the relationship between things in terms of time, space or direction, e.g. *the toy was in the box, he's behind you*.

prescriptivism The attitude that language should have a strict set of rules that must be obeyed in speech and writing.

primary auxiliary verbs **Auxiliary verbs** that can also occur as **main verbs** (*do*, *be* and *have*).

pronoun A word that can take the place of a **noun**, e.g. *he, she, it*.

proper noun A **noun** that is the name of a specific person, place or brand.

prosody **Non-verbal** aspects of speech like pace, stress, pitch, intonation, volume and pauses.

proto-word A combination of sounds that a child uses that actually contains meaning, rather than just being a random utterance like **cooing** or **babbling**.

pun Replacing a word or phrase with one that sounds the same or similar for creative or humorous effect.

quantifier A word that gives information about the quantity of a **noun**, e.g. *there are a few cardigans*.

Received Pronunciation (RP) An **accent** traditionally associated with educated people and the upper class. It's characterised by lots of long vowels and the pronunciation of /h/ and /t/ in words where people with regional accents might leave them out.

referential language Spoken language that gives information by referring to objects or concepts. It usually only makes sense if the listener understands the context, e.g. *the vase is over there*.

register A type of language that's appropriate for a particular audience or situation, e.g. formal language is appropriate for a political speech.

rhetorical language Language with phonological or structural features used to provide extra effects or meanings.

sans-serif typeface A typeface where there aren't any fine 'strokes' attached to the tops and bottoms of letters.

schwa A generic vowel sound ([ ]) that is usually pronounced in unstressed syllables e.g. the e in *system* or the a in *alone*.

semantics The study of how the meanings of words are created and interpreted.

sentence An independent grammatical unit made up of one or more **clauses**.

serif typeface A typeface where fine 'strokes' are attached to the tops and bottoms of letters.

similes Comparisons that use the words *like* or *as*.

simplification When a child learning to speak drops consonants or consonant clusters to make words easier to pronounce, or swaps the consonants for others that are easier to pronounce.

slang Informal, non-standard vocabulary used in casual speech.

sociolect A variety of language used by a particular social group.

split infinitive When the base form of a verb is separated from the word *to* by another word — usually an adverb, e.g. *to quickly run*.

Standard English A **dialect** of English considered 'correct' and 'normal', because it has distinctive and standardised features of spelling, vocabulary and **syntax**. It's the form of English usually used in formal writing.

standardisation The process by which grammarians and prescriptivists attempted to structure and influence English usage according to what they believed constituted 'correct' or 'incorrect' usage of the language.

sub-genre A group of similar texts that combine with others to create a complete **genre**, e.g. tragedy and comedy are types of drama.

subject The focus of a **sentence** — the person or thing that performs the action described by the **verb**, e.g. *Billy ate a sandwich*.

subordinate clause A **clause** that gives extra information about the main clause, but can't stand alone and still make sense.

subordinating conjunction A linking word like *although* or *because* that connects a subordinate clause to the main clause, e.g. *I'm off work because I feel sick*.

substitution When a child replaces a consonant in a word with one that's easier to say, e.g. saying *dot* instead of *got*.

subtext The implied meaning behind what's actually being said or described.

suffix An **affix** that comes after the base form, e.g. *sadness*.

superlative An **adjective** that states the **noun** it's describing is beyond comparison. It's formed by adding *-est*, e.g. *fastest*, or using the word *most*, e.g. *most beautiful*.

syllables The individual units of pronunciation that make up a word.

symbolism When a word or phrase represents something other than its literal meaning.

synonyms Words that have the same or very similar meanings.

syntax The order and structure of sentences.

tag question A question added to the end of a statement to encourage a response, e.g. *don't you think so?*

telegraphic stage The stage of language acquisition at which children begin to create three- or four-word utterances containing mainly **subjects**, **verbs**, **objects** and **complements**.

tense Grammatical **inflections** on verbs that show the time an action took place, e.g. in the past or present.

th-fronting When a speaker replaces *th*-sounds with *f* or *v*, e.g. *think* as *fink* and *them* as *vem*.

transactional language Spoken exchanges aimed at making some sort of deal.

turn-taking A feature of orderly conversations when the chance to speak switches back and forth between the participants.

underextension When a child uses words in a very restricted way, e.g. using a word like *hat* to refer only to the one the child is wearing, not to other hats too.

uptalk / upspeak When the intonation rises at the end of statements rather than just questions.

verb A word that describes the action or state that a **sentence** refers to.

vernacular The commonly-spoken language of a country or region.

word classes How words are categorised according to the function they can perform in a **sentence**.

Zone of Proximal Development Vygotsky's (1978) theory that when caregivers help children with verbal responses, they provide a model that the child can copy and apply when they're in other situations.